DATE DUE			
Jan 28 '74			
Mar 4 '74			
Apr 30 '82			

The Politics of Defence

The Politics of Defence

DAVID OWEN

TAPLINGER PUBLISHING COMPANY
NEW YORK

FIRST PUBLISHED IN THE UNITED STATES IN 1972 BY
TAPLINGER PUBLISHING CO., INC.
NEW YORK, NEW YORK

Library of Congress Catalog Card Number: 72–76256

ISBN 0–8008–6406–9

PRINTED IN GREAT BRITAIN

Contents

1. The Smell of Burning   9
2. The Machinery of Defence Decisions   20

PART ONE: CRISIS DECISION-MAKING

3. The Cuban Missile Crisis   35
4. The Gulf of Tonkin Incident   52
5. The 1967 Arab-Israeli War   64
6. The *Pueblo* Incident   76

PART TWO: POLITICAL DECISION-MAKING

Political Issues   89
7. East of Suez   94
8. The African Continent   109

PART THREE: MARITIME DECISION-MAKING

9. Maritime Strategy   127
10. International Maritime Law   136

PART FOUR: STRATEGIC DECISION-MAKING

Strategic Issues   147
11. The Evolution of NATO's Nuclear Strategy   151
12. National Deterrents   168
13. European Defence   193
14. The Control of Defence Decisions   225

REFERENCES   237
INDEX   245

To G.W.R.

Chapter 1. The Smell of Burning

The whole process of defence decision-making is dangerously deficient throughout the world. The documentary evidence that exists points to serious errors and omissions in actual defence decisions in all the countries of the Western Alliance, and particularly the United States. It is clear that similar deficiencies also exist in the Warsaw Pact countries. Yet these errors occur at a time when men's powers of self-destruction are greater than ever before. Statistics of megatonnage of nuclear weapons have almost ceased to shock — we have learnt to live with nuclear weapons, and their terrifying powers of devastation now numb rather than excite. The arms race has become almost an accepted fact of twentieth-century life. Even after the Second World War there was only a temporary lull. From 1949, at the start of the Korean war, world military expenditure doubled in three years. A further rise of about 50 per cent occurred between 1965 and 1970, the largest part of this being accounted for by the Vietnam war and increased Soviet defence-spending. Overall world military expenditure at the start of the 1970s was around $200 billion, absorbing 6–7 per cent of all world output.

The most frightening aspect of the arms race is the rate at which the Soviet Union and the United States continue to acquire nuclear weapons. The arms race is fed not only by the ever-increasing advances in weapons technology, but by the fostering of military attitudes that are calculated to play on the emotions of pride and fear. Too frequently, such emotions lead to the search for parity of weapons for its own sake. The pursuit of parity, itself an almost indefinable objective, with scant regard to the costs involved, has resulted in absurdly high levels of overkill as measured by megatonnage, warheads or by the actual number of delivery systems. An understandable emphasis on the need to maintain a high level of military

9

technology has developed into a passionate belief that national security dictates the matching in all circumstances of other countries' weapons systems. The new doctrine of sufficiency appears to have only a semantic difference from the old doctrine of superiority.

The politicians' unceasing role in the defence field should be to question the central assumptions on which defence policy lies, to reduce where possible expenditure and to explore the decision-making process through which any policies will be exercised. Two years as a politician with responsibilities for the British Navy does not entitle me to pose as a military strategist. Yet the vantage point of the British Defence Ministry gives a politician valuable information on world defence issues. I found it fascinating to witness and participate in the day-to-day decision-making process that controls the military complex, particularly since the Royal Navy has the responsibility for maintaining Britain's strategic deterrent.

The actual mechanics of the decision-making process is a crucial area on which the politician inside the defence ministry of any country should concentrate. It is easy to be carried away by the pomp and pageantry of the services, to delve ever deeper into the intricacies of weapons systems and to become fascinated by military discipline and tradition; but for the serious politician these should only ever be fringe activities.

Public attitudes towards defence are strongly influenced by politicians, yet politicians' rhetoric is all too rarely based on reality. Right-wing politicians too frequently exaggerate the military threat; while for left-wing politicians it is easy to focus attention not on the actualities of the arms race but on the so-called measures of disarmament that have been enacted over the last decade. Politicians have been guilty of distracting attention from the unpleasant facts and of making extravagant claims for what have at best been only partial measures of arms control, and unhappily, far too often, purely 'cosmetic' treaties. To put these treaties in their right perspective is emphatically not to argue that the effort in obtaining even this limited agreement has been wasted. The reality behind the various disarmament treaties serves only to underline how important it is to educate world opinion into demanding more effective measures.

In 1959, it was typically the Antarctic which was demilitarized, not the Arctic – the short way round between the Soviet Union and the United States. Similarly, the Sea Bed Treaty, which needs to involve general disarmament of the oceans, only bans fixed weapons on the ocean floor. Far from being a major breakthrough, as it was hailed, it merely signified that the important major powers had already decided that fixed sea-bed bases were too vulnerable to detection and had therefore started to invest in deep-diving, slow-moving platforms designed to launch even larger rockets than Poseidon.

The Latin American nuclear-free zone is an undoubted advance, but again reservations need to be recorded in that none of the countries involved had previously shown evidence of possessing either the inclination or the knowledge to become nuclear powers.

In 1963, the Partial Test Ban Treaty led to a very worthwhile reduction in atmospheric testing and subsequent radioactive pollution, but the French and Chinese governments have ignored the treaty and continued to test. There have also been frequent atmospheric leaks from the continuing underground tests. It is arguable whether this treaty can really be seen as genuine disarmament or as enlightened self-interest on the part of countries who had already done a great deal of atmospheric testing and were prepared to forgo such tests in future only because they had already developed underground testing techniques. In fact there has been an actual increase in the number of nuclear tests since the treaty was signed.

The Outer Space Treaty of 1967 has the effect of banning orbital weapons systems, although the fractional orbital bombardment system (FOBS) of the Soviets since it is not stationed in space is not effectively covered by the treaty. But as yet there are no significant advantages for orbital systems compared with continental ballistic missile systems.

The Non-Proliferation Treaty of 1968, which came into force

on March 5th 1970, potentially could represent a considerable advance and the decision of the West German government to ratify it was an important and hopeful sign. But many potential nuclear powers such as Israel, India, Pakistan, and South Africa have refused to sign or ratify the treaty, and the French and Chinese have once again taken no part in it.

The only major measure of actual disarmament has been the treaty banning the use of biological weapons and the decision not to hold any stocks of such weapons. There has also been some limited progress on drafting a treaty involving chemical weapons but the Soviet Union may well refuse to give up her extensive chemical weapon stocks.

This depressing analysis shows how very limited and extremely partial most of the measures so far negotiated have been. It does the cause of disarmament a disservice to exaggerate their scope or their effectiveness.

The Strategic Arms Limitation Talks (SALT), first proposed by President Johnson in 1964 and which actually began in 1969 in Helsinki, offer the greatest hope for the future; but, once more, an attitude of cautious optimism is all the watching world can reasonably adopt. The politicians have again tended to oversell the limited achievements to date and to boost false hopes for the immediate future. Progress should be possible, but it will be slow and, because the talks are now confined to the United States and the Soviet Union, eventually China, France and Britain will have to be involved. The mood of détente which is now clearly evident on all sides in Europe is the most hopeful development in the whole history of East–West relations since the Iron Curtain fell after the Second World War. Although the events of Hungary and Czechoslovakia still haunt the memory, there are reasonable grounds for believing that the coming decade may show a real improvement in relations. But it would be absurd to believe that such advances can come without difficulties and setbacks. It is vital therefore, that central issues are faced and decisions taken against the background of our actual situation and not the situation that politicians hope may come about. If the present nuclear arms race maintains its momentum, then the likelihood of nuclear weapons being used substantially increases. But nuclear limitation agreement may come only after conventional troop reductions have been negotiated and it may be necessary for the West to make a gesture in the shape of unilateral troop reductions in the hope that self-adjusting balanced force reductions will follow. It will be difficult, and perhaps unwise, to negotiate significant reductions in troop levels and actual reductions in strategic nuclear weapons simultaneously (though this need not apply to tactical nuclear weapons, where a reduction could be offset against a reduction in tank numbers). Realism points to a continuation of the present slow trend towards any meaningful reductions. It is against this background that it becomes increasingly important to develop far better control mechanisms than currently exist to cover all areas of defence decision-making. It is no good waiting for some idealistic solution to present itself. Too many critics of the defence field and advocates of détente and disarmament allow their aspirations for the future to deflect them from serious examination of existing imperfections.

Writers and commentators frequently claim that there is no effective control over the whole military complex, both industrial and strategic. Yet sustained enthusiasm for demanding greater control and subjecting the military to consistent examination comes to the fore only when major military spending programmes are under scrutiny. Only when parliamentarians are confronted by crucial choices on the allocation of financial resources do military activities become a subject for public debate. Even then it is rare for such debates to focus on the all-important control mechanisms. There is a reluctance on the part of most politicians to become involved in what they believe is a specialized area. They are content to leave to the experts, or to a small number of their colleagues, policies which may critically affect the lives of everyone in the world. As a direct consequence of this neglect, major politicians often have a hopelessly inadequate conception of both the limitations and the capacities of military power. History has shown that it is the politicians who regularly undertake commitments incompatible with resources, and who put forward propositions which are at times dangerous as well as irresponsible.

Working within a defence ministry one becomes increasingly aware that the military are reluctant to accept guidance in the detailed process of decision-making. Yet this is the very area which should be the major concern of a politician. The fundamental questions at the root of any effective control system become centrally important when faced by a crisis. To my own shame it was only when faced by a particular incident that I began to question the philosophical basis that underlies military attitudes, postures and policies. One afternoon in the Ministry of Defence, without any warning build-up, I faced the breakdown of a highly sensitive intelligence mission which I had only recently authorized. Suddenly the whole tempo of life changed. A fairly detached, almost routine, outlook was replaced by an acute awareness of how close to the knife edge so much of our military activity has become.

The insidious process of military indoctrination, a heady mixture of pomp and secrecy to which most politicians involved in defence are susceptible, tends to blunt one's normal sensitivity. One can easily become a part of the very military machine that one is supposed to control. In the wake of this incident – the outcome of which was fortunately not serious – I began to question not only the real evidence on which I had agreed to the particular mission, but also how much evidence I had or was ever likely to have on the formulation of the all-important risk evaluation. Political authorization is essential, yet to be effective it has to know the real value of the intelligence information that is likely to come from any particular mission. The touch of drama that accompanies these top secret submissions can lead to one relaxing the discipline of demanding detailed justification. The Intelligence people argue, perfectly legitimately, that they rely on putting together a series of small pieces of information, which individually are of no great importance. For the politician in the midst of this somewhat alien world, authorization means undertaking a difficult assessment, and the temptation not to intervene is immense. Yet in view of the undoubted risks of some of these missions it is worth questioning how long the politicians can continue to rely on a hostile nation responding to incidents in the rational manner that has largely characterized their response in the past. Everyone knows and accepts that spying does go on, and that other nations react to it in a similar way. But the question remains: how long before a combination of accident and ineptness, risk and chance, acts as the trigger for a military response which would threaten the world's very existence?

After living through this and other incidents, with the agonizing personal reappraisal that followed, the moral imperative to voice one's anxieties is too compelling to ignore. One of the central aims of this book is to attempt to eschew generalizations and to bring together specific facts relating to the process of decision-making from a number of military incidents which took place during the 1960s.

The details of the *Pueblo* mission and its authorization are discussed since they reveal the weakness of the whole intelligence procedure in the planning and conduct of a highly sensitive mission. The actual intelligence gain to the Communists from the seizure of the *Pueblo* was a major coup, but no one reading the record of the first few hours, with its demonstration of total lack of any political control, can doubt that the incident might have escalated into a major East–West confrontation.

At the time of the Cuban missile crisis the whole world sensed that civilization was perilously close to the nightmare of self-destruction. It was a time, in Khrushchev's evocative words, 'when the smell of burning hung in the air'. Yet the smell of burning is not just confined to the dramatic headline-catching situation. It hangs threateningly but inscrutably over every military strategy and operation.

The Gulf of Tonkin incident shows how President Johnson and a small group of his closest advisers misled Congress into giving the President blanket authority to wage war in South-East Asia. It also demonstrates how insidiously even in a democracy a government can pass through the thresholds of military escalation unchecked.

The Arab-Israeli war highlights the dangers of escalation inherent in a military situation in which the super-powers are involved but in which they do not control all the key military decisions.

These episodes are described in detail in the belief that, if only the facts surrounding them were more widely known, the present complacency in the Western Alliance surrounding defence decision-making would be shattered. These particular examples all cover the area of crisis management. Crisis decision-making, though the most dramatic, is only one aspect of defence decision-making. All defence decisions have a high political content, but in artificially isolating decisions where the political content and involvement is high, one is able to examine the extent to which politicians' prejudices and personalities affect the eventual decisions. This study has deliberately excluded any detailed examination of the industrial-military complex, because this area has been fairly widely discussed and analysed. The recently revealed Pentagon Papers on the origins of the Vietnam war give a fascinating glimpse into political decision-making. It is important to realize that it is only by analysing actual incidents retrospectively that politicians will learn how to control not just the military but also themselves. It cannot be stressed enough that it is not sufficient for politicians simply to blame their military advisers. The real need is for politicians to examine their own impact on defence decision-making and to improve not only their understanding but also their performance.

Strategic decision-making is studied solely in the context of Western Europe. It has important long-term implications for world security and national expenditure priorities. In Europe, NATO's performance during the 1960s, particularly in developing a coherent policy for nuclear deterrence, has clearly revealed the extreme difficulties of achieving a rational policy within a multinational framework. The sheer waste of resources in human and financial terms that has resulted from France's decision to develop her own independent nuclear deterrent is one striking example. It is vital that France resumes her role as an active member of the Alliance and that her present exclusion from Anglo-American nuclear collaboration is replaced by a freer exchange of information and a move towards joint targeting and an integrated allied command and control system.

The need is not now for bilateral Anglo-French nuclear collaboration, as is so frequently suggested, but trilateral collaboration with the United States.

This book is written not to pillory but to persuade the military — not that all senior officers even need persuading — that it is in their own interest to subject their affairs to greater outside scrutiny. To persuade the politicians that they have a high constitutional duty to examine far more closely than hitherto the fundamental basis of defence policy and the decision-making structure which implements such a policy. Finally, to persuade the citizen that the control of the military is ultimately his responsibility, and that the risks of failing to exercise that responsibility are far greater than he seems to realize.

No one writing with such recent experience of the defence world is a totally free agent. Bound by the provisions of the Official Secrets Act, one is prevented from writing in too great detail of any recent experience, such as the events of August 1968 in Czechoslovakia. The sources for this book are, therefore, published documents, and for the details concerning the Gulf of Tonkin incident and capture of the USS *Pueblo*, the main source is the Congressional Record. This Record documents the findings of the most important public forum in any democratic country which systematically subjects the military to public scrutiny. Yet even Congress does not always break through the barrier of undue secrecy, for it is bound by law and convention to uphold state secrecy. For example the powerful Foreign Affairs Committee chairman, Senator Fulbright, was given the opportunity to publicize the Pentagon Papers well before they were given to the *New York Times*. Despite the all-out opposition to publication from the Nixon Administration, it was important for the Pentagon Papers to be published. At long last, ordinary people can read documents which not only reveal the facts but give an insight into the strange isolated world of defence decisions. In the words of Justice Hugo Black, one of the members of the Supreme Court who made the favourable majority decision to allow publication:

> In the First Amendment, the Founding Fathers gave the free press the protection it must have to fulfil its essential role in our democracy. The press was to serve the governed, not the governors. The government's power to censor the press was abolished so that the press would remain forever free to censure the government. The press was protected so that it would bare the secrets of government and inform the people. Only a free and unrestrained press can effectively expose deception in government.[1]

There are real dangers in governments applying press censorship. President Kennedy later regretted that his Administration had intervened to prevent the publication by the *New York Times* of a story about the planned invasion of Cuba which led to the humiliation at the Bay of Pigs. If publication had gone ahead despite pleas to safeguard the national interest, there can be no doubt that a sufficiently large section of public opinion would have denounced the policy for the folly that it was and that the operation would have been called off. History abounds with similar incidents where secrecy has been a shroud to hide errors and incompetence. In the United States, the facts surrounding military incidents tend to emerge rather quicker than in Britain, where the rule banning all publication of official documents until thirty years have elapsed has only recently been changed from a fifty-year period. The existence of the 'D' notice procedure in Britain and the absurdly out-dated Official Secrets Act combine to make it difficult to obtain information. The extent of Britain's real involvement with troops on the ground in Indonesia, for example, was unreported for years, although the facts were well known to newspapers. Even in the United States, documents dealing with clandestine operations are not de-classified and are not even published under the State Department's twenty-five-year rule for releasing all documents. Yet publication of the Anderson disclosures on the Indo-Pakistan war has eroded legitimate confidentiality.

The United States is almost inevitably the major focus of much of the criticism of this book. This does not stem from any anti-American feeling, for the lessons of these incidents are of universal application and, as the book argues, the Western countries have still much to gain from a genuine reconstruction of the defence partnership with the United States.

Western Europe has still to establish a viable defence posture in relation to nuclear weapons for the 1980s and beyond. Against the background of SALT, Britain has to decide whether to ensure the future viability of her present force of four Polaris submarines. France, now established as a nuclear power, faces similar problems in relation to her four submarines, three of which are now being built and which, when completed, will give her a second-strike nuclear capability. Dominating any discussion of Anglo-French nuclear cooperation is the problem of the two countries' relationship to NATO, of West German attitudes and of the appalling difficulties of unified command and control when dealing with more than one nation. But to develop a rational defence policy for the 1970s one needs to understand and scrutinize the process of defence decision-making as it developed in the 1960s. It is also necessary to judge the likely political developments in Europe. Too often, the noble ideal of European unity has stimulated the projection of wildly optimistic time-scales for the development of a federated state. Even if a federated Europe were desired – and there is little evidence that this is yet the case – its attainment is at least two decades away. The prospect of such a European state becoming a fourth nuclear power is even further away. A Western European deterrent strategy can therefore only be sensibly discussed in terms of the United States, Britain and France as independent nations working within the framework of a defence alliance.

Chapter 2. The Machinery of Defence Decisions

Any objective assessment of the decade from 1960 to 1970 shows that the existing national security machinery of the major powers is gravely defective and that the sophisticated procedures designed to ensure sensible defence decision-making are in urgent need of reform.

The record of events speaks for itself. The Russians risked nuclear war by putting missiles into Cuba and in the process made a serious error of judgment, not only of American resolution, but of their own capability to respond. American military involvement in Vietnam will be judged by history as disastrous. The United States and the Soviet Union have progressively adopted policies which have involved them more deeply in the Middle East, the consequences of which remain to be seen. Repeatedly throughout the decade there have been incidents which show a profound inability among national governments to make realistic assessments of present and future problems. The Americans' endorsement of the invasion of Cuba at the Bay of Pigs, their decision to put troops into Santa Dominica and the British handling of Anguilla are striking examples of the more extravagant follies. Such incidents not only reflect the inadequacy of the existing defence decision-making procedures, but raise questions as to whether experiences like Suez and the Lebanon in the 1950s have had any really profound impact on the way defence decisions are reached.

Defence decisions, at every level, contain the potential for serious escalation. A fact of life that needs to be stated repeatedly, for all its apparent simplicity, is that a small number of men in both Russia and the United States, and to a lesser extent in Britain, France and China, have it in their power to destroy human civilization. The apparatus through which these individuals at present exercise and control that power should be of immense importance to the world. It is not so much the actual trigger mechanism for controlling the forces of thermo-nuclear devastation that needs to be studied as the whole process of decision-making that lies behind such forces.

To state the realities so baldly is not to invoke the prospect of nuclear war lightly. A sensible attitude to these issues can and should be based somewhere between the two poles of 'sabre-rattling' and complacency. As the world lives with nu-clear weapons, so the super-powers seem to grow in maturity. As the nuclear arsenal of the two super-powers has grown, so has their caution. The chances of an irrational act or response are less now than in the past. In the 1950s, for all the absurdities of the then current nuclear strategies, the risk of accidental nuclear war was probably always exaggerated by the critics. Yet the effect of such criticism has been wholly beneficial, for purely technical risks have been markedly reduced. There is still a real need for the greatest vigilance, particularly on the part of the politician in remorselessly challenging and scrutinizing existing procedures for the control of nuclear weapons. The tendency in government is to draw the definition of a 'need to know' too tightly and so deprive all but a very few politicians of access to highly classified information. Only politicians can accept ultimate responsibility for the detailed safety procedures and controls, and yet their tendency is to take such detail too much for granted and to be restrained by the demands of security from probing what is admittedly a very sensitive security area.

A nation's control of its own defence forces is seen throughout the world as a hallmark of a true democracy. National parlia-ments and politicians have over the years shown themselves nominally extremely zealous in upholding their constitutional rights for controlling the military. Yet despite this concern, which is both genuine and well-founded, it is striking how little effective parliamentary machinery exists for controlling or scrutinizing the defence forces of most democratic countries. While the need for public scrutiny of all spheres of government activity is a basic tenet of modern democratic government, the case for particularly vigilant scrutiny of the area of national security is overwhelming.

The defence area in government is necessarily rather diffuse, involving more than the Department of Defence, and is certainly not the preserve of the military. Defence should be the servant of a nation's foreign policy and so the department with responsibility for dealing with external affairs rightly has a crucial formative role in establishing defence policy. This division of responsibility between two departments is only one of the multitude of divisions which characterize defence decision-making. The division between formulation and execution of policy in a field of ever-increasing complexity, is itself almost impossible to achieve. A further division which bedevils the process is that any issue which fundamentally affects national security tends to involve the head of the government. In theory, this involvement is strictly that of the final arbiter, but in practice the head of the government – as has happened most strikingly with the President of the United States over Vietnam – becomes effectively the initiator, controller and even executant of quite detailed defence decisions.

The process of decision-making in government, the inter-departmental influences and rivalries, the impact of politicians, their personalities and capabilities has fascinated academic theorists. Much has been written in many different countries highlighting the machinery of government, its techniques and disciplines in all sectors, not least in defence and foreign affairs. It is not necessary to examine the detailed departmental committee structures to understand the process of defence decision-making. It is nevertheless a fascinating subject. There have been major organizational changes in the American and British military establishment since the Second World War, all aiming in the direction of a greater unification. Yet it is important to realize that almost every evolutionary step towards greater unification has been opposed by the individual services, and in consequence most changes have been critically weakened compromises.

It is necessary, however, to understand that the defence

ministries in the Western Alliance are all organized in a fundamentally different manner to other government departments. There is also evidence that similar organizational differences exist in the Warsaw Pact countries. The major difference is that the serviceman enjoys a power and freedom of action that is never given up by politicians to civilians within the same government machine. It has been accepted over decades that military personnel within defence departments are not even subject to the same decision structure as governs civilians

The reasons for these differences are in part obvious and stem from the disciplined nature of the armed forces. Yet many of the differences are not easily explicable and are rooted in outmoded social attitudes and deep-seated traditions which have been built up over the centuries, but which have little relevance to twentieth-century living.

Differences can be identified at all levels of decision-making, and though these can best be illustrated by reference to the position of the head of individual services, the same pattern can be found throughout the structure. In the United States, the Joint Chiefs of Staff have a statutory role as principal military advisers to the President and Secretary of Defense. The Secretary of Defense does not speak for them on the National Security Council, for they serve that body in their own right and so have direct access to the President. In the Soviet Union, the military are not represented on the eleven-man Politburo where all the important decisions on defence and foreign policy are made. A small inner group of the Politburo controls the nuclear trigger. But the military are represented on the Central Committee. The Supreme or Higher Military Council is composed of Politburo members and senior officers. In the United Kingdom, the Joint Chiefs are not formally members of the Defence and Overseas Policy Committee of the Cabinet. Though they attend all its meetings, they do not take part in discussions on policy. In this forum the Secretary of State for Defence speaks for the Department, but the Service Chiefs have the right to appeal to the Prime Minister above the head of the Secretary of State. Although seldom resorted to, this power has been used at least three times over the last ten years – if to no real effect – on final decisions whether to phase out aircraft carriers or cancel the F-111. Their mere presence at Committee meetings is, however, psychologically an important factor.

No senior civilian official in government service in the United States or the United Kingdom has the same power of access to the head of government, and it would be considered unworkable if it was suggested that this access should be granted.

It could be argued that this access is merely a symbolic power, but the facts show that an equivalent degree of independence is given to servicemen at almost every level. The serviceman retains an alternative command structure in most cases, even when nominally serving in a position under civilian command. It is the exception to find a situation where a serviceman works under a civilian without some form of appeal mechanism which can circumvent the civilian decision structure. In many cases, defence and foreign ministries work closely together, but the divisions which exist between the military and the civilians inside government can impair rational decision-making. For example, the Ministry of Defence was in favour of Britain withdrawing from Aden long before the Foreign Office came round to this view, yet it was the Ministry of Defence that foolishly decided to increase the previously small military presence in the Persian Gulf following the Aden withdrawal. In the United States, the State Department appears to have had a major influence in maintaining a balance in American relations between Egypt and Israel and in curbing the Department of Defense from actually intervening on the side of Israel. These divisions of view are both natural and beneficial and there are dangers when genuine divisions are compromised away at official level and never surface for open discussion at the political level.

A more serious division, however, is that which flourishes between the individual services. Inter-service rivalries still bedevil decision-making procedures, for each service has its own command structures, its own traditions and goals. It is not surprising that, given the intensive one-service training and conditioning in his early service years, a senior officer finds it extremely difficult to see his own service's role as part of a balanced contribution to national defence. This problem becomes particularly relevant in circumstances which demand that he makes a critical assessment of overall defence priorities and of the allocation of resources to his own service.

It is an interesting commentary on the actual working of most defence departments that what evidence there is points to there having been no substantial change over the last two decades in the percentage share of the defence budget allocated between the three main services.

Dissatisfaction with the procedure for making sensible decisions in the area of defence policy has been widespread in both the United States and the United Kingdom since the Second World War. In July 1970, the Blue Ribbon Defense Panel reported to the President of the United States that, 'The President and the Secretary of Defense do not presently have the opportunity to consider all viable options as background for making major decisions, because differences of opinion are submerged or compromised at lower levels of the Department of Defense.'[1] They went on to say that the present arrangements for staffing the military operations activities provide 'a forum for inter-Service conflicts to be injected into the decision-making process for military operations; and it inhibits the flow of information between the combatant commands and the President and the Secretary of Defense, often even in crisis situations'.

Serious criticisms of the American military establishment are not new: they stimulated the 1947 National Security Act and were emphasized in the Hoover Commission's Task Force on the National Security Organization which led to the 1949 Amendments to the National Security Act.

In 1953, further reorganization took place and in 1958 substantial changes in the military organization were reflected in further amendments to the 1947 Act. The 1960s were marked by repeated efforts by both the executive and the legislative branches to strengthen civilian control. In the United States, the Joint Chiefs of Staff give testimony before Congressional committees and traditionally give an annual posture statement on their service. In the course of testimony, clear differences of opinion have emerged between the professional and the political heads of the services, which can produce not only personal tensions but divided loyalties within the department. In the Soviet Union, senior officers appear to have a surprising degree of freedom to criticize policy and this was most marked after Khrushchev's fall from power.

In Britain, the military have no such access to an open forum for dissent, but the military viewpoint is given wide publicity. Whereas in other sectors of governmental activity differences of viewpoint between a department and its political head are rarely revealed, the opposite seems to be the rule in defence departments. In the United Kingdom there have been for many years single-service public relations departments, staffed in part by their own serving officers, inevitably owing their primary allegiance to their service head rather than to their political head. It can be argued that, where the national security is involved, it is right that the public should be aware of differences of opinion, but such a procedure is fundamentally different from that which governs the behaviour of other sectors of government activity. It inevitably leads to tensions between the civilians and the military and the politicians and military. If not restrained, it can lead to far too great an identification and involvement of parts of the military with the industrial lobby. It can and does result in a distortion of sensible defence decision-making, when the public are conditioned to demand greater spending on particular military programmes.

To point out these facts is not to argue against greater public involvement, for there is undoubtedly a need for far greater awareness of why governments spend money on defence. The aim should be to ensure a balanced and well-informed public opinion. Essentially, this is the job of democratic parliamentary institutions which have largely failed to stimulate informed public discussion.

Since the Second World War, the reorganization of the Ministry of Defence in Britain has followed much the same evolutionary path as taken in the United States. The aim in both countries has been to achieve a far greater degree of unification of the three single services. This was highlighted by changes in 1964 abolishing single-service ministries such as the old Admiralty and the War Office to form a Navy Department an Army Department and an Air Force Department as single-service departments within the Ministry of Defence. The position of the political head of a service, such as the First Lord of the Admiralty, or the Secretary for War with a seat in the Cabinet, was progressively eroded, first by the appointment of a coordinating Minister of Defence who sat in the Cabinet, followed by the emergence of the Secretary of State for Defence, answerable for the entire department with junior ministers for the individual services.

In the United Kingdom, as in the United States, the Chiefs of Staff have three main roles. They supervise their individual service, they participate in advising and planning in the nation's defence strategy and they participate by delegation in matters of operational command.

In both countries recent reports have strongly criticized this tripartite role. The Blue Ribbon Defense Panel suggests that the Joint Chiefs should be 'relieved of the necessity of performing delegated duties in the field of military operations and Defense Agency supervision', and goes on to recommend that, to highlight such a change, consideration should be given to changing the title of, for example, Chief of Naval Operations, the present title of the head of the United States Navy, to the Chief of Staff of the Navy. In the United Kingdom, a high-level departmental working party, called the Headquarters Organization Committee, with some outside members drawn from accountancy, industry, and commerce, made somewhat similar criticisms and suggestions for change. In both countries, servicemen's hostility to change is likely to obstruct any reform. They have in the past opposed the abolition of single-service ministries, the development of an integrated defence ministry, greater powers for the chief of the defence staff and almost any dilution of single-service authority. The main criticism from an organizational standpoint of defence decision-making is that the structure in most countries has created too great a reliance on the 'committee'. The Blue Ribbon Defense Panel put the issue squarely when they postulated that 'the basis of such recommendations and advice is mutual accommodation of all Service views, known in some forums as "log rolling", and a submergence and avoidance of significant issues or facets of issues on which accommodations of conflicting service views are not possible.'[2]

In the United Kingdom, the 'committee' nature of the process is heightened by the continued existence of the Admiralty, Army and Air Force Boards,[3] which are supposedly the main focus of decision-making for each service and which are chaired by a politician. Decisions are then formally made not in the name of an individual but in the name of the board for which all members nominally bear collective responsibility. It is an absurd system.

The arguments for fundamental reform eventually persuaded the Canadian government almost in desperation to integrate the three services completely. This revolutionary reform could and probably should have been avoided, for the ends of unification can be achieved while retaining single-service identities and need not involve such drastic measures as imposing the same military uniforms and titles. The problem is to force through any changes against the wishes of the military, for they represent in every country a formidable pressure group that has repulsed the forces of change even when led by such politicians as Winston Churchill and Dwight Eisenhower.

The defence departments in most nations operate to a far greater extent than other departments in a milieu which actively fosters a process of inadequate decision-making. The fragmentation of power and authority, the conflict of loyalties and the division between civilian and military personnel that currently exist are the culture on which the present deficiencies in decision-making thrive.

The events of the 1960s clearly show that the era of East–West crises is not over. Changes must be made in defence departments in all Western countries. It appears that only when confronted by the actual workings of the decision-making procedures in real situations will enough public interest be generated to demand change.

Ever since the Second World War there has been an inevitable movement towards applying the techniques of quantitative analysis to defence decision-making. The development of the computer has opened up the possibility of automatic decision-making at a strategic level as well as the operating of actual weapons systems. There is an urgent need in the whole area of defence policy for the greater use of the powerful techniques of statistical analysis, comprehensive information systems, systems analysis and simulation modelling techniques capable of answering theoretical 'what if' questions in the context of computer-based war games and other simulated situations. Yet there is a danger that the introduction of these techniques will be used merely as a substitute for avoiding the greatest need, which is for fundamental questioning of the overall political and military priorities that determine policy and the control mechanisms that ensure correct application. The United States Defense Department has pioneered many of the latest quantitative aids to decision-making, conscious of some of the deficiencies in the quality of many defence decisions. But the application of these techniques cannot be said to have resulted in a marked improvement in performance. The Soviet Union has also become deeply interested in applying modern management techniques, and the SALT discussions are based to a great extent on the varying interpretation of the latest quantitative assessments. These innovations have immense potential and their application should be welcomed. But they are not, and never can be, a substitute for decision-makers. Furthermore, the basic structure and framework within which these techniques operate has to be closely related to the ideals, aspirations and judgments of the individuals who will use the information that they provide. The greatest weakness of the decision-making revolution that has followed the introduction of the computer is the mistaken belief that the computer is a substitute for vigorous intellectual analysis on the part of people who use its information.

It is dangerous folly to superimpose on a defective decision-making structure techniques which can all too easily give a superficial impression of mathematical certainty. The actual decision-making process has first to be defined, and this means a behavioural analysis of the characteristics of existing and future decisions with an awareness of the human values and judgments that interrelate to form a balanced decision. This problem has been explicitly recognized by McGeorge Bundy, who was a close adviser to President Kennedy and President Johnson on strategic matters. Writing about the background to SALT, he warned:

> There is an enormous gulf between what political leaders really think about nuclear weapons and what is assumed in complex calculations of relative 'advantage' in simulated strategic warfare. Think-tank analysts can set levels of 'acceptable' damage well up in the tens of millions of lives. They can assume that the loss of dozens of great cities is somehow a real choice for sane men. They are in an unreal world. In the real world of real political leaders – whether here or in the Soviet Union – a decision that would bring even one hydrogen bomb on one city of one's own country would be recognized in advance as a catastrophic blunder; ten bombs on ten cities would be a disaster beyond history; and a hundred bombs on a hundred cities are unthinkable. Yet this unthinkable level of human incineration is the least that could be expected by either side in response to any first strike in the next ten years, *no matter what happens to weapons systems in the meantime.* Even the worst case hypothesized in the ABM debate leaves at least this much room for reply. In sane politics, therefore, there is no level of superiority which will make a strategic first strike between the two great states anything but an act of utter folly.[4]

In the crucial areas of strategic policy no responsible politicians should ever be prepared completely to automate the decision process. The advocates of a nuclear deterrent strategy based on a launch-on-warning system are to be found in both the United States and the Soviet Union. It is a matter of fundamental public interest that such advocacy should be rejected. The degree to which many of the present-day military weapons systems are already geared to an automated response mechanism needs to be exposed publicly.

There can be no substitute in this crucial area of human affairs for the judgment of individuals, even though the evidence of history is that the manner in which these judgments are formed and exercised is gravely defective.

Part One Crisis Decision-Making

Chapter 3. The Cuban Missile Crisis

The Cuban missile crisis demonstrated clearly – even to the reluctant dreamers of the Western Alliance – the harsh realities of the new super-power structure which had become increasingly apparent ever since the end of the Second World War. President Kennedy's opening words in his broadcast to the American people on October 22nd, 1962 – 'Good evening, my fellow citizens' – had a meaning for many more people listening throughout the world. Suddenly, the personality, character and judgment of the President of the United States was as important for the people of Paris, London and Bonn as for their counterparts in New York, Washington and San Francisco.

Yet the crisis was not a sudden, unpredictable event. It had been building up slowly ever since Fidel Castro came to power in Cuba in 1959, after overthrowing the corrupt and largely American-backed Batista regime. From the outset, the United States administration had overreacted to Fidel Castro's revolutionary Marxism. Finally, on July 6th, 1960, a year and a half after Castro had come to power, the United States took reprisal actions against Cuba. President Eisenhower initially ordered an embargo on sugar and this was followed by an oil embargo, which was successfully countered by a Russian supply of oil. In April 1961, the newly elected President Kennedy was humiliatingly implicated in the Bay of Pigs fiasco, where an attempt at invasion, clandestinely sponsored by the United States government, was routed. The cumulative effect of all these policies was only to strengthen Castro's military power and political control, and to heighten Russian influence. In the United States, where Cuba was an intensely emotional issue, militant Senators constantly called for direct armed intervention. Both Nixon and Kennedy had taken a tough line on Cuba in the presidential elections, and most Democratic and Republican politicians were deeply committed

35

to a whole series of attitudes and policies incomprehensible to most Europeans who saw no reason why trade should not continue between Cuba and themselves.

It is important to analyse America's domestic political situation in the autumn of 1962. President Kennedy's legislative record had been extremely disappointing, both the Senate and the House of Representatives were hostile to most of the policies of the Administration, and mid-term elections were coming in November. The whole subject of missiles was also very sensitive. As a Senator, Kennedy had campaigned on the issue of a 'missile gap' which he alleged had been allowed to develop under the Eisenhower Administration. On becoming President by an extremely narrow margin, Kennedy soon discovered that his allegations had been totally wrong, and that he had allowed himself to be misled by the propaganda of the Air Force and the military industrial complex. The true situation was completely the reverse. The United States had an overwhelming superiority over the Russians in practically every parameter of missile comparison. Yet even two years later it was still politically difficult to admit the real position. So, in September 1962, an oppressively image-conscious Administration found itself confronting a new Cuban situation with memories of its earlier humiliation, and bound to a mythical missile gap. In retrospect, it is really remarkable how little this past history affected the ultimate decision-making, and how realistic most of the crucial decisions were.

On March 22nd, 1962, the question was first raised in the House of Representatives as to whether Russia was building missile bases in Cuba. The official view was, and remained, that this was not a likely Russian intention. On September 4th, President Kennedy discussed in some detail the anti-aircraft defence missiles with a range of twenty-five miles that were known to exist in Cuba, and this speech was widely reported as being confirmation of the defensive weapons systems but specifically excluding the possibility of a build-up of an offensive military capability by the Russians. At this time, however, there were informed reports that certain Washington strategists were not too sure of Russian intentions, and saw the arms build-up in Cuba as the first step towards the eventual construction of intermediate-range ballistic missile emplacements. It was felt that the defensive missiles were there to prevent photographic aerial reconnaissance, by having the ability to shoot down overflying aircraft, and that when this intelligence avenue was closed to the United States, the Russians would be able to build missile sites without being discovered. Comment was also made on the growing number of Soviet ships sailing into Cuban ports.[1] The Administration continued to deny that there was any serious danger, and George Ball, the Under Secretary of State, told the Select Committee on Export Control on October 3rd that the build-up 'does not constitute a threat to the United States'.[2] Yet, on October 4th, the Administration introduced measures to tighten up the economic blockade, and to put pressure on those countries which continued to trade with Cuba. American ports were to be closed to all ships of any nation that permitted its vessels to carry military equipment and who, on a non-continuous run, carried any non-military Communist cargoes to Cuba. It also excluded foreign ship-owners whose vessels were engaged in trade between Cuba and the Soviet bloc from carrying American government-financed cargoes on any of their ships.

The real mystery is why the missile sites were not discovered sooner than the night of October 15th. Robert Kennedy stated that, 'No official within the government had ever suggested to President Kennedy that the Russian build-up in Cuba would include missiles,' and said that the United States Intelligence Board had advised on September 19th, without reservation, 'that the Soviet Union would not make Cuba a strategic base'.[3] We now know that there were earlier reports from within Cuba about the delivery of larger missiles than the surface-to-air missiles already known to be present, and that people in Washington were becoming highly suspicious. The Deputy Secretary for Defense, Roswell Gilpatric, has said that he does not think we will ever know the exact sequence of events during those six weeks from the end of August, when photographs showed no missiles, until the middle of October. Clearly, the failure to obtain aerial photographs of one major portion of Cuba for a whole month was a quite extraordinary omission which owes much to the basic American misjudgment of Soviet intentions.

The time from the moment the missile sites were discovered to the President's broadcast to the nation has been well chronicled by Elie Abel,[4] Robert Kennedy and numerous American journalists, whose main concern has been the various positions adopted by the individuals in the group which later took the formal title of Executive Committee of the National Security Council. To the outside world, and particularly to those who have served in government, these titbits of information have a macabre fascination, as it becomes increasingly and horrifyingly obvious that decision-making at this superior level is beset by the same passions and jealousies with which one is all too familiar in everyday life.

The key facts are not now in dispute. There were only two courses of action seriously contemplated; one was bombing by a 'surgical strike' against the missile bases in Cuba and the other, some form of naval blockade. In the words of President Kennedy:

> During that period, the 15 people more or less who were directly consulted frequently changed their view, because whatever action we took had so many disadvantages to it, and each action we took raised the prospect that it might escalate with the Soviet Union into a nuclear war. Finally, however, I think a general consensus developed, and it certainly seemed after all alternatives were examined, that the course of action that we finally adopted was the right one.[5]

The key decision made by the President was to use sea-power as the military response most appropriate in the circumstances. The sea, it was felt, would be the least provocative and the most flexible medium in which to exercise the considerable military power of the United States. It was particularly effective in this area close to American naval ports and far away from any concentration of Russian naval forces. Initially it was decided to intercept all ships within 800 miles of the Cuban coastline. This limit was later reduced to 500 miles by the President on the suggestion of his friend David Ormsby-Gore, now Lord Harlech, who was then the British Ambassador to the United States. This concession, which was opposed by the Navy, reflected the President's genuine desire to give the Russians as much time as possible to withdraw.

The proclamation formally establishing the quarantine was signed by the President on October 23rd. It was decided not to halt the supply of oil, petrol, foodstuffs and other materials necessary for a normal civilian life in Cuba. The actual wording of the proclamation read:

Any vessel or craft which may be proceeding towards Cuba may be intercepted and may be directed to identify itself, its cargo, equipment, and stores and its ports of call, to stop, to lie to, to submit to visit and search, or to proceed as directed. Any vessel or craft which fails or refuses to respond or comply with directions shall be subject to being taken into custody.

Any vessel or craft which it is believed is *en route* to Cuba and may be carrying prohibited material or may itself constitute such material shall, wherever possible, be directed to proceed to another destination of its own choice and shall be taken into custody if it fails or refuses to obey such directions. All vessels or craft taken into custody shall be sent into a port of the United States for appropriate disposition.

In carrying out this order, force shall not be used except in case of failure or refusal to comply with directions, or with regulations or directives of the Secretary of Defense issued hereunder, after reasonable efforts have been made to communicate them to the vessel or craft, or in case of self-defense. In any case, force shall be used only to the extent necessary.[6]

Prohibited material was defined as surface-to-surface missiles; bomber aircraft; bombs; air-to-surface rockets and guided missiles; warheads for any of the weapons; mechanical or electronic equipment to support or operate any of these items.

On the evening of October 23rd, Defense Secretary McNamara said that about twenty-five Soviet cargo ships were moving towards Cuba and that armed boarding parties would be ready to search them. At this time the complete photographic evidence was released, showing medium-range ballistic missiles sites whose missiles were thought to have a potential range of 1,100 miles.

It was felt unlikely that a sustained airlift involving the transport of ballistic missiles could be carried out between the Soviet Union and Cuba, whether non-stop or involving intermediate staging points, mainly because of the absence of suitable large aircraft. Nevertheless, the United States requested Jamaica, Trinidad, Guinea and Senegal to deny landing rights to Soviet planes bound for Cuba. Not surprisingly, the Russian news agency Tass described the American action as a provocative move and said that, 'Peace-loving states cannot but protest against these piratical actions declared by the United States President with regard to the ships heading towards Cuba's shores and against control over ships of sovereign states on the high seas.'[7] While the United Nations Security Council met there was some discussion, particularly amongst other Western maritime nations, as to the legality of the imposed quarantine. The ultimate question was posed by a journalist who asked an American Defense Department official, 'Are you prepared to sink Soviet ships?'[8] When given the straight reply 'Yes', it was not only the journalist who began to wonder what could happen next.

U Thant, the United Nations Secretary-General, in an attempt to avoid just such an eventuality, sent identical letters to Khrushchev and Kennedy urging an end to the blockade and the avoidance of shipments for two to three weeks. Intervention by the United Nations was urged by many people, probably without any expectation that in this particular confrontation the United Nations would have much chance to act as go-between, since the super-powers were already dealing directly with each other. Strictly speaking, the United States had acted in contravention of the United Nations Charter by failing to submit notice of a threat to peace to the Security Council before taking action.

On October 25th, the Russian ship *Bucharest* was intercepted at sea. She declared that she was carrying petroleum and was allowed to proceed. At about the same time Adlai Stevenson was challenging the Russian Ambassador Zorin in the Security Council, who had refused to answer his questions on the missile sites. He was prepared, he said, to wait for his answer 'until hell freezes over'.[9] Continual reports on the positions of the Russian ships steadily approaching Cuba intensified the situation. On Friday 28th, a Panamanian vessel under Soviet charter, the *Marucla*, was boarded and then allowed to proceed.

Throughout this period a series of strange contacts was established and messages passed between Russia and the United States using unconventional intermediaries. The press was also used as an agent of communication between the governments.

In a letter replying to U Thant, Khrushchev said that he had ordered the masters of Soviet vessels bound for Cuba, but not yet within the area of the American warships' piratical activities to stay out of the interception area, but he emphasized that this was a purely temporary order.[10] Meanwhile, the Americans continued to provide evidence from surveillance flights that the building of the ballistic missile sites was going on at a rapid pace.

President Kennedy had already sent Khrushchev a private letter warning him of the hazards to world peace and to the safety of the Soviet Union itself. In reply, Kennedy received a long private letter in which Khrushchev talked of the horrors of the last war and said that Russia would remove the missiles if the United States lifted its quarantine and promised not to invade Cuba. While the Americans were still deciding on their response to this letter, a second, far less hopeful message was received from Khrushchev and publicized. President Kennedy wisely decided to ignore the second public letter and replied instead to the first private letter, stressing that work must cease on the sites and that bases must be made inoperable; if this was done, the United States would then remove the quarantine and promise not to invade Cuba. On October 28th, Khrushchev sent his reply agreeing to dismantle the arms and to crate and return them to the Soviet Union. At the same time, he complained of violation of Soviet airspace by an American plane, and of violations of Cuban airspace where an American plane had already been shot down. Kennedy replied immediately, taking his previous letter, and Khrushchev's reply, as firm undertakings on the part of both governments which should promptly be carried out. He explained that the aircraft which had violated Soviet airspace was on an air-sampling mission, and had made a serious navigational error. It has still never been satisfactorily explained how, at a period of the highest tension, any such mission could have been risked, and whether or not the plane was on an essential overflying mission of surveillance.

The crisis was over. But the settlement dragged on. Castro, angered by negotiations which virtually ignored the Cubans laid down his own terms on October 28th. He demanded the end of the economic blockade, of subversive activities, pirate attacks, violations of air- and naval space – and withdrawal from the Guantanamo base in Cuba, to which the United States had treaty rights for an indefinite period. He also refused to have American observers on his territory.

The Russian withdrawal, in the event, was slower than expected. On November 2nd, President Kennedy announced that the missile bases were being broken up, but that the United States would continue air surveillance until a satisfactory international means of verification was in operation. He said that the International Red Cross would be an 'appropriate agent'[11] for this purpose. On November 9th, the United States fleet off Cuba was reinforced because of Soviet delays. Then, on November 20th, Kennedy lifted the blockade after Khrushchev had given his pledge to remove the missiles in thirty days.

Castro, who had previously objected to their withdrawal, now agreed.

Even today, looking back on the Cuban missile crisis, it is hard to be sure of Russian motives and to what extent the sending of missiles to Cuba had been a deliberate plan. The official Russian explanation by Tass was that the action was simply defensive. They claimed that it had been envisaged in the joint Soviet-Cuban communiqué of September 3rd, as a result of the Cuban mission to Russia. That communiqué had said that the arms and military equipment were designed exclusively for defensive purposes. Soviet assistance in strengthening the defences of Cuba, it was argued, had been necessitated by the fact that the Cuban Republic, since its very inception, had been subjected to continuous threats and provocations from the United States. The United States, the Russians alleged, would baulk at nothing, including organization of armed intervention in Cuba, as in April 1961, to deprive the Cuban people of the freedom and independence they had gained, and to place them again under the domination of American monopolies and make Cuba a United States puppet.[12]

The Russians also claimed that they did not need a base. 'Our nuclear weapons are so powerful in their explosive force, and the Soviet Union has such powerful rockets to carry these nuclear warheads, that there is no need to search for sites for them beyond the boundaries of the Soviet Union,' alleged the *Soviet News*.

The Soviet Union, it claimed, would continue to help any 'peace loving state' that requested aid, but

How are the preparations for aggression against Cuba being justified? By saying that the Soviet merchant ships carry cargoes to Cuba, and the United States considers them to be military cargoes. But this is a purely internal matter of the states which send these cargoes and those which buy and receive them.

The whole world knows that the United States of America has ringed the Soviet Union and other socialist countries with bases.[13]

It was never established that the Russians *had* sent nuclear arms to Cuba and certainly, in view of the increasing Chinese influence there, the Russians might have been understandably reluctant to send nuclear warheads. Nor has it ever been explained why the Russians did not take more trouble to hide the building of the missile sites. They should have expected an American reaction far earlier than they eventually received it, for it is doubtful if the Russians had the low opinion of American surveillance activity that ensuing events might have justified. On this basis, some people have postulated that the whole operation was a deliberately provocative action to test American reactions in the tentative hope that the missiles might remain once established and thereby strengthen the Russians' image in South America.

The idea that the Russians were using the situation to persuade the Americans to remove their missile bases in Turkey does not stand serious examination. Turkish missiles were on known sites and effectively neutralized by the targeting of missiles in Russia. The missiles in Turkey were known to be out of date and President Kennedy had previously given specific instructions that they were to be removed. The Cuban crisis only served to uncover their presence and to demonstrate that even a direct order by a President can fail to be implemented by the government machine.

It was postulated at the time that the Soviet Union was attempting to use Cuba as a bargaining position to force negotiation over the status of Berlin, but this is unlikely.

The most persuasive explanation of Russian intentions centres on the known attitudes and personality of Khrushchev. He had for some years fought off vigorous claims by Soviet military commanders for increased defence expenditure. He had relied on a policy of minimum deterrence and had rejected the demands for matching every single American missile and warhead. He believed that war with the United States was extremely unlikely, but that if it came it would lead to catastrophic nuclear devastation and that all the Soviet Union needed was to pose a viable prospect of being able to devastate a large portion of the American population, hence a targeting strategy aimed at cities not at missile sites. But by 1962, Khrushchev's strategy was in danger of being undermined by constant criticism and he badly needed to achieve a military success. Typically, he gambled. By putting the missiles into Cuba he hoped that, for the minimum of cost and effort, he might obtain maximum military and diplomatic effect, silence his critics inside the Kremlin and strengthen his position. To some extent, the gamble had been forced on him by President Kennedy's own indefensible decision to speed up American missile deployment, despite knowing full well that his much trumpeted election allegations of a 'missile gap' were totally false.

Khrushchev's choice of Cuba, so close to the United States and already an intensively sensitive political area, was a flagrant case of overbidding. The gamble failed. But when Khrushchev had his cards called he revealed in the manner of his withdrawal the shrewd, hard-headed realism that lay behind the bombastic image.

In retrospect, one of the most interesting aspects of the crisis was how successful the quarantine operation proved to be. President Kennedy said that the quarantine 'had much more power than we first thought it did, because I think the Soviet Union was very reluctant to have us stop ships which carried with them a good deal of their highly secret and sensitive material'.[14]

At this time the Russian Navy, though it had been steadily expanding since 1947, had still not appeared in force outside Russian waters, and was not yet the obvious world maritime power that it was to become by the end of the 1960s. The United States naval forces were able in this case to operate within a short distance of their home ports, and force could be applied subtly, steadily and with a degree of central control and discrimination that would have been difficult to achieve elsewhere.

The legality of the quarantine has frequently been challenged and Khrushchev, not unnaturally, referred to it as an act of piracy. In international law, a naval blockade which interferes with traffic on the high seas between the world at large and a specific state is only a belligerent right. It is, in effect, an operation of war, and as such relies for its validity on a state of war existing between states. It was because of this interpretation that the United States never mentioned 'blockade' and in all official pronouncements kept strictly to 'quarantine'. In the past, the term 'pacific blockade' had been used to describe a form of blockade short of a state of war, but the occasions on which this term had been used – most recently Greece in 1916 – offered no direct comparison to the Cuban situation.

The American quarantine was specifically directed against third-country shipping, which was suspected of carrying cargoes that might add to the offensive capability of Cuba. The difficulty of proving that a weapon is offensive or defensive prior to its use is obvious, especially at a time when defence strategy is mainly based on deterrence. The claim by some commentators in the United States that only the surface-to-air missiles on Cuba could be termed 'defensive', and that missiles with a range such as to reach other states were automatically offensive, is much too simplistic an argument to sustain. It would certainly have been impossible for the United States, with their own missile sites in Turkey, to argue this case at the United Nations. Arguing from the Cuban point of view, the so-called 'offensive' missiles could be just as fairly termed defensive, and in the light of the American involvement in the 1961 invasion it is not hard to see why the Cuban government wanted some form of missile capability. Having them Russian-manned would simply make even the more hawkish American advisers hesitate before recommending a further military action.

It has been argued that the quarantine did not fall into the category of 'use of force' but was instead 'preventive force' in keeping with Article 2 (4) of the United Nations Charter, and that it could be regarded as consistent with the peaceful means of settling disputes envisaged by the Charter, which does provide for the collective use of military and economic sanctions. Though it did not report the missiles to the Security Council prior to enforcing the quarantine, the United States did use the regional security arrangements which are recognized under Article 51 of the Charter as being in harmony with collective security as a supplement to the United Nations. The Organization of American States, acting in accordance with the 1947 Rio Treaty, met and passed without dissent a resolution recommending member states to take all measures, including the use of armed force, to ensure that the government of Cuba could no longer receive military material and related supplies from the Sino-Soviet powers.

It is clearly within the principles of the United Nations Charter for the Organization of American States to take peaceful measures to maintain peace and security within its own region. The United States naval quarantine was, therefore, a collective action which did not involve a declaration of belligerency, and did not interfere with normal commercial maritime traffic. Given the limitations of Security Council actions – with the power of the veto ever-present – it can be argued with some justification that the United States did everything possible to remain within the principles of the Charter.

After the crisis was over, and the initial feelings of relief had subsided, the questions began. What was the quality of the advice available to the President? How much control could he exert over the military in the United States? Robert Kennedy has written of his brother's distress that the military representatives he met, with the exception of General Maxwell Taylor,

seemed to give so little consideration to the implications of steps they suggested. They seemed always to assume that the Russians and the Cubans would not respond or, if they did, that a war was in our national interest. One of the Joint Chiefs of Staff once said to me that he believed in a preventative attack against the Soviet Union. On that fateful Sunday morning, when the Russians answered that they were withdrawing their missiles it was suggested by one high military adviser that we attack Monday in any case.

Robert Kennedy had also said that 'if our deliberations had been publicised, if we had had to make a decision in twenty-four hours, I believe the course that we ultimately would have taken would have been quite different and filled with far greater risks'.[15] In the various revelations about the position of the individual advisers to the President, the most striking and probably the most important in terms of influencing the discussions – and subsequently the President – was Robert McNamara, the Secretary of Defense. Here was the political head of the military, consistently arguing against his own top military advisers that a surgical air strike was militarily impractical and also seeking to challenge the view that a missile base in Cuba was very different from one in Russia. He even went so far as to attack the argument that a Cuban missile base would upset the strategic balance between the Soviet Union and the United States, dismissing the loss of a few minutes' warning time of a pre-emptive strike as being of little real consequence, particularly bearing in mind the increasing presence of Soviet missile-carrying submarines only some few miles outside American territorial waters. Unfortunately, it is all too rare for a Secretary of Defense to take up such a position, because of the continual pressures to go along with and support all military advice. Some idea of the personal animosities that the Defense Secretary's position involved can be gathered from Elie Abel's account of McNamara's stormy meeting with Admiral Anderson, Chief of Naval Operations, which also gives an insight into how resentful some of the military are at having to explain themselves to their political masters.[16]

It is now quite clear that McNamara's assessment of the military significance of such a missile base was correct. To argue from this that the Administration should therefore have done nothing is to ignore the real political consequences – not just the approaching November mid-term elections and possible tarnishing of the Kennedy image. A failure to react would have had serious repercussions, within the NATO Alliance, raising doubts about the United States' will to stand by the allied position over Berlin, and allowing the Russians to adopt a more aggressive stance unopposed. The Berlin crisis of 1960–61 was still in 1962 marked by incidents in the land and air corridors to the city. It is easy to belittle the argument of prestige, but the prestige of nations can be an important issue. At the time of the Bay of Pigs Kennedy had shown glimpses of real statesmanship, for while his advisers worried about the political consequences he courageously took sole responsibility for the decision, realizing that the damage to his reputation and standing would be short-lived. The introduction of the missile base was, he correctly judged, an issue of a quite different dimension. This was not just a case when failure to act would lead to national humiliation, but was, in his own words, 'a deliberately provocative and unjustified change in the *status quo* which cannot be accepted by this country, if our courage and our commitments are ever to be trusted again by either friend or foe'.[17]

The possibility of negotiating a face-saving settlement involving the withdrawal of the two American missile bases on the Turkey–Russia border in exchange for a Russian withdrawal from Cuba was actively canvassed by Adlai Stevenson and called for in the second Russian letter. But this would never have been seen as an equal settlement politically, for in this case the Russians had clearly taken the initiative, and would have been seen to have negotiated something of importance on the basis of threat. The effects of allowing such a precedent to be established might have been felt from Formosa to Berlin. The greatest concession Russia could have reasonably expected was the one they eventually obtained, namely the open American pledge not to invade Cuba; and one should not underestimate the value of this pledge to Russia. They knew not only that such an invasion was a real possibility, but that if it had taken place they would have been militarily powerless to intervene; like the West over Hungary, and later over Czechoslovakia, they would have had to stand helplessly by. President Kennedy again showed statesmanship by not gloating over his triumph and by allowing Khrushchev to withdraw without public humiliation.

The major error in the handling of the crisis by the United States Administration was their quite reckless dramatization of the issue. During the early days they did seriously consider making private diplomatic representations to the Russians. They seemed to accept from October 18th, however, that the only way of playing the crisis was to put it on the world stage, to make known to the world and to the Russians simultaneously that they knew about the missile sites, and to conduct all the subsequent negotiations on the basis of a public Russian withdrawal. President Kennedy never disclosed his knowledge when the Soviet Foreign Minister Gromyko visited him in the White House on Thursday October 18th; he never used the possibility of instant communication to Khrushchev. To negotiate by public ultimatum in the era of nuclear warfare was an act of recklessness for which neither President Kennedy nor his friends have ever even attempted to give any explanation. In a decade which had seen the emergence of the summit conference, with the personal meeting as its very raison d'être, in an atmosphere where Khrushchev was able to write the personal letters he did, and where Ambassador Dobrynin had a quite intimate personal relationship with Robert Kennedy, the Attorney General, it is all the more extraordinary that diplomacy should have been suspended. Once the President had decided on his eventual course of action — even if it had been decided only a few hours before his announcement to the world — he should have given Khrushchev the chance to withdraw quickly and quietly.

In fact, Robert Kennedy has revealed that the quarantine decision was taken on Saturday, October 20th, two days before the President's broadcast. Relief at the successful outcome of the crisis, personal grief at the assassination of President Kennedy, and the false magic of the 'Camelot' public relations operation combined to produce the impression of a crisis handled with unparalleled skill by a group of brilliant men headed by a statesmanlike President. The truth is harsher, but the men involved emerge in some respects all the stronger for that. The world came very close to the brink during those few days. We do ourselves and the real record of President Kennedy a grave disservice by failing to analyse as objectively as possible the decision-making process that made us all horrifyingly aware of the risks of nuclear war.

Robert Kennedy, in an interview given two days before his assassination, gave his own account:

> The fourteen people involved were very significant, bright, able, dedicated people, all of whom had the greatest affection for the United States – probably the brightest kind of group that you could get together under those circumstances. If six of them had been President of the United States, I think the world might have been blown up.

It is a truism that it is in the interests of the world that people with the attitudes represented by those six should not become President of the United States, Premier of the Soviet Union or Chairman of the People's Republic of China.

Chapter 4. The Gulf of Tonkin Incident

The Gulf of Tonkin incident in August 1964 is important to any current assessment of defence strategy, not just because it gave rise to the famous wide-ranging Congressional resolution of August 7th, 1964, but because it raises fundamental questions as to how one of the world's great powers made what its own Administration acknowledged was the 'functional equivalent' of a declaration of war. The resolution was itself frequently cited by President Johnson as his authority from Congress to conduct war operations against North Vietnam, and though on August 5th, appearing before the Security Council of the United Nations, Adlai Stevenson declared that American reprisals were 'limited in intention', few people would deny that the decision to continue escalation of the war into North Vietnam territory stemmed from the Tonkin incident. The resolution itself is worth quoting in full, for it was passed unanimously in the House of Representatives and with only two dissenting voices in the Senate, those of Senators Morse and Gruening.

> Whereas naval units of the Communist regime in Vietnam, in violation of the principles of the Charter of the United Nations and of international law, have deliberately and repeatedly attacked United States naval vessels lawfully present in international waters, and have thereby created a serious threat to international peace; and
>
> Whereas these attacks are part of a deliberate and systematic campaign of aggression that the Communist regime in North Vietnam has been waging against its neighbours and the nations joined with them in the collective defense of their freedom; and
>
> Whereas the United States is assisting the peoples of southeast Asia to protect their freedom and has no territorial, military, or political ambitions in that area, but

desires only that these peoples should be left in peace to work out their destinies in their own way; Now, therefore, be it

Resolved by the Senate and the House of Representatives of the United States of America in Congress assembled. That the Congress approves and supports the determination of the President, as Commander in Chief, to take all necessary measures to repel any armed attacks against the forces of the United States and to prevent further aggression.

SEC 2. The United States regards as vital to its national interest and to world peace the maintenance of international peace and security in southeast Asia. Consonant with the Constitution of the United States and the Charter of the United Nations and in accordance with its obligations under the Southeast Asia Collective Defense Treaty, the United States is, therefore, prepared, as the President determines, to take all necessary steps, including the use of armed force, to assist any member or protocol state of the Southeast Asia Collective Defense Treaty requesting assistance in defense of its freedom.

SEC 3. This resolution shall expire when the President shall determine that the peace and security of the area is reasonably assured by international conditions created by action of the United Nations or otherwise, except that it may be terminated earlier by concurrent resolution of the Congress.[1]

It was not terminated until January 12th, 1971, when President Nixon signed an Act formally repealing the resolution which had given virtually unlimited authority to an American President to intervene in South-East Asia for six years.

The facts on which the Senate decided to pass the resolution are still hotly disputed, not least by Senator Fulbright, who played such a crucial role in persuading his fellow-Senators to pass it. He now believes that he was misled by the Administration into believing the hurried initial presentations that this was a deliberate and unprovoked attack on American ships on the high seas.

Clearly, the matter was not as straightforward as it at first seemed, and even from the start there was doubt whether the North Vietnamese had attacked the destroyers *Maddox* and *Turner C. Joy*, on August 4th.

Senator Fulbright's initial account to Congress was, however, quite straightforward:

> ... On August 2 the United States destroyer *Maddox* was attacked without provocation by North Vietnamese torpedo boats in international waters in the Gulf of Tonkin. The American vessel, with the support of aircraft from the USS *Ticonderoga*, fired back in self-defense and drove off the attackers. The United States thereupon warned the Hanoi regime of 'grave consequences' in the event of further military attacks on American forces. On August 4 the *Maddox* and another destroyer, the *Turner C. Joy*, were again attacked by North Vietnamese torpedo boats in international waters. The attack which lasted for over two hours was without any doubt a calculated act of military aggression. The United States thereupon responded with air strikes against North Vietnamese torpedo boats and their supporting facilities at various points on the coast of North Vietnam.[2]

This account from an experienced Senator, with the benefit of a full and comprehensive briefing from the Administration, was bound to carry very considerable weight with his fellow-Senators. Yet even given this account it is arguable whether the incident was really sufficient to justify Congress giving the President such wide-ranging powers.

Many people have argued that the Administration was at the time desperately searching for a pretext for escalation of the war into North Vietnam, and it was alleged that President Johnson and his aides had been carrying around copies of the resolution supporting any action he might take for some weeks. The detailed Pentagon study published in the *New York Times* on Sunday June 12th, 1971,[3] reveals that a Congressional resolution was discussed in the State Department in mid-

February 1964 and prepared on May 25th. This only confirms the suspicions of Congressional dissenters who had at the time alleged that the Tonkin Gulf incident was merely the pretext which the Administration used to push a ready-made resolution through a compliant Congress.

It is necessary to study the overall political background in the summer of 1964 to form a judgment of the prevailing climate. Appeals in July by President de Gaulle, Secretary-General U Thant and even from North Vietnam for the reconvening of the Geneva Conference had been summarily dismissed in both Washington and Saigon. Lyndon Johnson, in a presidential election year, was clearly wary of taking a posture which might support the Republican charge that he was 'soft on Communists'. Meanwhile the faltering regime in South Vietnam was clamouring for a step-up of the war. General Khanh led a mass meeting with a shout of 'To the North' and made a speech urging this very policy, no doubt in the hope of reducing Communist pressure in the South. All these events could not but influence the United States Administration, which had for some time been under pressure from their military advisers to hit back into North Vietnam. On March 17th, 1964, President Johnson authorized the military to plan for retaliatory air strikes on seventy-two hours' notice and for full-scale air-raids on the North on thirty days' notice.[4]

The Gulf of Tonkin incident, as the world now knows, was no more than an extenuating circumstance which enabled the President to obscure the real significance and ease the shock for the benefit of American public opinion of carrying the war into North Vietnam.

This was thought to be especially important in pre-election time. However, the bombing did not help General Khanh. Public disapproval, culminating in a series of student demonstrations in Saigon, Hue and other cities, soon forced him to step down. It is worth noting not only that the CIA had frequently challenged the domino theory as applied to the possible fall of South Vietnam, but that it had also advised that the bombing of North Vietnam would not cause Hanoi to stop supporting the insurgency in the South. Yet the Joint Chiefs of Staff and the politicians ignored this advice.

It is an interesting fact that, all along, Hanoi has never denied the first attack on the *Maddox* on August 2nd. It was, they said, a reprisal for the amphibious raid on the North Vietnamese islands that had taken place on July 30th, which we know now was part of a series of clandestine operations carried out by the South Vietnamese but under the control of the United States Military Assistance Command. It is also clear that North Vietnam, who observed a twelve-mile limit, felt that they were provoked by the sailing of American naval ships in what they considered to be their territorial waters. The United States, who observe a three-mile limit, claimed they were 'lawfully present in international waters'[5] and this key question was raised by Senator Morse in the Tonkin Gulf debate, alleging that the United States government knew that the matter of national and international waters was a controversial issue in Tonkin Bay, and that the United States also knew that the South Vietnamese vessels planned to bomb, and did bomb, two North Vietnamese islands within three to six miles of the coast of North Vietnam. In view of this, he asked why vessels of the United States were in the vicinity of that bombing.[6] This was the key question and we know now that the destroyer patrols in the Gulf of Tonkin (code-named De Soto patrols) were part of the covert military pressures against North Vietnam that had been taking place with the full knowledge of the President and his advisers.

Senator Fulbright, not knowing the real situation, explained at the time that three miles was the established limit the United States recognized, and that one of the reasons for sending the *Maddox* in closer than twelve miles from the shore after August 2nd was to demonstrate that the United States did not recognize the twelve-mile limit.[7] It is clear that, since the ships were involved in electronic intelligence-gathering related to future raiding parties, they had to sail in as close as possible to the shore in order to pick up the messages, or to test the enemy radar. The Pentagon study denies deliberate provocation, but the *Maddox* should not have been collecting such intelligence at such a time and in such a place if provocation was not intended. It is undeniable that, in the patrolling operations, American destroyers in Tonkin Bay had patrolled within eleven miles and not less than three miles off the coast of North Vietnam, and that North Vietnam claimed that her territorial waters went out twelve miles – a claim by no means unique in the world.

Senator Morse said in the debate that, though he thought the United States had the international right to patrol within the twelve-mile limit, such patrolling 'ought to be done with discretion'.[8]

On September 1st, 1964, North Vietnam issued a statement giving her own views on territorial waters, saying that the question of defining the breadth of the territorial waters was strictly within the sovereignty of each country. The United States government, they claimed, had absolutely no right to decide the breadth of the territorial waters of the Democratic Republic of Vietnam (DRV). The government of the Democratic Republic of Vietnam declared that the question of defining the breadth of its territorial waters as twelve miles was in accordance with the laws of the country, within its sovereign rights and in keeping with international juridical custom. They angrily denounced a speech by the American Under Secretary of Defense as being obviously intended to justify the repeated intrusions into the territorial waters of the DRV by the destroyer *Maddox* and other war vessels since July 31st, 1964, and to corroborate in a clumsy manner what they claimed was the imaginary story of a so-called attack on American warships in international waters.[9]

On February 20th, 1968, Robert McNamara, who was still Secretary of State for Defense, in a closed session of the Senate Foreign Relations Committee, said that the United States recognized no claim of a territorial sea in excess of three miles, and that this was the consistent position of the United States re-emphasized at the 1958 Convention on the Law of the Sea in Geneva. He claimed that there was no basis in fact in statements reported in the press that the *Maddox* had entered into waters claimed by North Vietnam as territorial. At no time prior to the August 1964 Tonkin Gulf incidents, he asserted, did the North Vietnamese government claim a width of territorial sea in excess of three miles. The North Vietnamese government had succeeded the French government, which had adhered to the three-mile limit, and under the rules of international law no claim by North Vietnam in excess of three miles would be assumed unless specifically made and published. He went on to say that Cambodia, a sister successor state, publicly adopted the French three-mile rule on achieving independence, and only later proclaimed a five-mile limit.

McNamara asserted that the first statement of North Vietnam which approached a claim in excess of three miles occurred on September 1st, 1964, well after the attack, in the orm of a broadcast from Radio Hanoi in which it was stated that the Democratic Republic of Vietnam declared that the territorial sea was twelve miles.' Taking his position on the basis that no official documentary confirmation of the claim asserted in the broadcast was known to exist, he argued that the United States should not even have assumed as a practical matter a claim of twelve miles since this was not the uniform position of the Communist countries. For, whereas Cuba and Poland adhere to the traditional three-mile limit, Yugoslavia and Albania claim ten miles.[10]

What is odd about McNamara's statement is the fact that the existence of a North Vietnamese claim to a twelve-mile limit seemed to be accepted as fact by Congress and was referred to by Senator Morse during the August debate on the resolution. No one has denied that the alleged attacks on the *Maddox* took place outside the twelve-mile limit – about thirty and sixty miles off the coast. But it is now clear that the *Maddox* deliberately, at a time of considerable tension, sailed within twelve miles of North Vietnam knowing that there was doubt over the exact definition of territorial waters.

The build-up of events leading to the first admitted North Vietnamese attack on the *Maddox* on August 2nd appears to have been that on July 25th, 1964, Radio Hanoi alleged that American ships had fired on North Vietnamese sailing vessels. On July 29th, South Vietnam's Air Force Commander Ky, stealing a march on General Khanh, announced that South Vietnamese commandos had been parachuted into North Vietnam.

On August 3rd, 1964, the North Vietnamese protested to the International Control Commission about an attack by the United States and South Vietnam on North Vietnamese islands. They claimed that, on July 30th, South Vietnamese patrol boats had raided North Vietnamese fishing vessels in the Tonkin Gulf. This was quite true, and also early on July 31st, under General Westmoreland's command, they had bombarded the North Vietnamese islands of Hon Me and Hon Nieu.

We now know that McNamara's claim in his 1964 testimony that the United States Navy had played no part in the attack was dangerously misleading.[11] On August 3rd, President Johnson had himself ordered that the *Maddox* and *Turner C. Joy* should return to the Tonkin Gulf and the Commander-in-Chief Pacific (CINCPAC) Fleet had sent a message suggesting that the *Maddox* and *Turner C. Joy* should draw the North Vietnamese patrol boats away from the islands. The task group commander had also already warned that the North Vietnamese considered the American ships as enemies because of their involvement. It is now clear from the Pentagon study that McNamara had received reports on the clandestine attacks and that Dean Rusk had also been kept informed.

It is to the credit of Senator Morse that, even in 1964 during the debate on the resolution, he realized that the Administration's denial of a link with the South Vietnamese attack was highly suspect. He stated then that, 'On Friday, July 31st, South Vietnamese naval vessels – not junks but armed vessels of the PT boat type made available to South Vietnam by way of our aid programme – had bombed two North Vietnamese islands. One island is approximately three miles and one approximately five miles from the main coast of North Vietnam.'

He went on to argue that the United States had been in close advisory relationship with the South Vietnamese and that the bombing of the islands was a well thought out military operation, and that, while these islands were actually being bombed, American destroyers were on patrol in Tonkin Bay.

During the debate, Senator Fulbright admitted that the United States was supplying the South Vietnamese with ships, saying that the North Vietnamese had two major ways of approaching South Vietnam, one by sea and one by land, and that the sea approach was in his view the easiest way to supply the Mekong Delta, and that this justified helping the South Vietnam government to try to interrupt the transfer of men and supplies to the Mekong Delta. The boats that may have struck at the coastal areas of North Vietnam might, he admitted, have been supplied by the United States.[12] We now also know from the Pentagon Papers that on August 3rd, while the destroyer patrol was resumed, two further clandestine attacks were authorized involving bombardment of the Rhon River estuary and a radar installation at Vinhson. This followed air strikes on August 1st and 2nd across the Laotian border. The second alleged North Vietnamese attack took place on August 4th, a moonless night; but despite all the investigations of this attack, no clear facts have emerged to discredit totally the North Vietnamese denial of any offensive action.

The *Maddox* was not the innocent ship on a routine patrol that at the time it claimed to be. The *Baltimore Sun* had reported that shortly before it was attacked on August 2nd, 1964, the *Maddox* had taken aboard at Formosa a large 'black box' of electronic equipment operated by a special crew of about a dozen men and that the black box contained equipment for monitoring North Vietnamese radio and radar signals.[13] We also know that the *Maddox* was authorized to stimulate a North Vietnamese electronic action.

At 6.00 p.m. on August 4th, following the alleged attack by North Vietnamese patrol boats and reports of five, seven, and eventually twenty-two torpedoes having been fired, the *Maddox* sent the following message: 'The first boat to close the *Maddox* probably fired a torpedo at the *Maddox* which was heard but not seen. All subsequent *Maddox* torpedo reports are doubtful in that it is suspected that sonar man was hearing ship's own propeller beat.'[14] Subsequent investigation showed evidence of considerable confusion on board the two American ships; at one stage they only narrowly avoided actually shooting at each other.

Immediately following the attack, the Task Commander to CINCPAC Fleet sent this message: 'Review of action makes many recorded contacts and torpedoes fired appear doubtful. Freak weather effects and over-eager sonar men may have accounted for many reports. No actual visual sightings by *Maddox*. Suggest complete evaluation before any further action.'

The Pentagon study[15] reveals that McNamara returned from the second National Security Council meeting on August 4th, at which the President had authorized the reprisals, only to hear on the telephone from CINCPAC that there was confusion as to whether an attack had actually taken place. McNamara told CINCPAC to check and make certain that an attack had really occurred before launching the planes, and within two hours CINCPAC confirmed that the attack was genuine. The study also reveals that McNamara and the Joint Chiefs of Staff examined intercepted radio messages from the North Vietnamese, saying that their vessels were engaging the destroyers. It would undoubtedly clear up much of the mystery over whether this alleged attack really did take place if the United States would now reveal the text of these intercepts. What worries many people who have examined the Gulf of Tonkin incident is that, despite all these messages, despite doubts sufficient to request absolute confirmation that they had been attacked, despite the fact that no injury had been caused, the United States decided to take immediate further action. That evening, President Johnson broadcast to the nation. 'The US response', he announced, would be 'limited and fitting'.[16] The following day, Secretary of State McNamara declared that reprisal raids had destroyed twenty-five enemy torpedo boats, and fuel bases on the mainland of North Vietnam.

It has since been claimed that the raids of August 4th and 5th caused Hanoi to lose one half of its naval force, while the United States lost about three planes and one pilot.[17]

Yet the North Vietnamese did nothing militarily in return. Their government, however, claimed that the air attack had caused loss and damage to the local population. In the attack on August 2nd, they said that the *Maddox* had fired first. On August 3rd, they claimed that the United States and South Vietnamese ships had shelled Quang Binh province, and the second attack on August 4th they dismissed as an 'imaginary story'.[18]

The true facts concerning the Gulf of Tonkin incident may never be known. What has caused increasing concern as more facts have emerged is how any American Administration could have based the firm belief that their forces had been subjected to deliberate attack on such sketchy intercept, radar and sonar evidence. That they should have acted on the basis of such evidence, within twelve hours, raises fundamental questions relating to command and control, many of which are posed by John Finney in his article, 'A Case Study in How Not to Go to War',[19] and even more questions arise from the Associated Press inquiry into the incident.

The most favourable interpretation, from radar tracks and other reports, is that PT boats were engaged in harassing the *Maddox* and the *Turner C. Joy*; but the evidence that they actually launched a torpedo attack is far from convincing (see Chapter 9). The charitable interpretation of the politicians' decision to accept the kind of evidence they appear to have been presented with, is that it fitted in with all their preconceptions that open war with the North Vietnamese was inevitable. What should be asked — and not just by Senator Fulbright, but by politicians in every country — is whether this form of military decision-making is tolerable. In the United Kingdom and other NATO countries, there is no such Congressional committee inquiry to reveal the paucity of the evidence on which important defence decisions are made, and but for the revelations of the Pentagon study much would still be unknown.

The warning implicit in the Tonkin incident should be clear to everyone. No democratic government should attempt to involve its nation in a major war on the basis of lies, half-truths and deliberate deception.

Chapter 5. The 1967 Arab-Israeli War

The Gulf of Aqaba runs into the Red Sea through the Straits of Tiran, which divide the Egyptian territory of Sinai from the Saudi Arabian island of Tiran. At its narrowest point, the strait is a mere 3·3 nautical miles from Johnson Point on Tiran Island to the signal station on Sinai's shore.

In June 1967, a dispute over these straits triggered off the 'Six-Day War', and thus intensified the long Middle East crisis. What had previously been a straight Arab-Israeli problem became one which involved – to an extent hitherto unimagined – a direct confrontation between Russia and the United States.

The Gulf of Aqaba's importance is that the port of Eilat gives Israeli shipping access to the area east of Suez, without going round the Cape of Good Hope, since the ships cannot use the Suez canal. Two weeks after the 1949 armistice was signed, Israel had seized Eilat and as a result the port was immediately blockaded by Egypt, and remained virtually unused for six years. In 1956, one of the reasons for Israel's starting the Sinai campaign was her wish to break the blockade on Eilat. A major achievement of that campaign from Israel's point of view was that the terms of the settlement specifically allowed for the opening of the Gulf of Aqaba to her shipping. This 1956 settlement resulted in the stationing of a United Nations Emergency Force (UNEF) on Egyptian territory, with the permission of the Egyptian government, to help maintain the cease-fire called for by the United Nations in November 1956. But the Israelis left the fort of Sharm el-Sheikh, which commands the Straits of Tiran, only in March 1957, and at that time the Israeli government made it plain that their withdrawal was conditional on the continued movement of Israeli ships down the Gulf and through the Tiran Straits. Israel noted then that the maritime nations, including the United States and Britain, supported free movement of shipping in the Gulf of Aqaba. The Israeli government also reserved the right to act in what they termed 'self-defence', under Article 51 of the United Nations Charter, should there be any interference with Israeli shipping.

From being a small, run-down port, Eilat was then built up so that, by 1967, it was a flourishing port. A pipeline was built from Eilat to the refinery at Haifa, which carried Iranian crude oil, so as to by-pass the Suez Canal; the pipeline's capacity of about $4\frac{1}{2}$ million tons a year was well in excess of Israel's own domestic needs. Excluding oil, Eilat handled only about 12 per cent of Israel's other trade, but it was an important and potentially expanding trade, coming from the Far East, East Africa, New Zealand and Australia.

The growth of hostilities during the early part of 1967 to the Six-Day War was only the culmination of many years of repeated border incidents and political tension. On April 7th, 1967, Israeli forces made a serious attack on several Syrian villages. Mounting tensions led Syria to seek President Nasser's help under their Mutual Defence Pact of 1966. All through this period, the growth of the Arab guerrilla movement and of the Palestine Liberation Army in Jordan and Syria was putting increasing pressure on President Nasser to reassert his leadership of the Arab world. The continued presence of the UNEF on Egyptian territory was frequently criticized by Arab guerrilla leaders and questions were being asked as to why greater pressure was not being put on Israel across the Egyptian frontier.

On May 16th, President Nasser asked that the UNEF should withdraw from the border and concentrate instead inside the Gaza Strip. At this time no mention was made of the forces at Sharm el-Sheikh.

U Thant, the United Nations Secretary-General, sent for El Kong, Egyptian representative at the United Nations, and told him that a partial withdrawal of the force was impossible. If the withdrawal was to take place, it would have to be total. The United Nations, he explained, could not be asked 'to stand aside in order to enable the two sides to resume fighting'.[1]

There was some uncertainty about Egypt's right to request

withdrawal. The former Secretary-General, Dag Hammar-skjöld, had claimed when the initial settlement was negotiated after the 1956 hostilities that he and President Nasser had reached a private agreement that there should be no with-drawal until the 'task' was accomplished.[2]

On May 18th, after receiving the formal request, U Thant, acting with a speed for which he has since been criticized, gave orders for the UNEF to be removed. Much of the criticism ignores the fact that he had to protect United Nations lives and that the Egyptian government had a complete legal right to insist on withdrawal. No one, however, had expected the removal to be immediate. It was a surprise when U Thant's action was announced to the General Assembly on May 19th.

On May 20th came the first reports that Egypt had occupied Sharm el-Sheikh, thereby giving her command of the outlet of the Gulf of Aqaba. On May 21st there was a partial mobiliza-tion of troops on both sides. Israeli ships were reported to be steaming towards the Tiran Straits. This immediately raised the whole question of whether Egypt would reimpose the ban on Israeli shipping in the Gulf of Aqaba which she had given up since the 1956 war.

Only the installation of medium-range guns was necessary for an effective blockade to be imposed, and on May 22nd it was reported that Egyptian guns had closed the vital waterway of the Straits of Tiran.

Command of the waterway was easy to achieve since all ships had to pass within half a mile of the Egyptian outposts in the narrow channels which are the only safe route among the coral reefs.

President Nasser then announced that the UAR had closed the Gulf of Aqaba to all ships flying the Israeli flag or carrying strategic materials. He claimed that in recent days Israel had been making aggressive threats and boasts, and that she was planning to attack Syria on May 17th, and so he had requested the withdrawal of the UNEF: 'It is obvious that the UNEF entered Egypt with our approval and therefore cannot continue to stay in Egypt except with our approval.'

He went on to say that the armed forces had occupied Sharm el-Sheikh and that this was 'affirmation of our rights and our sovereignty over the Gulf of Aqaba which constitutes Egyptian territorial waters. Under no circumstances will we allow the Israeli flag to pass through the Gulf of Aqaba.'[3]

This Egyptian action met with an immediate response. Israel's Prime Minister, Mr Eshkol, declared it an act of war. President Johnson claimed the blockade was illegal, U Thant flew to Cairo for talks, and George Brown, the British Foreign Secretary, flew to Moscow. At that time the Russian news agency Tass warned that any aggressor against the Arabs would have to face Russian resistance.[4] President Nasser's attitude to the closing of the Gulf was realistic, and he was described as seeing it as 'a symbolic Arab victory – a revenge for 1956 – rather than a crushing act of economic warfare'.[5]

The Arabs were not so naive as to suppose that the economic threat to Israel of blockading Eilat was likely to force the Israelis into making political concessions, particularly when Israel had already survived a complete Arab trade boycott and the closure of the Suez canal.

If the blockade was intended only as a humiliation of the Israelis, the question was whether ships of other nations would be searched. On May 24th it was reported that a Panamanian freighter had arrived at Eilat the previous day without a search. It was clear that an effective blockade could not be enforced without searches, and, if necessary, the seizure of any foreign ships which might be carrying strategic goods to Israel. It seemed as if there might well be a possibility of negotiating some form of compromise settlement. But then *Al Ahram* reported that nine entrances to the Gulf had been mined.[6] This information at once made the blockade potentially a more serious issue. The *Al Ahram* report was then denied by the Egyptian Ambassador in Washington, but it was known that *Al Ahram* was editorially very close to President Nasser.

At this time President Nasser had all thirteen Arab states – including Tunisia – behind him. The Arabs, however, could not present a totally united front, Syria and Jordan having broken off diplomatic relations because of terrorist activities. It was widely believed that Egypt would not go to war without Russian backing, and it was difficult to determine any Russian interest in pushing for a war when they must have been well aware of the deficiencies of the Arab armies. Some people felt that the Russian strategy was clear from the outset: that they planned to oust all Western interests and influence from the Middle East so as to gain control of the oil market and become the dominating influence in the area.

But even if this was the Russian aim, they almost certainly did not want war, for it would have been too near their southern flank. There is some evidence that at this stage the Russians failed to see the dangers, and possibly over-emphasized the controlling influence that the United States had on Israel.

The United Nations itself was virtually helpless. On May 24th, the Security Council debate on the crisis ended indefinitely after Communist and Afro-Asian delegates refused to join private discussions. The Security Council was also painfully aware that the Russian veto would prevent its taking any specific action and other members of the Security Council would have probably supported the UAR on the Gulf question.

The United States and Britain – although they both declared the blockade illegal, and were concerned about the threat to freedom of shipping – were, when it came to the point, unwilling to act. At one stage the British Prime Minister, Harold Wilson, and the Foreign Secretary, George Brown, advocated a much more active role for Britain than most of the Cabinet were prepared to underwrite. On June 4th the *Observer* commented 'it was only with the greatest reluctance ... that the Cabinet as a whole agreed at its long meeting on 23rd May, the day Mr Brown flew to Moscow, that Britain should take such an active part in the dispute'.[7] The interventionist idea was to send a small naval force under the cover of an international air-strike force operating from the eastern Mediterranean, but it was eventually vetoed, underlining the strength at times of crisis of Cabinet rather than prime-ministerial government.

Mr Eban, the Israeli Foreign Minister, found the United

States also reluctant to act. In his talks with President Johnson on May 26th he produced documents intended to prove an American commitment to aiding Israel. But President Johnson held out firmly against involvement. The war in Vietnam was his major commitment, and he was unwilling to be dragged into another potential war situation.

The proposal which was then being discussed in London and Washington was for the maritime force to sail through the Straits of Tiran and assert their rights to what was being claimed as an international waterway. The proponents of the policy were hoping that the force would be able to fly the United Nations flag, but were still prepared to advocate sending the force, provided a number of the major maritime powers were prepared to support the proposal. The scheme was never based on Britain 'going it alone', nor even for proceeding solely with the backing of the United States. It was felt that, without a number of nations contributing their forces, any initiative was doomed to be misrepresented and misunderstood.

But it is in just this type of situation in the Middle East that the credentials of Britain and France are so suspect. The Arab world has not forgotten the outrageous duplicity of the two nations during the 1956 war; and a change of government from Conservative to Labour in Britain and the emergence of General de Gaulle in France were not of themselves sufficient to curb suspicion of the two countries. Arab opinion makes little distinction between governments. What is not forgotten by the Arabs is that Britain and France had repeatedly lied to the world about their relationship with the Israelis over the Suez intervention. They see this episode as the most cynical and disreputable act in a long history of British double-talk over a whole period of Middle East diplomacy. The mistrust Suez created, understandably, still lives on.

In many ways it was strange that the Labour government in Britain should have been even considering a policy which touched on the old Imperialist slogan of sending a gunboat. It is worth analysing what contribution such a maritime force could have effectively made to the situation. Firstly, Israeli ships were not essential to keep the oil flowing through Eilat. Provided that tankers flying non-Israeli flags could enter the Gulf, there was no oil supply reason for risking an escalation of the crisis. The number of vessels flying the Israeli flag which normally passed through the Straits of Tiran was also disputed, with the Israelis claiming a larger number than American official sources were prepared to concede. Intervention by Britain and the United States would have put at risk valuable assets in other Arab countries, and at this time, because of the general economic situation, Britain was particularly vulnerable to any large-scale withdrawals of sterling by Arab countries such as Kuwait.

Eventually, these and other military arguments prevailed. There was also no enthusiasm for intervention from the other European countries in NATO. It is hard to be sure what would have been the result had the interventionists' argument won. Certainly intervention would have reassured the Israelis that they were not alone, but there would have been the serious risk of direct confrontation arising between the United States and Russia. It has never been fully established whether the Straits had in fact been mined by the Egyptians, though it seems in retrospect unlikely. Apart from the political issue, there were technical difficulties involved in mining the passage because of the depth of the water and the great strength of the current. Yet a maritime force would have been extremely vulnerable to attack, not just from any mines, but also from shore-based missiles. The possible sinking of one of the vessels could not have been completely ruled out, and presumably this eventuality must have been considered. Under such circumstances what retaliation, if any, would then have been available – short of a land invasion? The answer is probably none. So for an uncertain gain the interventionists were putting themselves in a ludicrously vulnerable position. It is true that the rejection of the idea of maritime intervention inevitably increased the pressure on Israel to take independent action. Yet what needs to be asked is how such a potentially dangerous intervention came to be considered so seriously by the British Cabinet.

Mr Eban said on May 30th that Israel was prepared to accept any solution — presented within a time limit — which guaranteed free passage for *all* ships, but he warned that 'we will act alone if we must.'[8]

On May 27th, U Thant made his report to the Security Council. He said that President Nasser had assured him that Egypt would not 'initiate offensive action against Israel'.[9] The Egyptians, he reported, wanted 'a return to the conditions prior to 1956 and to full observance by both parties of the provisions of the general armistice agreement between Israel and Egypt'.

President Nasser had meanwhile been sent warnings not to act rashly by President de Gaulle, President Johnson and the Soviet leaders. But on May 28th, he was threatening to close the Suez canal if war broke out between Egypt and Israel, and if, in consequence, any other nation felt it necessary to intervene.

Nasser repeated his previous claim that the Tiran Straits were Egyptian territorial waters over which Egypt alone exercised sovereign rights.

On May 29th, at an emergency session of the United Nations Security Council in New York, the United States proposed a temporary lift of the blockade to give the United Nations time to resolve the crisis. But the Egyptian delegate claimed that the control of the Straits belonged historically to the Arabs and, as a result, the proposal collapsed.

Then on May 30th came the turning point — Nasser and Hussein signed a Defence Pact. This was of strategic importance for it was along Israel's frontier with Jordan that she was most vulnerable.

A few days later, on June 5th, 1967, war broke out, and an initial maritime incident became a full-scale land battle. The outcome of the six-day battle with its overwhelming victory for the Israelis was a short-lived triumph, for it heralded — and, some argue, necessitated — a full-scale commitment on the part of Russia to the Arab cause.

The dramatic events of the Six-Day War have tended to

overshadow the Israeli attack on the USS *Liberty* which took place on June 8th. This incident is, however, of considerable interest since it was the only one which directly involved a super-power and was, therefore, potentially the most serious of all incidents. This was recognized by President Johnson's decision to use the 'hot line' to Moscow to keep the risk of any misunderstanding to the minimum in the first few hours of confusion. It is interesting looking back to speculate whether the United States government would have acted as tolerantly as it did if the aggression had come from the Egyptians. Certainly the cool response would have been difficult if only because of the virulent criticism which would have been directed at the Administration from the Jewish community inside America for a policy of inaction, particularly when faced with such heavy American casualties.

The USS *Liberty*, although the Pentagon has never admitted it, was clearly a communications ship on an intelligence-gathering mission. Its electronic equipment was capable of picking up all messages passed between Egyptian and Israeli field commanders and headquarters in Sinai, and as such was in a critical position to determine the course of the war, pin-point missile sites and also produce concrete evidence on which side had instigated the initial attack. Since most battlefield communications depend on short-wave and short-range frequencies, the ship had to cruise near to the coast. The USS *Liberty* was an old ship and hundreds of similar vessels had been used by the United States Navy during the Second World War, so that its outline should have been easy to recognize, which makes the Israeli claim of mistaken identity all the harder to sustain. It was also a clear day, the ship was in international waters and was well marked with its name painted on the stern and United States letters and numbers printed on the bow. There has been some question as to whether the American flag was flying throughout the incident, but this can never be taken as the only source of identification. Given these facts it is quite extraordinary that the incident ever took place. Recon-structing the sequence of events as best one can from the information available, it appears that the *Liberty* left Rota, its base in Spain, on June 2nd, officially to 'assure communications between United States Government ports in the Middle East and to assist in relaying information concerning the evacuation of American dependents and other American citizens'.[10]

On June 8th, the *Liberty* was situated some fifteen nautical miles north of El Arish, clearly outside the territorial waters claimed by either Egypt or Israel, and this question has never been disputed. It is also clear that she had been under surveillance from the air for some time. At 2.03 p.m., Israeli aircraft flying in fast and low attacked the *Liberty* with cannon and rockets and scored numerous direct hits. It appears that five or six attacks were made on the ship and that two fuel tanks and ammunition from its four machine-guns exploded. Following the air attacks less than half an hour elapsed before Israeli torpedo boats arrived and challenged the *Liberty* to identify herself. Apparently the captain of the *Liberty*, unable to read the signal because of the smoke and flames from the initial air attack, signalled back to the Israeli ships to identify themselves. The Israelis must have felt that this was the response indicative of an Egyptian ship, particularly since the starboard machine-gun on the *Liberty* fired a short burst and the rearward gun also began firing. The Israelis fired their torpedoes; the first one missed the *Liberty*, but the second torpedo hit her in the starboard side below the waterline causing a four-metre hole and immediately killing twenty-five men.

As a result of the whole action, thirty-four American servicemen were tragically killed and seventy-five men wounded. The *Liberty* did not sink and managed to reach Malta on June 13th for extensive repairs. On June 9th the Israeli apology sent out by Premier Eshkol to President Johnson was published and on June 15th the Israelis again expressed their deep regret and offered to pay compensation for the loss of American lives and for the damage to the ship.

Since the incident there has been considerable speculation over the Israelis' motives. Their explanation that it was a simple case of mistaken identity has also been challenged. The

Israelis claimed to have believed that the *Liberty* was the Egyptian troop transport vessel, the *El Quesir*, which was known to be in the vicinity. What is most alarming about accepting the mistaken identity theory is that Russian ships were also known to be in the vicinity. If a mistake of such a magnitude could have taken place involving the *Liberty*, how much more serious it might have been if a Russian vessel had been involved. Speculation has also centred on whether the attack had been deliberate and whether the Israeli high command feared that the *Liberty* might have obtained damagingly revealing evidence identifying Israel as the aggressor.

A detailed, and probably well-informed sequence of events appeared, however, much later.[11] Apparently, Israeli forces having captured El Arish thought that they heard naval gunfire which later turned out to be exploding ammunition dumps. In the excitement, an Israeli radar operator misread or misreported the speed of the *Liberty*, which was some fourteen miles offshore, as being twenty-two knots when it was in fact half this. On a crude judgment that ships steaming at more than twenty knots must be presumed to be warships, it was assumed that the *Liberty* was an Egyptian vessel on a combat mission. So the fateful attack was launched without any really effective reconnaissance information to ensure accurate identification. The whole incident confirms the well-known difficulty of obtaining accurate information if one is relying solely on electronic data, and this difficulty is particularly marked in a maritime situation. The error was all the more ominous since at the time it was known by the Israeli command that a Russian vessel was in the area.

A summary of the United States Navy Board of Inquiry's findings were published on June 28th by the Defense Department. It showed that the *Liberty* had been under orders not to approach closer than 12·5 nautical miles from the shore. It had, however, apparently been decided by the Joint Chiefs of Staff before the attack took place that the *Liberty* should move even farther from the coast, though it was realized that such a move would make it harder to collect intelligence information.

The inquiry clearly revealed that the all-important message from the Joint Chiefs of Staff never reached the *Liberty* before the attack, the message having been misrouted and delayed. To add to this picture of confusion in the higher command there is also some evidence that the Israelis had identified the *Liberty* on an earlier aerial reconnaissance mission but that the information had not been transmitted to local Israeli commanders.

This whole incident yet again shows serious failures of military communication; it highlights the inadequacy of the command and control procedures and raises fundamental questions on how the process of decision-making really operates under war conditions. Commentators at the time were deeply critical of the inquiry's report, saying that it had not explained why the ship was directed to operate in such close proximity to waters known to be hazardous; or why there was no acknowledgment or explanation of what happened to the message reported from the American Embassy in Tel Aviv inquiring about American ships operating in the area. Nor had the inquiry any explanation of why orders directing the ship farther away from danger, which had been sent prior to the attack, were not received until after the attack. The *Washington Post*[12] summed up the situation in words which cannot be lightly dismissed.

> The prompt transmittal of orders in this nuclear age, is the first essential of effective military command. The inexplicable failure of this order to arrive nearly cost a ship and did cost the lives of many Americans. A similar lapse could end in the destruction of the Nation itself. If this is a representative performance of naval communications, the country is running risks that make the dangers to the *Liberty* seem minimal.

These risks become all the more relevant as the extent of American and Russian involvement in the Arab-Israeli conflict increases.

Chapter 6. The *Pueblo* Incident

Throughout 1967 the North Koreans had been pursuing a much increased campaign of violence against South Korea. The Americans themselves reported to the United Nations a rise from fifty breaches of the armistice in 1966, to 543 in the first ten months of 1967, and raiding teams had been regularly sent on sabotage missions, penetrating the cease-fire line. On a number of occasions they had clashed with South Korean and American soldiers in the demilitarized zone. On January 19th, 1968, a thirty-one-man team of North Koreans had penetrated South Korean territory as far as Seoul with the intention of murdering the President of the Republic of Korea. Then on January 23rd, 1968, the United States intelligence ship *Pueblo*, manned by a crew of six officers, seventy-five enlisted men and two civilians, was seized by North Koreans off the North Korean coast. Suddenly, the Korean question became an important one, for the first time since the signing of the 1953 Korean Armistice agreement.

It was, and still is, difficult to assess North Korean motives for the seizure, or for the stepped-up activity across the cease-fire line. It seems highly improbable that the North Koreans really wished to restart the Korean war and, even if they did, it was most unlikely that they would wish to signal their intentions beforehand and in such a clear way. Like so many border incidents all over the world, the most likely explanation was that the incidents owed much to the need to bolster morale on the home front: to show the North Korean people that the South Koreans, who were then enjoying a higher standard of living, were still very vulnerable to attack from the North Koreans, despite American help in patrolling the demilitarized zone. Whatever their motive for seizing the *Pueblo* the North Koreans had chosen to challenge the United States in an area of great sensitivity. There are few nations in the world who

76

have such a strong vested interest in ensuring the freedom of the seas, and a maritime episode had already been used by the same United States Administration as the trigger for the escalation of the war into North Vietnam. The United States Navy was particularly concerned at that time about its intelligence ships, for only a few months before, in June 1967, the USS *Liberty* had been attacked by Israeli patrol boats and aircraft off the Sinai peninsula.

In this case, emotion was especially aroused because only two ships had ever been boarded and captured in the entire history of the American Navy. For this and other reasons the public outcry which followed the incident centred mainly on why the *Pueblo*'s captain, Commander Lloyd M. Bucher, had not used his guns to fight off the initial challenge, and why he had not scuttled his ship rather than allow it to be captured along with valuable intelligence materials. Members of the captured crew, who had been ill-treated and tortured, were eventually forced to sign confessions, and these confessions were the subject of much criticism inside the United States Navy, on the basis that servicemen should withstand such mental and physical pressures.

After a period of ceaseless diplomatic activity aimed at freeing the crew, the United States government agreed to go through the mockery of signing a confession prepared by the North Koreans, a confession which, with the North Koreans' knowledge, they had already repudiated in advance. As a result of this extraordinary procedure, on December 23rd, 1968, the North Koreans released the crew after nearly a year in captivity. In January 1969, a naval court of inquiry was opened, hearing evidence in an atmosphere which many feared would result in the captain of the *Pueblo* being made a public scapegoat. On April 14th, the court found Commander Bucher innocent of wrong-doing in surrendering his ship, but noted that he deserved a reprimand for inadequate destruction of documents on the ship. This finding was followed in May by the extremely sensible decision of the Secretary of the Navy, John Chafee, to take no disciplinary action against anyone involved in the capture of the *Pueblo*, and in consequence there was no reprimand or court martial for Commander Bucher. A decision which, not surprisingly in view of the emotion generated, was immediately attacked as being spineless. Yet the central importance of the *Pueblo* incident was not the behaviour of the captain and crew of the ship.

The central issue was highlighted in the Congressional Committee Report, which states that the inquiry into the USS *Pueblo* incident

has resulted in the unanimous view that there exist serious deficiencies in the organisational and administrative military command structure of both the Department of the Navy and the Department of Defense. If nothing else, the inquiry reveals the existence of a vast and complex military structure capable of acquiring almost infinite amounts of information but with a demonstrated inability ... to relay this information in a timely and comprehensive fashion to those charged with the responsibility for making decisions.[1]

This is a devastating critique of the central control in a potentially very serious situation, and there is every reason to believe that the British Ministry of Defence and other Western defence ministries would make many of the same mistakes in a similar crisis. It is all too easy for countries who do not have such an open inquiry system as the United States to sit back and dismiss the revelations about the *Pueblo* incident as being of little concern to them. There is certainly a lesson in these incidents for every citizen, whether in the Western Alliance or the Warsaw Pact countries, for only by a widespread awareness of how vulnerable and deficient is the central process of defence decision-making will it ever be improved. In most countries there is an understandable though regrettable tendency for the problems of national defence and security to be shielded from the normal processes of scrutiny. It is to the immense credit of the American Constitution that it does not allow the military establishment to escape from Congressional challenge and inquiry.

A striking aspect of the whole incident was, as in the Cuban crisis, the failure of American Intelligence to foresee the possibility of a North Korean response to the *Pueblo* mission. As in the Gulf of Tonkin, the United States was deliberately sending a ship into an area of high exposure which, in view of the progressive heightening of tension, could not be regarded as a purely routine intelligence exercise. It is probable that despite the initial confusion as to whether she was twenty-five or 15·4 miles offshore when seized, the *Pueblo* did not enter North Korean territorial waters, but the area was highly sensitive.

In 1968 the North Koreans were clearly becoming more aggressive. On January 11th, two North Korean patrol boats had raided a group of 200 South Korean fishing boats, after a somewhat similar action on January 6th. On both occasions the North Koreans publicly announced that, as long as 'imperialist aggressors' conducted reconnaissance by sending spy boats, their ships would continue to take determined counter-measures. On January 21st, the North Korean delegate at Panmunjom, General Pak Chung Kook, protested formally against American infiltration of their coastal waters with armed spy boats.

In view of all these incidents it is extraordinary that, according to the inquiry, neither the Commander-in-Chief Pacific Fleet Headquarters nor the Commander Naval Forces Japan had been aware of these North Korean threats of retaliation prior to the seizure of the *Pueblo*. The inquiry revealed that a warning message from the National Security Agency on December 29th, 1967, had urged the consideration of protective measures for the *Pueblo* mission, but the message never reached any responsible authority. The copy which was sent to the Joint Chiefs of Staff was retransmitted on January 2nd for information to the Commander-in-Chief Pacific, and was never acted on, since his staff did not consider it contained any new information. It never reached even the Commander Naval Forces Japan, who was responsible for the mission. His initial message to the Commander-in-Chief Pacific Fleet, concerning the proposed mission, spoke of the 'estimate of risk: minimal since *Pueblo* will be operating in international waters for entire deployment'.[2] The copy of the warning message sent to the Chief of Naval Operations never reached its destination, being lost in transmission in the Pentagon.

So it was that a lightly armed vessel under orders to manœuvre its guns only when absolutely necessary, and whose gun covers were caked in ice at the time of seizure, was sent unescorted on its intelligence mission. Even though the *Pueblo* was under instructions not to go within thirteen miles of the North Korean coastline, it should have been clear to anyone who had seriously studied the available intelligence that this was a high-risk operation. It is worth examining how the all-important risk evaluation was made, the procedures being remarkably like those used in other Western countries.

The *Pueblo* mission was only one of hundreds of missions which had to be reviewed and approved by the Joint Chiefs of Staff. In theory, before the monthly schedule of missions was approved, other interested or affected government agencies were given the opportunity to comment. The Joint Chiefs of Staff in this case never met, as it was the week of the Christmas holiday and two of the Chiefs of Staff were away from Washington. Since none of their staffs raised any objection, approval was granted on December 29th without any formal meeting. It was then politically approved by the Deputy Secretary of Defense that same day. The inquiry was unable to establish how long the Deputy Secretary of State took in his review of the monthly reconnaissance schedule, but for anyone who has been exposed to similar submissions it is easy to understand how approval would be readily given without any serious questioning for all missions other than the acknowledged high-risk missions. The major error, therefore, was in the initial risk evaluation, and the inquiry seriously questioned whether any of the commanders or their staff were even aware of the specific criteria put out by the Joint Chiefs of Staff as the basis of assessing the risks of such missions.

The sub-committee was also very concerned by the handling

of the National Security Agency warning message, and particularly by the lack of candour of witnesses on the subject. They
commented that

> Pentagon representatives who testified or briefed Congres-
> sional Committees immediately after the *Pueblo* incident
> and up until March 4th, 1969, never hinted that such a
> message ever existed. As a matter of fact, there appeared
> to be a deliberate effort to bury and obfuscate the fact by
> discussion solely of 'warnings' allegedly issued by the North
> Korean Government.[3]

Senator Fulbright commented soon after the *Pueblo* was
seized that he was only then learning what actually happened
in the Gulf of Tonkin and that he did not expect to learn the full
facts of the *Pueblo* case for another two or three years. This
attitude typified much of the initial Congressional reaction,
and a marked scepticism was noticeable throughout the early
stages, with many people even questioning whether the *Pueblo*
had penetrated the twelve-mile limit.

The lack of any ship protection measures was also seriously
questioned by the inquiry, which found indications that there
was a reluctance at many levels of the military command
structure to commit and assign specific forces to reconnaissance
missions. This, they argued, placed pressure on the officer
originating the mission to give it a minimal risk categorization,
since it was the only risk evaluation which could easily be
approved by higher command.

Against the background of a well-known reluctance to
assign specific forces for protection, it seems even more surprising that the Navy had no contingency plans whatsoever
for going to the rescue of the USS *Pueblo* in an emergency. The
Commanding General of the Fifth Air Force had queried
whether special air support for the *Pueblo* mission was necessary,
and had been told that such support was not being requested.
Yet, when the emergency did arrive, the senior staff officers of
the Commander Naval Forces Japan seemed wholly unaware
that no contingency plan existed, and seemed to think that the

Fifth Air Force could in any case produce a suitable emergency response without any prior discussion or planning. The actual request for assistance took forty minutes to reach the Commander of the Fifth Air Force, mainly because the two commands had never previously exercised emergency telephone procedures. Even after this delay it is clear that the operational aircraft were not in a high state of preparedness. The 18th Tactical Fighter wing at Okinawa launched the first aircraft in response to the order of the Fifth Air Commander one hour and twenty-three minutes after it was received, which only underlined the error of not having alert forces at instant readiness. The USS *Enterprise*, a nuclear-powered aircraft carrier, was at the time of the seizure approximately 550 nautical miles away, and for three hours it steamed steadily away from the scene of the crisis. Again there was evidence of serious delay. Forty-five minutes passed from a message originating with the Commander Seventh Fleet to change course until it had actually been executed by the *Enterprise*. It is now known that the aircraft on immediate readiness were armed only with nuclear weapons, not conventional weapons, and this explains some of the delay. It is a shattering indictment of the actual manner in which McNamara's flexible response strategy had actually been implemented by the United States Air Force that, over five years after it had been established as policy, nuclear weapons should be the main immediate armament in a part of the world well known for its instability.

The key decisions subsequent to the seizure were also all authorized before President Johnson was even informed. It was not until early on January 24th that higher authority in Washington put a hold order on all the forces in the area. The sub-committee, in commenting on the response to the seizure, said that they were well aware of the terrible implications involved in ordering fighter aircraft to fly to the assistance of the *Pueblo*, and that they were open-minded on the question of the advisability of sending such aircraft. Their concern was not, therefore, whether aircraft should or should not have been dispatched, but over the sequence of events that followed the seizure. The sub-committee found that there were 'intolerable delays in the transmittal of important messages', and that the operational commanders were apparently not precluded from exercising their own judgment in providing some assistance to the *Pueblo*. The 'operational commanders had both the authority and the opportunity to act if they had been able to do so immediately'.[4]

In retrospect, it is clear that all the early decisions were made by the military initially at a relatively local level to allow the *Pueblo*'s captain to handle the incident in his own way. The later decision to answer the incident with a show of force by calling out Air Force fighters which, due to darkness, never flew over Wonson where the *Pueblo* had been taken, was made at area command level. The rerouting of the *Enterprise* was also made at area command level.

President Johnson was, therefore, presented with a situation in which he had very little room for manœuvre, either militarily or politically. The same day he decided to take the politically demonstrative action of calling up reservists, and he called for an urgent meeting of the Security Council in an attempt to bring diplomatic pressure on the North Koreans. The United States Administration was by then in a difficult position, since there was no effective way in which it could respond short of a direct attack on North Korean territory. The North Koreans had no similar intelligence ship which might be seized as a quid pro quo, nor were they dependent on sea-going traffic to supply their coastline, so a naval blockade would have had little effect. The President, too, was well aware that he would be risking the lives of the captured crew if he took any overt retaliatory action. It is clear that the opportunity for American counter-action existed for only a short time after the *Pueblo* had been challenged. If aircraft had been immediately available on instant readiness to overfly the *Pueblo*, the North Koreans might have been forced to call off their harassment, but even at that early stage it would have been a risky and provocative action.

By the time President Johnson was involved he was in a

position where he could only threaten. Wisely, within the limits of his own domestic political situation he did not attempt to make too much of any possible aggressive counter-response, and only concentrated fighter aircraft in South Korea. The Secretary of State, Dean Rusk, made the legitimate point that even if the North Korean allegation that the *Pueblo* had contravened the twelve-mile limit – which he denied – was true, then their response was still illegal. He rightly claimed that, under the 1958 Convention of Law at Sea, if a warship sailed into territorial waters, then the coastal state had the right to require the warship to leave, but had no legal right to seize it. Dean Rusk pointed out that on two occasions in 1965, and once in 1966, Soviet naval vessels had penetrated American territorial waters. All three ships were, he claimed, general intelligence ships, and the United States had required them to leave but had never seized them. The whole issue of the real value of intelligence missions is difficult for governments to discuss publicly. The *Pueblo* was concentrating on intercepting VHF and UHF short-range communications, and had to be close to the shore in order to pick them up. Such information can, if skilfully interpreted, give an early indication of enemy strategy. However, it has to be carefully judged whether the inherent risks of such intelligence missions are justified by the potential value of the information likely to be collected. There is substantial evidence that such detailed military and political assessment and justification takes place all too rarely and that the value of the expected information is often trivial in comparison to the political risk being undertaken.

One good outcome of the incident was the overall tightening up of United States naval security that followed, the revision of communication procedures, provision for an improved weaponry for the intelligence ships and better destruction equipment for documents. It is also likely that protection for isolated ships will be provided more freely in future and some form of contingency planning will probably become mandatory to cover intelligence missions.

The risk evaluation of intelligence missions is obviously the key issue, and for a time the procedure is likely, particularly in the United States Navy, to be more thorough. One lesson from this incident is that the political heads of the armed forces in all countries must exert greater control over such missions. There is already in existence in many countries a well-defined procedure for political authorization. It is clearly necessary, however, for the politicians to ask more fundamental questions not only on risk evaluation, but in the crucial area of assessing the real value of the intelligence information. Shrouded in secrecy, the intelligence community is too often able to escape the degree of objective scrutiny that their activities demand. It is high time, if politicians are to ensure tight control of the military, that they should undertake regular, detailed reviews of the activities of the intelligence community and refuse to allow this area to hide behind a carefully contrived veil of secrecy. They should not be frightened off by believing this to be too technical an area. It is essentially a field for the exercising of good judgment. The military have a tendency, particularly in times of peace, to justify all too easily the taking of risks and to be insensitive to the overall situation between countries. They are too used to seeing ideological differences solely in terms of black and white values. They are trained to think in terms of threats and enemies which are not always the most appropriate background for an objective assessment.

Part Two Political Decision-Making

Political Issues

It would be foolish to imply that the defects of defence decision-making are due solely to the military and their procedures. In fact, politicians must accept a major responsibility for many of the more extraordinary decisions that have occurred in the 1960s.

The Vietnam war is certainly the most important example of how an initially small and tentative commitment can escalate into a massive military operation. It is easy to criticize merely, with the benefit of hindsight. The problem is that each decision taken in isolation can often be shown to have had an inherent logic at the time. Inexorably, in such situations, pressures build up and reactions to circumstances begin to beget whole new situations which themselves demand an increased reaction. This process occurs in practically every field of governmental activity. But in the defence field, there are unique features which bedevil the systematic application of sensible decision procedures.

The most important psychological factor, particularly in the initial phases, is secrecy. The extent of the commitment, whether the wording of an existing treaty or pledge, or the actual troop levels involved, is far too often disguised from the general public under the overall cloak of national security. Hand in hand with security goes the extraordinary unwillingness of many informed people to criticize the military. When military matters are under discussion, too many non-military people suddenly lose confidence in their normal critical faculty. It becomes all too easy to argue that one is not aware of all the facts; and that clearly the government would not be taking a particular action if it was not for the existence of some undisclosed circumstance. Many people tend to identify military decisions with vague patriotic concepts and feel that to be seen to question a particular decision may, in some strange way, raise doubts about their own patriotism. All these factors coalesce to form uneasy non-specific pressures. The way to counter these pressures is to develop a political structure which encourages and sustains scrutiny of the defence budget and military decision-making, a structure which actively fosters a climate of critical but concerned comment.

Informed discussion would also do something to ensure that politicians understand the implications of their decisions. The principle of the abolition of conscription, for example, is rightly favoured by most politicians, who see compulsory service as an interference in an individual's liberty. But few realize the extent to which service manpower levels impose their own strategy. Under present strategies there is a point at which unilateral troop reductions can undoubtedly raise the threshold at which one might be forced to use nuclear weapons. The actual level at which this might occur is debatable and a good deal of exaggeration and deliberate over-bidding takes place, but this type of dilemma is rarely faced with complete honesty by commentators or politicians. The movement inside the United States towards volunteer forces is now certain to result in the cessation of compulsory military training. The removal of the Vietnam commitment will mean that initially the fall in troop numbers will not have any appreciable strategic consequences, but it could have a profound long-term impact on Western strategy. There are no easy answers. The 'numbers game' over troop levels can be played with many permutations, but it is foolish to ignore the interrelationship between relative troop levels and the ability to ensure that any future strategy rests at least initially on a response relying solely on conventional weapons.

It is probable that the Vietnam war has resulted in more day-to-day political decision-making over military operations than ever before in world history. To assess the impact of this involvement at this stage is extremely difficult. Many military commanders would argue that the outcome would have been very different had they been delegated a greater degree of control. Others will argue that, given such military control, the risk of escalation into a third world war would have been far greater. Robert Kennedy's remark about the type of advice he experienced when in his brother's Administration shows how one politician felt.

> One member of the Joint Chiefs of Staff, for example, argued that we could use nuclear weapons, on the basis that our adversaries would use theirs against us in an attack. I thought, as I listened, of the many times that I had heard the military take positions which, if wrong, had the advantage that no one would be around at the end to know.[1]

It is doubtful whether it will be possible to draw major conclusions on the conduct of the Vietnam war until a few more years have elapsed and a greater degree of objectivity can be focused on the whole issue. The Pentagon Papers will need to be supplemented by the personal accounts of such key decision-makers as Robert McNamara, Dean Rusk and, above all, President Johnson. The full release of all the relevant Presidential Papers and the as yet unpublished volumes of the Pentagon study dealing with the secret diplomacy of the Johnson period will be crucial to any analysis of real motives and aspirations.

It is important to recognize that these papers were not all available to the authors of the Pentagon study, nor were State Department and Central Intelligence Agency files. Yet enough is revealed in the Pentagon Papers to show how dominant was the view that, since the United States was the most powerful nation in the world, the outcome in South Vietnam would demonstrate the will and ability of the United States to have its own way in world affairs. The double-talk of the politicians, with their public statements emphasizing the obligations of the United States to help their friends and ensure freedom for the South Vietnamese, is starkly revealed by a memorandum from John T. McNaughton, Assistant Secretary of Defense for International Security Affairs to Robert McNamara. Written on March 24th, 1965, it defined United States aims:

70% – To avoid a humiliating US defeat (to our reputation as a guarantor).

20% – To keep South Vietnam (and the adjacent) territory from Chinese hands.

10% – To permit the people of South Vietnam to enjoy a better, freer way of life.

ALSO – To emerge from the crisis without unacceptable taint from methods used.

NOT – To 'help a friend', although it would be hard to stay in if asked out.[2]

The Vietnam war has led to public cynicism and resignation to the workings of the United States defence policy which will bedevil any sensible public dialogue for decades to come. This is not just the famous 'credibility gap'. A degree of detachment has followed the initial anger and frustration over the Vietnam revelations. This detachment makes it difficult to discuss defence issues sensibly. A whole generation of young Americans has opted out of even thinking in terms of American military responsibilities being world-wide. It is this generation which could redirect American policy away from military aid and towards civil aid to the underdeveloped world. The less attractive alternative is a return to isolationism. One effect is certain – the old attitudes and postures will not remain.

The 1960s have been marked by a number of small military incidents in different parts of the world. Russian involvement in Cuba has been the most dramatic, and the invasion of Czechoslovakia the most offensive and brutal, use of military power.

The Russians have also demonstrated in the 1960s how they can successfully use military power in a flexible and diverse way. In June 1967, after the Arab-Israeli war, they quickly deployed ships and submarines from the Mediterranean squadron to Egyptian ports – a clear demonstration of involvement and a dramatic way of bringing aid and comfort to their friends. However, at that stage it was predominantly a political gesture with no serious intention of military involvement. With the decision to install Russian surface-to-air missiles in the Canal zone following the negotiated cease-fire, the Russian presence in Egypt became more sophisticated and more permanent. Taken with the emergence of a naval base at Alexandria, it betokens a degree of military involvement for the 1970s that was not envisaged in 1967.

It is interesting to look in detail at some of the most important of the incidents in the 1960s in which military force has been used primarily in furtherance of political objectives, and it is fair to draw the conclusion that what the Western powers have done in the past, Russia will do in the future.

The area loosely described as East of Suez and that of the African continent have both been important centres of change throughout the 1960s. Lessons for the future can be drawn from studying the political background to the military decisions that were taken in these areas, and following their eventual outcome.

Chapter 7. East of Suez

The British military presence in the Far East has been a controversial issue in British politics for some years. Bedevilled by a chronic balance-of-payments deficit which owed much to the considerable costs of her overseas military forces, Britain was particularly vulnerable to the high costs in terms of foreign exchange which such commitments involved. The crucial and overwhelming argument for withdrawal was nevertheless political, not financial, and this should be stressed. However, it is naive to dismiss completely some of the valid arguments that can be deployed for retaining a military presence, provided that this presence is sufficiently strong to match its commitments. The mere retention of a presence without the necessary financial backing to provide adequate force is extremely dangerous.

INDONESIAN CONFRONTATION

In 1963, Britain possessed considerable forces in the Far East and these were used in the operation which became known as the Indonesian confrontation. Confrontation was an extremely successful use of military power in support of British interests. It is an example of the deterrent use of military power for achieving political objectives which, though costly in financial terms, achieved a measure of stability in the area for the 1970s without fortunately developing into a Vietnamese type of guerrilla war.

Indonesia broke off economic relations with Malaysia on September 21st, 1963, following the proclamation of Malaysia on September 16th. The main aim of Indonesia was to damage the trading centre of Singapore, but it was bound to have a serious effect on its own exports, since the countries which were now part of Malaysia accounted for nearly half of Indonesia's export trade.

President Sukarno adopted a militant posture from the outset, announcing his intention to crush Malaysia, while the British and United States governments responded by cutting off military aid to Indonesia, which only served to increase the aid and supplies to Indonesia from Russia and China.

All through 1964 Indonesian guerrilla activities intensified, and Malaysian fishermen were being harassed by Indonesian gunboats. But their overall activities at this stage, though frustrating, were not such as to pose a threat to Malaysia and in many ways they had the effect of unifying the new state. In July 1964 Malaysia's naval expansion programme was launched, and in September the British moved more naval ships from the Mediterranean to the Singapore base as the situation had deteriorated. It was becoming vital to ensure that sea-borne Indonesian guerrillas were prevented from landing. In August and September 1964 a small group of regular Indonesian forces was landed on the coast of Johore, and some were parachuted with the aim of linking up with Malayan Communist groups. Though the intruders were successfully exposed, the danger was clear. It was obvious that Indonesia, with its large army and common frontier with Sabah and Sarawak, themselves several hundred miles from the Malayan mainland, posed a real threat to the new state. The Indonesian military forces were also superficially fairly well equipped with MiG-21s, Badger bombers and missile-carrying destroyers. If Malaysia was to resist not only the economic confrontation but also the military confrontation it had to rely on British support — mainly the army, but also naval forces capable of patrolling the Straits of Malacca and other Malaysian waters.

By the start of 1965 Britain had assembled her largest outside military force since the Korean war in the Far East. A force of V bombers was stationed in Singapore; the Far East Fleet had been built up to a strength of some eighty vessels, which included aircraft carriers, destroyers, frigates and supply ships, and at one time more than six infantry battalions were stationed in Borneo. It was an impressive display of military strength aimed at deterring Sukarno and his military advisers from mounting an invasion of Malaysian territory. Steadily through 1965 the Indonesian internal situation deteriorated. The economy was in difficulties. Exports had declined and the existing development programme was in disarray. President Sukarno had courted the Chinese and thus angered the Russians, so that he could no longer rely on receiving more weapons. The American ban on spares was beginning to hinder the operational effectiveness of American ships and aircraft which had been supplied in the past. The military themselves were starting to become restless under the Sukarno regime. In October 1965 a successful anti-government coup took place in which the armed forces played a dominant role. The new government had no enthusiasm for Sukarno's policies, and confrontation officially ended on August 11th, 1966.

The whole episode was a triumph for the controlled use of deterrent forces, amassed deliberately in overwhelming numbers so that there could be no question in the Indonesians' minds as to British intentions. The strategy of deterrence without dropping a single bomb enabled Britain to leave most of the internal governmental problems to the Malaysians, yet to remain poised for action along a thousand miles of jungle frontier should the external situation have deteriorated. It is not too fanciful to imagine a situation occurring in other parts of the world – for instance, in South Africa – where a Russian deterrent presence could be used to ensure that South Africa did not invade an African country which was harbouring and encouraging guerrilla action. It is not the continued presence of a military force that is a necessary precursor of effective action, but the ability to deploy and sustain a fighting force away from the home base. It should be the aim of a flexible military strategy to organize logistic support so that, with the full backing of a friendly power's albeit limited facilities, it can sustain a military presence.

At the time of confrontation, Britain was inevitably very dependent on her fixed military bases in Singapore. For the future, even allowing for the minor modifications to the 1968 Far East withdrawal plan that have been announced through the 1970s, any world-wide military power that Britain will be capable of deploying will have to be far more self-sufficient than has been the case in the past. The United States Administration appears also to be moving towards a more flexible deployment policy, less dependent on fixed bases and believing that intervention can occur only when a friendly power is prepared to make facilities available.

It is also interesting that in the 1970s the whole basis of interventionist military policies is being challenged. It has become increasingly obvious that involvement in nationalistic struggles and guerrilla warfare can debilitate even a superpower. It has been interesting to see the United States using the afloat power of the Sixth Fleet in the Mediterranean to counteract the growing Soviet presence in Egypt. This was shown in a most striking way in 1970 when the internal situation in Jordan deteriorated and Syrian involvement could have threatened the security of Israel. The ability of the United States to react without utilizing bases in other Mediterranean countries and of being able to respond quickly and flexibly is of major political importance in the maintenance of an uneasy balance in the Middle East.

THE BRITISH WITHDRAWAL FROM EAST OF SUEZ

An interesting case history of political decision-making is the manner in which the British government through the 1960s decided eventually to withdraw from the Far East. It will be judged by history as a major change in British foreign policy, comparable in some respects with the decision to give India independence. In a democratic country it is doubtful whether any government could have balanced all the conflicting advice on the desirability of withdrawal so as to make a single decisive decision. Yet the opportunity was present in 1964 for the new Labour government to make such a strategic decision. It took office, however, with attitudes to Britain's role in the world that owed more to nostalgia than to reality.

The Macmillan era had been marked by 'top table' posturing and bogus 'summitry' conducted, albeit with great panache, against a progressive decline of Britain's actual power and influence. It took a few painful years before the Labour government was able to shrug off the comfortable illusions fostered in opposition and to come to grips with the real position of the Commonwealth and of Britain in a world greatly changed since many of the key ministers had last held power.

The decision to withdraw was forced out of a reluctant and divided government, and the manner in which the decision was made had an important impact on the British armed services, the Commonwealth and Anglo-American relations. In retrospect, it is clear that it would have been far better had the decision been made and implemented as part of an overall strategic policy, but this would have required a greater unanimity on the actual merits of withdrawal than existed within the Labour government then in power.

In the early 1960s Britain once again began to encounter serious balance-of-payments problems and a significant number of economists started to argue that the cost in foreign exchange of military bases, particularly those in Malaysia and Singapore, represented an unjustifiable financial burden which should be substantially reduced.

Taking office after an absence of thirteen years, a Labour government was returned to power in Britain, pledged to reduce defence expenditure and to adopt a more realistic foreign policy. However, at that time Britain was heavily committed to confrontation with Indonesia, which involved at its height more than 59,000 military personnel. This meant that, despite the large balance-of-payments deficit which the Labour government inherited, there could be no question of immediate defence savings. The February 1966 Defence Review set out the policy of the new government:

It is in the Far East and Southern Asia that the greatest dangers to peace may lie in the next decade, and some of our partners in the Commonwealth may be directly threatened. We believe it is right that Britain should continue to maintain a military presence in this area. Its effectiveness will turn largely on the arrangements we can make with our Commonwealth partners and allies in the coming years. As soon as conditions permit, we shall make some reductions in the forces which we keep in the area.[1]

In July 1966 the Labour government faced yet another financial crisis with a seriously deteriorating balance-of-payments situation. The Cabinet decided mistakenly to defend at all costs the existing parity of the pound, and a decision was taken to resort to the classical cyclical deflationary policies of previous Conservative governments, which the Labour Party in opposition had so frequently attacked. Again, defence cuts were urgently needed; fortunately by now the new government in Indonesia was already discussing with Malaysia the possibility of ending confrontation and so, in July, as part of the announced savings in foreign exchange, it was decided to reduce troop levels in the Far East.

By February 1967, British troops were almost out of Borneo, and by April 10,000 men had been returned from the Far East to the United Kingdom. All this time, pressure on the government from economists outside and from MPs within the Parliamentary Labour Party was building up for yet more substantial reductions in force levels. Many of the critics did not accept the basic arguments for the then defence policy in the Far East and questioned the entire principle of keeping British forces east of Suez.

By March 1967, the government was seriously considering a policy of complete withdrawal from the mainland of Asia not later than 1975-6, and of reducing by half the existing force levels and locally employed civilians in Singapore and Malaysia by 1970-71. This new policy was discussed in Washington at the April meeting of SEATO and met strong opposition from America, Australia and New Zealand, who were particularly concerned by the British government's intention actually to leave the Persian Gulf, Singapore and Malaysia within a specific time-scale. But the government was already committed to the concept of withdrawal, despite widespread recognition of the achievements of confrontation: 'Our aim is that Britain should not again have to undertake operations on this scale outside Europe. The purpose of our diplomacy is to foster developments which will enable the local peoples to live at peace without the presence of external forces.'[2]

Similar statements were expressed by President Nixon in 1969, spelling out the new American policy in the Far East following the decision to withdraw combat troops from Vietnam. However, in 1967, Dean Rusk and President Johnson saw the British withdrawal as undermining the American position in Vietnam and leaving them vulnerably exposed, as the only foreign power with overseas military bases in the Far East. To them the British were failing to live up to their commitments and relations between the two countries became very difficult.

All this time the British government was under conflicting pressures. The arguments of Malaysia, and particularly of Lee Kuan Yew in Singapore, against total withdrawal were strengthened by the consistent advocacy of what was termed a 'residual capability' from a small permanent British force by the government's own military advisers. It was argued that an actual British presence could make a unique contribution to the stability of the area, and this was also the view of the Americans. It was clear too at this time that force-level reductions on the scale envisaged by the government would mean that Britain would no longer be able to meet her force-level declarations to SEATO. Politically, however, internal pressures within the Labour Party and the deteriorating financial situation were influencing government ministers. It was decided that the greatest reductions would be concentrated on the Army, with the Navy and the Air Force contributing most of the servicemen planned to be in the Far East for the first half of the 1970s.

In May 1967 the instability of the Far East was demonstrated by rioting in Hong Kong, which was repeated again in June, and continued through the next few months. This led the

British government to change again its plans for garrison reductions in Hong Kong.

On July 18th, 1967, the British government published a supplementary White Paper on Defence, which announced that the total of men and women working in or for the services in Singapore and Malaysia was about 80,000 and that this would be reduced by 1970–71 to about 40,000, half of which would be civilians. It went on to say that, 'We plan to withdraw altogether from our bases in Singapore and Malaysia in the middle 1970s, the precise timing of our withdrawal will depend on progress made in achieving a new basis for stability in South East Asia and in resolving other problems in the Far East.'[3] The statement said that the government would continue to honour its declarations to SEATO and the Anglo-Malaysian Defence Agreement, and went on to say:

> We cannot assume that once we have left Singapore and Malaysia we shall never again have to use our forces in the Far East, since we shall have dependencies and other obligations there for the foreseeable future. We are, therefore, planning to maintain a military capability for use, if required, in the area, even when we no longer have forces permanently based there.[4]

At this stage it was still planned to maintain two operational aircraft carriers until the middle 1970s, and this fact, along with a decision to keep amphibious land forces until the final withdrawal, influenced the military planning of the rundown. On November 18th, 1967, the government was finally forced to devalue the pound, just at the moment when the most recent rundown plan for total withdrawal was finally approved. This latest plan was based on Prime Minister Harold Wilson's interpretation in the House of Commons of the phrase 'middle 1970s' as being as early as 1973 or as late as 1977.

The defence expenditure reductions which were announced to the House of Commons immediately following devaluation on November 22nd did not have any immediate effect on the Far East rundown, and the decision to give up the construction of an airfield on the island of Aldabra did not have any real impact on the viability of the concept of retaining a capability for reinforcement in the Far East. But it was now clear that the new Chancellor of the Exchequer, Roy Jenkins, was determined to make the fundamental reassessment of British foreign and defence policy that had been progressively fudged over in a series of compromised decisions for the previous three years. The Cabinet had been under continuous pressure from the Parliamentary Labour Party to withdraw. In Britain the fusion of the executive and the legislature in Parliament ensures a greater sensitivity to party feeling than in the United States, with its separation of powers. The Chancellor was now determined to challenge the whole concept of the 'East of Suez' posture that had led to the heavy foreign exchange costs of permanent British bases in Malaysia, Singapore and the Persian Gulf. He also challenged the concept, not just from a narrow Treasury accounting viewpoint, but on the central issue of whether a military presence in these areas was of primary importance to Britain's national interest.

Devaluation had the long overdue effect of concentrating the minds of the British Cabinet on long-term foreign policy decisions. It soon became clear that there were only two main issues on which there was disagreement. The first was whether to withdraw from Far Eastern political and defence commitments by the end of the financial year 1970–71, or one year later 1971–2. In the event the Cabinet compromised following representations from Lee Kuan Yew and its own Foreign and Defence Ministers, and decided to withdraw at the end of 1971. This date was noted with satisfaction in Singapore and inside the Ministry of Defence as being well after the latest date for a general election. Theoretically, therefore, there was still time for a Conservative government to reconsider withdrawal, should they be returned to power. This was made easier by the odd decision to conduct a 'cliff-edge' rundown with a force of some 10,000 remaining behind until the very end, supposedly to cover the final withdrawal on the dubious basis that withdrawal might itself trigger not only an internal security situation but external attack. Largely because of this supposed external threat the aircraft carrier *Ark Royal* was allowed to continue its refit in order to be able to fly Phantom aircraft capable of dealing with the most sophisticated Russian-produced aircraft. It was, as events have shown, an absurd scenario; yet the argument was used and presumably believed.

The second major issue which the Cabinet faced went to the very root of the whole controversy. An immediate decision was necessary on whether to cancel the F-111 aircraft. The Chancellor of the Exchequer, a previous Minister of Aviation, was adamant that the F-111 should be cancelled. There had been considerable escalation in its cost, and he knew that real economic savings only come from making major strategic decisions, for a series of minor cuts would in the end produce no real savings. But the F-111 was supported by the entire Ministry of Defence, despite the fact that cuts would have to be made by both the Army and the Navy in order for it to be retained. The Defence Secretary, Denis Healey, was prepared to offer exactly equivalent cuts in defence expenditure in order to save the F-111. A rather unconvincing case was made out for the F-111 operating entirely within Europe, but the real reason why so much importance was attached to this particular aircraft's retention was that, with its long range, Britain could support her claim to be retaining a general world-wide military capability. As is usual in such circumstances, the conventional military arguments were all deployed with great vigour and emotion, including the powerful argument that to forgo the F-111 would be to put servicemen's lives at risk. Usually this of all arguments is the one most likely to be accepted uncritically, but on this occasion it was not a trump card, since a majority of the politicians were determined to ensure that no British servicemen were permanently in the area for their lives to be put at risk.

At last ministers were determined to challenge the prevailing defence and foreign policy judgment and to cut political commitments at the same time as military resources. Too often in the past British politicians had accepted the commitments and the responsibilities without assuring the resources in terms of manpower and equipment. In consequence, overstretched, undermanned and ill-equipped British forces had often been exposed to unacceptable risks. Politicians had been frequently pushed into accepting such commitments by their senior military advisers, who were incapable of accepting the reality of the financial constraints within which they would have to operate. It is certainly not unknown for the Chiefs of Staff to advocate policies leading to overstretch which could themselves be challenged on the grounds of putting the lives of servicemen at risk. It would, of course, be the height of irresponsibility for any politician to ignore the advice of his senior military advisers when they allege that pursuing a certain policy will put the lives of servicemen at risk, but equally no such advice should be accepted automatically. Some of the most costly – and, it transpires, mistaken – decisions have been taken acting on such advice which, because of its high emotional content, can all too easily be accepted uncritically and unquestioningly.

In view of the subsequent failure of the F-111 aircraft to live up to its specification, it is fortunate that the Cabinet did decide to cancel. Subsequent events have also clearly shown how the estimates of the costs of cancellation were greatly exaggerated. The lesson of this episode is to realize not only how wrong the military and the politicians responsible for them can be in their assessment of critical military equipment, but also how necessary it is for governments to make far-sighted strategic decisions at a time of their own choosing, not waiting to face harsh reality in times of financial disaster.

So it was that on January 16th, 1968, to a packed House of Commons, the Prime Minister announced details of a wide-ranging expenditure review which included such politically sensitive items as the postponement of the raising of the school-leaving age and the reintroduction of prescription charges for National Health Service medicines. The date for a complete withdrawal of British forces from Malaysia, Singapore and the Persian Gulf was fixed for December 31st, 1971, and the government had accepted that it would not be able to fulfil its obligations to SEATO and that it would have to renegotiate the Anglo-Malaysian Defence Agreement. The decision was received badly by the Americans, who particularly resented the withdrawal from the Persian Gulf. It also undoubtedly severely damaged Britain's relations with Australia, New Zealand, Malaysia and Singapore. It was seen by officers in the British services as a betrayal of obligations and commitments that led to a short period in which service morale sank lower than it had done since the abortive invasion of Suez in 1956.

In retrospect, if a firm decision to withdraw had been made at the latest in the summer of 1966, millions of pounds would have been saved, the absurdity of transferring troops from Aden to the Persian Gulf would have been avoided and the re-equipment programme for the services could have been logically developed to support primary British defence interests within Western Europe. A major realignment of British foreign and defence policy would have been given an overall coherence and logic which would have shown it to be the historic and long overdue decision that it essentially was. In the event, the historic perspective was completely lost, the decision was seen by the world and presented inside Britain by a Conservative opposition as an undignified scuttle, a panic reaction to financial pressures, and as an example of incompetent and ill-considered government. The Conservative opposition rashly pledged itself to restore a British presence in the Far East, to reverse the run-down and to remain in the Persian Gulf. Slowly, as the election date drew nearer, political reality began to assert itself. The on-the-spot military presence began to develop instead into a contribution to a five-power force. A cost with an upper limit of £100 million a year became £10–30 million a year and the commitment on the Gulf became an intention to undertake a comprehensive review of the whole situation.

Elected on June 18th, 1970, the new Conservative government soon adopted policies remarkably similar to those of its Labour predecessors. It endorsed the total withdrawal from the Persian Gulf announced by the Labour government. This was facilitated by the 1969 United Nations settlement of the status

of Bahrein, which had been accepted by Iran in the belief that
Britain would be withdrawing. Suddenly, the fact that 40 per
cent of Britain's oil supplies came from the Gulf region was no
longer the crucial determinant. No longer were the risks of
intervention from foreign powers felt to be so menacing. Within
the space of three years all the old arguments were ruthlessly
abandoned. Policy statements once zealously espoused by
British Foreign Ministers and by Conservative opposition
spokesmen, as well as by Dean Rusk and the Pentagon, were
forgotten. The once vogue phrases about political and military
vacuums were forsaken only to gather dust with the still highly
classified documents inside the Ministry of Defence which
contained all these absurdities. Suddenly, aircraft carriers with
modern sophisticated Phantom fighters thought necessary to
cover the withdrawal in the Far East could be safely assigned
to the North Atlantic. The bitter controversy was over.

The only arguments to remain were whether the Labour
government's plan for a general capability for reinforcement
would be a more viable proposition if, as the new Conservative
government felt, it involved a small three-service British force
on the ground in the Far East as part of a five-power commitment. There can be few politicians who wish Britain to be
involved again in Malaya as she was during the post-war
emergency and as happened in the confrontation with
Indonesia. The lesson of the Americans in Vietnam, when a
super-power found itself bogged down in a civil war in the
jungle and forced to withdraw, only reinforces the French
experience there. In the racial riots in Malaya in 1969, Britain
stood by, hoping against hope that it would not be necessary to
intervene. British troops on the ground then undoubtedly made
it harder to envisage disengagement, the danger being of
involvement at a time not of one's own choosing. The deterrent
effect such a force has can be realized only against external
attack. For all the disavowals of the Five Power Conference in
London in 1971, an on-the-ground force makes it difficult for a
British government to escape involvement in a possible counter-
insurgency war in Malaya or Singapore.

The British force of 5,000 servicemen in the Far East planned for the 1970s could well carry the seed of an ever-increasing involvement in the area. Recent history has shown that in Malaysia and Singapore British forces on the ground have had to be expanded to 78,213 servicemen at the height of the Malayan emergency which then dropped to 44,710 in July 1960 at the end of the emergency, and rose again to 59,734 in December 1965 at the height of confrontation.

The fundamental issue is to define the functions, not the extent of the financial commitment or the size of a British presence in the Far East. Too frequently, the argument revolves around a rather artificial distinction between internal or external threats and vague assertions about ensuring the stability of the region. The need is to define exactly the circumstances in which it might be necessary for Britain to come to the aid of the Malaysian or Singapore governments. Where precisely will these circumstances be affected by having troops on the ground or on stand-by as part of a general deployment capability? Having realistically assessed the circumstances, Britain should then judge whether she would wish to be involved, knowing that involvement in the past has been a long-drawn-out process which inevitably means taking sides in an area where issues are confused. The main problem comes from within these countries, from the racial tensions that are generated by the presence of the 'overseas Chinese'. It has never been a simple question of democratic governments versus Chinese-inspired Communist movements, which is how the Western propagandists present the issue. There have always been superimposed on this naively conventional picture reflections of nationalism, socialism and internal political divisions. The more obvious external threats, such as those which could arise again from Indonesia, are likely to be preceded by a period of tension and could, therefore, be adequately dealt with if it was judged advisable by Britain, utilizing an overall reinforcement capability.

The real issue for the 1970s is the same as in 1966. Should Britain any longer attempt to involve herself in establishing permanent military bases in the Far East? There are no credible arguments to sustain the belief that a military presence can actually protect a nation's overseas trading position. All through the 1960s Britain paid a heavy financial price for an illusory defence policy that owed more to sentiment than to reality. A fixed military commitment should be to protect a nation's vital interests. Britain's vital interests are not in the Far East. Her prime national interest, and therefore defence interest, lies in Europe. She should maintain a military force capable of operating world-wide, but that force should be independent of fixed military bases.

The relevance of the British experience from 1966 to 1971 should not escape the politicians in Washington or their military advisers. For America faces remarkably similar issues in the 1970s. Any Administration, whether Democratic or Republican, will have to try to reduce defence expenditure as part of a systematic phased programme. Having withdrawn from Vietnam, it will have to disengage from the Far East as part of an overall strategic plan. The indications unfortunately are that the United States will reproduce many of the British mistakes on a larger scale. The Administration will reduce expenditure only in response to Congressional pressures, thus ensuring wasteful cancellations and abortive research and development costs. The Administration will quit foreign bases and countries in haste and under pressure, after episodes such as Cambodia and Laos, which ensure lasting damage to American prestige and standing. The United States armed forces will resist the inevitable reductions until the end and they will be left bitter and disillusioned. It is a sombre prospect, which only highlights the inadequacy of governments when faced with the need for making long-term decisions on foreign and defence policy. A mixture of compromise, sentiment and muddle seems to be the hallmark of military withdrawals. It is a mixture that has operated in Indochina, Cyprus, Algiers, Vietnam, Aden, the Persian Gulf and Malaysia and Singapore. It must be hoped that at least some lessons will eventually be learnt from such a dismal record.

Chapter 8. The African Continent

As each new decade starts, it has become fashionable to predict that the African continent will emerge as the area of central importance in world affairs. The start of the 1960s was no exception and, with the Congo in 1960–61, the East African mutinies in 1964, the Rhodesian rebellion in 1965 and the Nigerian civil war in 1968–9, world attention was certainly involved in Africa to a far greater extent than in the 1950s.

However, there can be few people who would doubt that the 1970s promise even greater attention being focused on Africa. The issue of apartheid is so central to human relationships that it cannot but dominate the coming decade. It is clearly essential that Western governments do not ally themselves with the present South African government and also that they fully endorse the United Nations Resolution calling on member nations to stop all arms supplies to South Africa. To do so is not simply to indulge in gesture politics but rather to foresee the long-term outcome of the present racialist policies and to ensure that Western governments are not seen by Black Africa to be supporting white minority groups. Already, the economic bargaining power of the governments of Black Africa is growing. If their own cohesion were greater, they would have the potential in combination to exert economic pressure on the West through trade embargoes and selective investment. Such economic sanctions could be far more damaging than any Western trading loss from retaliatory South African sanctions. It is probably only by Black Africa exerting such collective pressure that the West will ever realize that the pursuit of anti-apartheid policies is not only morally right but also a form of enlightened self-interest when viewed even in the time-scale of ten or fifteen years.

THE EAST AFRICAN MUTINIES

Russia, and to some extent China in Tanzania, have realized that Africa is an area of political importance. It is vital that the West should anticipate and check Russian influence in this area, and there is no more striking example of how an outside amphibious force can be used effectively to bolster friendly governments than the British response to the East African mutinies.

In the early hours of January 20th, 1964, troops of the 1st Battalion of the Tanganyikan Rifles arrested their British officers and moved into all the key military vantage points in the capital, Dar-es-Salaam. The main cause of the discontent was inadequate pay and the wish to have only African officers. Initial consultations with government ministers broke down, rioting took place in the streets and eventually the mutineers were appeased, but on the next day the 2nd Battalion also mutinied. The British government immediately ordered the aircraft carrier *Centaur* and the destroyer *Cambrian* to head for the trouble spot; a naval survey ship *Owen* was already off Mombasa, and the frigate *Rhyl* was near to Dar-es-Salaam. The 2nd Battalion of the Scots Guards was returned from Aden to Kenya to stand by in readiness for any possible call for assistance.

Meanwhile trouble broke out amongst African troops at Jinja in Uganda and Lanet in Kenya. Both President Obote and President Kenyatta asked for British assistance to help put down what looked like a chain of mutinies. Finally President Nyerere, understandably reluctant to call in the former colonial power, asked on January 24th for British help to regain control of his troops. At first light, HMS *Centaur* landed men of the 45 Royal Marine Commando by helicopter near the barracks of the 1st Battalion of the Tanganyikan Rifles, while HMS *Cambrian* fired blank shells as a diversion. The whole episode was quickly over – discipline was restored and the British troops withdrawn. It was by any standard an effective use of military power in support of governments who were pursuing policies broadly in line with British interests.

It is not too fanciful to imagine circumstances in the future where a Russian maritime force might be able to support a Marxist-orientated African government against a right-wing military coup in somewhat similar circumstances and so further their own interests. It is the flexible political use of military power in Africa which is the most likely outcome of the presence of the Russian Navy in the Indian Ocean. To combat this influence, the Western powers will have to be prepared to forestall what might appear to be a military threat with a mixture of political and military counter-measures. The first essential is not to become politically isolated in Africa, and this means rigorously eschewing policies which can be interpreted as giving aid and comfort to governments practising apartheid policies. If the Western powers are seen to be on the side of apartheid, it will only increase the tendency of African leaders to look to Russian military power in times of crisis and to offer Russia facilities and bases for the servicing of their ships.

ARMS SUPPLIES TO SOUTH AFRICA

A recent example of a politically misguided assessment of maritime strategy occurred when the new British government took office in June 1970. It seemingly arrived with military preconceptions which were still deeply rooted in the 1940s. Quite apart from the moral and long-term political arguments against supplying arms to the present South African government, the purely military case for such a decision was extremely thin. It rested pre-eminently upon the belief that the Russian naval presence in the Indian Ocean poses a major military threat as well as a political threat. The case for their being a military threat rests on the supposition that, under certain circumstances, the Russians might interfere with Western tankers sailing around the Cape. The importance of such a threat only began to be accepted in discussions once government ministers had become committed to its existence. Within a few months it had become almost an accepted strategic concept, and was written up as such in responsible newspapers.

Yet, prior to June 1970, the dominant professional view within the Ministry of Defence was that the Russian naval presence posed primarily a political threat. It was the political threat, not the military, which remained the accepted assessment in Washington and in the capitals of the other NATO countries.

It is important to assess the real extent of the threat which the Russian Navy does pose to the Western Alliance, and in order to do this it is necessary to examine the present size and strength of the Russian Navy (see Chapter 9).

The controversy over the Simonstown Agreement illustrates the problem, for it stems from a concern over the free passage of ships around the South African coast, which is one of the busiest of all sea lanes. It is argued almost exclusively by British right-wing strategists that the Cape route is vital for Western trade and that the growth of the Russian naval presence in the Indian Ocean is a military threat to this particular sea route. The strategic arguments for such an assertion are extremely dubious. The Russians are well aware that to interfere with Western shipping around the Cape would be a major act of hostility which would be immediately challenged militarily by the Western powers. The ever-increasing size of the Russian merchant fleet makes it an easy target all over the world and it would be for the Western powers to decide where to intervene militarily. In fact they would be certain to choose a maritime area where they were strong and could rely on land-based maritime air cover. There is no military or political reason why a hostile act at the Cape would have to be countered at the same geographical point.

The main value to Britain of the Simonstown Agreement has been that the fuelling facilities there have meant an economy of three to four Royal Fleet Auxiliary tankers; it also provides a convenient place where a ship's company can break its voyage with a period of relaxation ashore. However, it is significant that the United States Navy does not put in to any South African port and that it has not compromised with the artificial arrangements for multi-racial entertainment that exist for British sailors. Only the prior existence of the Simonstown Agreement stopped a British Labour government from cancelling all naval visits to South African ports. The Agreement covered the use of the base and limited joint British-South African anti-submarine naval exercises. It was kept by the Labour government for reasons that owed much to Britain's need to maintain all her traditional export markets. The only breach of the agreement has been the refusal of the South African government to pay workers at the base equal rates of pay for exactly the same work irrespective of race or colour. It is time the British adopted the same stance as the United States Navy, and stopped visiting South African ports. For the price of, at the most, four additional tankers, Britain could have a flexible afloat support system which would ensure complete freedom for the Royal Navy to exercise around the Cape and in the Indian Ocean.

The absurd legal arguments which threatened in 1971 to break up the Commonwealth about how many helicopters Britain should or should not supply to the South African Navy as a result of earlier sales of naval vessels have only been the smokescreen for a fundamental change of political attitudes to South Africa which followed the return of a Conservative government in June 1970. The exaggeration of the Russian presence in the Indian Ocean, the flouting of the United Nations Security Council Resolution banning the sale of arms to South Africa and the false claims for the military importance of Simonstown all reveal a wholly different political attitude to an issue which is about basic human rights. Many people in the world are rightly not prepared to see the evils of Communism countered by a defence alliance which in any way links the West with the evils of apartheid. Britain has compromised for too long with South Africa. South Africa needs Britain and her partners in the Western Alliance far more than they need South Africa.

The Russian Navy in the Indian Ocean does introduce a new factor into the military balance and it would be absurd to underestimate its importance. Its size and potential, however, need to be viewed with a historical and political perspective.

THE BEIRA PATROL

In 1966, the United Nations became involved in the use of force to support its principles on racial discrimination. It was a new initiative for United Nations activity which is likely to become a controversial policy option again in the 1970s. Judged in isolation the Beira patrol has been a remarkable demonstration of the effective use of naval power. But its effectiveness has been masked by the ability of the Rhodesians to develop alternative sources of supply overland through South Africa. The Beira patrol, in consequence, has been subjected to uninformed criticism on the naive basis that it has failed to stop petrol reaching Rhodesia. The blockade could only ever stop oil coming into the refinery at Beira, and in this task it has totally succeeded. It was the political decision not to extend the area covered by the maritime blockade or to disrupt the alternative land supply routes, whether by road or rail, which inevitably led to petrol reaching Rhodesia.

On November 11th, 1965, the Rhodesian regime under Ian Smith issued a unilateral declaration of independence. This was followed swiftly by Resolution 216 of the Security Council of the United Nations, carried by ten votes to none, with France abstaining. The Resolution condemned the unilateral declaration of independence made by a racist minority in Rhodesia and called upon all states not to recognize this illegal racist minority regime and to refrain from rendering any assistance to it.

The Beira patrol is a classic illustration of the failure of politicians to look realistically at the facts and of their tendency to rely on optimistic projections of that which they wish to hear. It is part of the whole tragedy of the handling of the Rhodesian rebellion that initially gesture politics was seen as a substitute for hard-headed realism. The justification for embarking on a naval blockade was the belief that the Smith regime was so weak that it would be toppled by even a temporary disruption of oil supplies. It is extraordinary that it was thought necessary to achieve this limited objective in such a flamboyant manner when a similar result could have been achieved by covert action, such as blowing up the pipeline or sabotaging the pumps. This would have avoided inducing the consequential pressures for escalating the military confrontation when no such action was ever contemplated. The British government had always been against taking any overt military action to disrupt road and rail communications from South Africa to Rhodesia. This action had been considered with the possibility of open military invasion, but the option had been dismissed as a result of a combination of military and political arguments. With the supporting attitude of South Africa and Portugal, it was felt that air strikes flown from Zambia aimed at disrupting supplies would have encountered the same difficulties that the United States faced in bombing North Vietnamese supply lines to the Viet Cong in the South.

There is little doubt, however, that these military difficulties were exaggerated in consequence of a combination of prejudiced military advice and the political reluctance of the then Labour government to risk civilian casualties which would have exacerbated the already strong 'kith and kin' arguments espoused by a largely hostile press. With a fragile majority of only five in the House of Commons, the government was understandably reluctant to antagonize public opinion by embarking on an operation that could have taken a week or more. To have landed troops would have necessitated first destroying the Rhodesian Air Force, and this would have meant extensive bombing of airfields close to civilian housing and inevitably leading to loss of life. This particular military action was probably wisely rejected as being politically unacceptable.

Commercial sanctions did not achieve any of the optimistic initial objectives. This result was predictable and inevitable, given the decision to exclude using any force even before independence was declared. The greatest error was never seriously to consider threatening a maritime blockade of any country which connived at sanction breaking. It is not justifiable, however, to argue that, because of the failure of sanctions to bite quickly, they should never have been applied in the first place, nor even that they should have been withdrawn. Sanctions in November 1971 were having sufficient effect on the Rhodesian economy, particularly with the shortage of foreign exchange, to influence the regime to negotiate a settlement with the Conservative government. Any settlement at this stage could only have been achieved by compromising with a racially motivated regime. No amount of constitutional juggling can avoid the fact that the 1971 settlement terms were worse than earlier offers. Yet sadly it has to be admitted that the opportunity existed, following the return of a Labour government in March 1966 with a large majority, to enforce a genuine solution compatible with the only defensible policy of not granting independence before majority rule. Moral outrage in 1972 should not be used as the cover for a failure of political will to match the problem with a credible solution in 1966.

A sensible objective now should be to analyse carefully and unemotionally the reasons for the failure of the overall sanctions policy. In particular, the quality of the advice from the Ministry of Defence, the Commonwealth Relations Office and the intelligence community needs to be assessed. Much of the unfair criticism of the Beira patrol stems from an awareness amongst its critics that the logical extension of the experience of the patrol is that a future maritime blockade covering either Rhodesia or South Africa would be effective only if applied to the entire coastline of southern Africa. The reason why the South Africans attach so much importance to the development of their own navy is that they are acutely aware of their vulnerability to a future naval blockade. By increasing their naval forces they hope to raise the price to be paid for any future policy of maritime sanctions to those nations that might ever contemplate such a strategy. Yet the number of naval ships necessary after the initial confrontation to enforce an extensive maritime blockade would not represent an insupportable burden, especially if shared between nations. The force could rely on afloat support. No loss of life need be involved, and the economic consequences would soon be established if strategic supplies such as oil were stopped completely. It cannot be stressed enough that a total maritime blockade of South Africa is a perfectly viable strategy provided the international will exists among the major powers in the United Nations to enforce it.

Apologists for the British policy in 1965 can fairly point out that although the United Nations was always ready to pass the most militant resolutions, it was far from certain that any military assistance would have actually been forthcoming from Britain's NATO allies. In this context, even though NATO's official responsibility does not extend to the sea area around southern Africa, the presence of Portugal within NATO was a constant bar to any supporting action from NATO countries even acting outside the Alliance. A democratic alliance should not continue to harbour within its structure undemocratic governments such as Portugal, nor should it tolerate the continued membership of countries such as Greece when controlled by a military dictatorship.

It also has to be faced that Japan, France and, to a lesser extent, West Germany did not wholeheartedly support commercial sanctions. Britain, as the administering power, was always far too keen to retain control over Rhodesian sanctions and limit United Nations action. By regarding the declaration of independence as an act of rebellion and announcing immediate economic sanctions, Britain emphasized her own primary responsibility. Accordingly, on November 20th, the Security Council passed Resolution 217, which stated that the declaration of independence had no legal validity and called on Britain to quell the rebellion. The Resolution also called on all states to refrain from any action which would assist and encourage the illegal regime and to desist from providing arms, equipment and military material and asked states to break all economic relations with Rhodesia, and specifically to put an embargo on oil and petroleum products.

In the first few months, sanctions did not have the sharp effect predicted by the British government, and the main concern centred on the future of oil supplies from abroad and the disposal of the 1966 tobacco crop. Petrol rationing was introduced and, on January 27th, Prime Minister Wilson, speaking in the House of Commons, said that despite the difficulties of enforcing oil sanctions because of circumventing action taken by oil companies in South Africa, the effect of the companies' action had been 'much less, thanks to the attitude of South Africa'.[1] At that time the official British view, surprisingly, was that the South African government would continue to act in a restrained manner and discourage sanction-breaking and that, though some petrol was coming in, it was not enough to enable the economy to survive. Such an optimistic assessment was not shared by many outside observers and pressure from African countries continued for the use of military force by the British government. At this time Britain should have accepted that she was not able to put down the rebellion alone and should have laid the responsibility fully on the United Nations.

On February 21st, the Rhodesian Minister of Commerce and Industry announced that a tanker with oil for Rhodesia would arrive at Beira in the foreseeable future, and this was followed by a report next day from Salisbury that the Portuguese government had agreed to the Rhodesian government leasing land on the dockside at Beira for building oil storage tanks. On March 2nd, the construction of six oil tanks with a total capacity of 18,000 tons was completed. The British government then put considerable pressure on the British directors of the Mozambique Rhodesian Pipeline Company, who owned the pipeline which ran from Beira to the oil refinery in Rhodesia. It became clear, however, that it might not be possible to prevent the Portuguese directors from pumping oil through the pipeline and that the only way of ensuring that oil did not reach Rhodesia was to prevent any tankers from reaching Beira.

The aircraft carrier *Ark Royal* and two frigates, the *Rhyl* and *Lowestoft*, were already stationed off the Mozambique coast and on March 8th it was confirmed that Britain had asked the Malagasy government for facilities for Royal Air Force reconnaissance planes. On March 15th, despite French objections arising from their defence agreement with Madagascar permission was given for five manned British aircraft to operate from Majunga in Madagascar.

Throughout the latter part of March there were rumours of tankers sailing for Beira and this was highlighted by the Greek government prohibiting the carrying of oil for Rhodesia to ports in Mozambique or South Africa. The Portuguese government began to complain about interference with merchant shipping and infringement of Portuguese territorial waters by British naval ships and aircraft, but the British merely apologized for any inadvertent breach of territorial waters and explained that they were only observing shipping and asking for their identity and destination. At all times the British government referred only to the Beira patrol and never used the word blockade. This distinction was made for reasons relating to international law.

It was now clear that two tankers, the *Arietta Venizelos*, which changed its name to the *Joanna V*, and the *Manuela*, had been chartered to bring oil to Beira. The Greek government twice warned the *Joanna V*, on March 26th and April 1st, not to proceed to Beira. On April 4th the Greek government, who had been under increasing pressure to allow Britain to use force to stop the *Joanna V*, said that if the United Nations authorized the British government to use force, then they would respect that decision, but that they could not give permission themselves without such a resolution. The *Joanna V* was sighted on April 1st by a Shackleton aircraft flying from Majunga and was intercepted by the HMS *Plymouth* on April 4th. The captain of the *Joanna* said she was destined for Beira for bunkering and provisions, and was allowed to proceed, arriving at Beira on April 5th. The situation was now very serious, with the Portuguese saying that they would not participate in sanctions against Rhodesia and that, while they would not take any initiatives, they would not interfere with the transport of any merchandise into Rhodesia.

In the United Nations, the Special Committee on Colonialism called on April 6th for the immediate use of force, and on April 7th the British government put a draft resolution to the

Security Council. On April 9th, after an inexplicable delay in calling a meeting by the President of the Council, who was the representative from Mali, Resolution 221 was passed with five abstentions. Bulgaria, Mali and the Soviet Union abstained because of the inadequacy of the measures. France abstained because she did not believe that there was a threat to international peace.

The Resolution said that the Security Council was gravely concerned by reports that substantial supplies of oil might reach Rhodesia as the result of an oil tanker having arrived at Beira, and that the approach of a further tanker might lead to a resumption of pumping oil from Beira to Rhodesia. The Council then declared that the resulting situation constituted a threat to the peace and called on the British government to prevent, by the use of force if necessary, the arrival at Beira of vessels reasonably believed to be carrying cargoes of oil to Rhodesia, and empowered Britain to arrest and detain the *Joanna V* upon departure from Beira if she had discharged any oil. The last time that Chapter VII of the United Nations Charter had been invoked was for military sanctions against North Korea on June 27th, 1950.

On April 10th the tanker *Manuela* was intercepted by HMS *Berwick*. She was boarded by two naval officers and two armed men, who informed the captain that, acting within the authority of the United Nations Resolution, they had been authorized by their government to use force to prevent oil being landed at Beira. The captain would not give the necessary assurances and so a further twelve armed men were put on board the *Manuela*, and the captain changed course away from Beira. The boarding party left for the *Berwick* next day when the tanker had steamed well south of Beira. That day the *Joanna V* actually berthed at Beira. She was struck off the Greek Register, given provisional Panamanian registration but told that it would be cancelled if she discharged oil. On April 15th, the Portuguese flew in paratroopers from Lourenço Marques to protect the pipeline, and tension mounted as the world watched to see what the Portuguese would do next. On April 16th Ian

Smith announced that, though the oil on the *Joanna V* was meant for his country, he had decided to forgo it in order not to involve other countries in his dispute with the United Kingdom.

It was possible for the Rhodesians to adopt this attitude to oil coming from Beira because an increasing amount of petrol was reaching the country by road and rail from South Africa and Portuguese Africa. Slowly over the next few months the South African government's support for sanction-breaking increased. Estimates differed as to the amount of petroleum products coming into Rhodesia, but the British government's earlier optimism concerning the South African government's attitude was soon shown to be completely unjustified. Though South Africa maintained her position of not offering overt assistance, the extent of covert assistance was considerable. Initial petrol rationing and higher prices for petrol were the main effects of the Beira patrol.

The United Nations had, however, activated a potentially powerful weapon for exerting much more than the mere moral pressure that can follow the passing of a Security Council resolution. Sanctions, in all their various forms, could give the United Nations the teeth that it needs if it is to have any real effect on governments insensitive to the normal diplomatic pressures. At present, the attitude of the major Western powers has been to argue that even trade sanctions cannot be used as a means of influencing the internal affairs and policies of another country. This dictum, sensible and pragmatic though it superficially appears, will not easily withstand the pressures that are building up over racial discrimination in Africa. As more African countries realize their commercial strength and bargaining power, particularly when they operate in unison, so the Western powers will find themselves under increasing pressure over their whole philosophical attitude to the use of sanctions.

The biggest challenge to the United Nations lies in the area of peace-keeping. This cannot be confined merely to command and control procedures for the use of conventional United

Nations forces. In the long term it will also need a coherent strategy for the application of sanctions upheld by United Nations peace-keeping forces. It will mean a reassessment of the use of maritime power, and an evaluation of the techniques used in the Cuban quarantine and the Beira patrol. A maritime blockade offers potentially one of the most effective ways of enforcing the authority of the United Nations with the minimum use of force, the minimum threat of escalation and the least political embarrassment. It is because the Beira patrol is seen as the first step towards such an interventionist policy for the United Nations that it has been subject to such virulent criticism. The lesson is not that the Beira patrol has been a failure, but that it was too limited in scope and wholly unsupported by an enforceable land-based strategy. However, it has demonstrated an application for limited force which the United Nations could develop. It is a form of sanctions which, for all the political pitfalls and technical problems, offers the United Nations a method of enforcement that it has hitherto lacked. Sanctions cannot and should not be introduced without first a realistic appraisal of possible reactions and without a realizable commitment to the application of readily enforceable measures to ensure success. Within these limits sanctions represent a policy option of far greater potential than most politicians care to admit. The legal problems posed by sanctions are extremely complicated but they are not as formidable as they are often made out to be.

The key status of a maritime blockade in which one nation, or group of nations, interferes with the free passage of ships of another nation upon the high seas depends for its legality on whether a state of belligerency exists between the nations concerned. The United States, at the time of the Cuban missile crisis, was careful only to refer to a quarantine which was limited in action to searching for offensive weapons. This wording never raised the legal issue of whether a state of belligerency existed between the United States and the Soviet Union. The United States also claimed that the quarantine was a preventative force and that it was multinational, being supported by the Organization of American States. It could not therefore be classified as a unilateral action.

The British government was determined to act legally over Rhodesia and so did not mount a wholesale maritime blockade of Rhodesia, or of any other countries, such as Portugal, thought to be breaking United Nations resolutions relating to sanctions. In consequence, at no time was Portugal blockaded, and at no time were cargoes specifically destined for Portugal stopped. The Beira patrol was only authorized to prevent cargoes reaching Portugal which were destined for Rhodesia in contravention of United Nations resolutions. Britain, prior to the passing of Resolution 221, had felt that she was not legally empowered to prevent *Joanna V* reaching Beira. It was not until the Security Council had agreed that, under Article 39 of the Charter, a threat to the peace existed, that it was possible to invoke military measures under Article 42. Whether the Security Council should have chosen to declare a rebellion by a colony against the administering authority as a threat to the peace is purely a question of judgment. Such a judgment is, however, exclusively left to the Security Council, though a check exists in that it is always open to one of the permanent members of the Council to cast the veto.

The important aspect of Resolution 221 is that the Security Council created a precedent on which future rulings may well become increasingly based. In the past, rulings concerning a threat to the peace have been interpreted very strictly along the doctrine of non-intervention and have been delivered so as to cover actual threats to international boundaries and international security. The Security Council made a political judgment over Rhodesia, as they were perfectly entitled to do, which gave a far higher priority to the long-term threat to peace from racialism than has hitherto been the practice. The Security Council used Article 39 in a positive sense to promote the values enshrined in the United Nations Charter rather than in a purely negative ruling to preserve the status quo. The Resolution should certainly be welcomed by those who believe that the United Nations should play a more active role, for it reactivates a hitherto largely unused power which could be developed in the world in much the same way as Supreme Court rulings on racial discrimination have been used in the United States. It could, for instance, be endorsed as the means of providing an external guarantee to any retrospective change in the Rhodesian constitution which was aimed at impeding progress towards majority rule; or, alternatively it could be used to force a change in the policies of apartheid in South Africa.

Part Three   Maritime Decision-Making

Chapter 9. Maritime Strategy

A striking feature of the world-wide military operations which have taken place during the 1960s is the high incidence of maritime involvement. Paradoxically, this has been occurring at a time when military strategists have been increasingly sceptical of the future relevance of maritime power.

Naval strategy in a thermonuclear age appears to some critics to be based on past maritime experience to a quite unrealistic extent. They do not dispute that during the 1970s the highest priority for the Russian, American, British and French navies will be the maintenance of the strategic deterrent. But they do question whether it is sensible to plan for the possibility of limited war at sea and whether it is conceivable that the escalation following an initial maritime incident could be contained within a maritime environment. Most advocates of limited war at sea pose a theoretical scenario that postulates interference with merchant shipping that, after a period of weeks, would begin to have a crucial importance to those countries dependent on their maritime links for fuel and food. Critics of such a scenario point out that inevitably any maritime involvement would lead to increased tension across existing land frontiers and put a high probability on border incidents occurring within days rather than weeks.

They also argue that no nation would be prepared to see their all-important sea trade life-lines cut without posing the threat of nuclear escalation, leading if necessary to the use of strategic nuclear forces. The difficulty of obtaining a sensible dialogue on the possibilities of limited war at sea is that both sides tend to overstate their case. For example, it is inconceivable that the super-powers will ever again face the same type of maritime warfare as they did in the two world wars. It is none the less a realistic planning assumption that an initial maritime incident could be contained with conventional weapons for many more days than is ever likely to be possible in an initial land-based incident. On land the boundaries are too clear-cut to allow much latitude for the interpretation of intentions. At sea, with no rigid boundaries, the probability is of slower escalation with more time for second thoughts and in consequence a higher nuclear threshold. To this extent limited war at sea is credible.

The proponents of extended war at sea over many months talk of the need for protection of world-wide sea lanes, and constantly reiterate import figures and merchant ship numbers to show the vulnerability of various nations to interference with their sea-borne trade. But these arguments are impossibly hard to sustain and the more sophisticated naval officers are themselves unconvinced that it is a sensible strategy on which to base their future policy.

It is clear that the realities of modern warfare rule out a protracted conventional war involving the super-powers, with one side sustaining severe loss of life and hardship to the civilian population. Limited war over many years will no doubt continue where a confrontation does not directly involve the super-powers. It is inconceivable, however, that Britain would ever involve herself alone in military action against the Soviet Union. On this basis, it is ludicrous to compare the size and strength of the British Navy with that of the Soviet Navy. A meaningful comparison will of necessity be between the navies of the two major alliances, NATO and the Warsaw Pact. Similarly, any strategic involvement with the Soviet Navy must be viewed globally and not on a purely regional basis or even after the initial period entirely within a maritime context.

The activity of the Russian Navy has been given increasing news coverage in the Western world. Its growing presence since 1967 in the Mediterranean and since 1970 in the Indian Ocean has focused attention on its potential. After that of the United States, the Soviet Navy, in both number and power, is the second navy in the world; but this is no new fact, though a casual reader of some of the world's newspapers might well think so. The Russian Navy has occupied that position for over ten years and it is absolutely clear from the statements of their politicians and naval leaders that the Russians intended to achieve a major maritime role many years ago. Yet they have not concentrated on building their navy to the detriment of their other fighting forces. Rather, they have corrected the imbalance that was so marked after the Second World War so that now all three of their fighting services are effective instruments of super-power. It was in 1948 that the Russians decided to become a major maritime power, and it is very necessary to put the recent publicity about the Russian Navy in its true perspective.

A country of over 200 million people with the resources that Russia has at her disposal cannot fail to become a major maritime power if she wishes to do so, and far too many people seem to have read into her growth sinister overtones which can all too easily be exaggerated. Until five years ago, although the Russians disposed of great maritime potential, they seemed reluctant to use it. They were thought of almost solely in terms of being a great continental power whose naval vessels were seldom seen outside home waters. Cautiously at first, but at what is overall an impressively rapid rate, this picture has been changed. Cuba may well have been the watershed or it might have merely hurried a process which had already started. The facts are that the Russian Navy now operates world-wide and is extending its maritime bases in foreign countries. It is starting to use the latest techniques of relying on afloat support, and its overall maritime proficiency has shown a marked improvement in recent years. Yet the overall size and shape of the Warsaw Pact naval fleets are not as formidable as they might appear. A recent comparison with NATO fleets based on a standardized cost has tried to take account of factors such as the greater degree of sophistication in smaller ships, the higher cost per ton of nuclear-powered submarines and the high proportion of old vessels in the United States fleet.[1]

A study[2] based on the situation in 1968 accepts that comparisons based solely on tonnage or the number of vessels is insufficient. It concludes that, on the value of the stock of fighting vessels, NATO has a superiority over the Warsaw Pact of about 2 : 1. It is a fair assumption that, despite valid criticisms of the valuation system that has been adopted, it will be some years before the Warsaw Pact navies can attempt to match the capability of NATO navies, even allowing for the current Russian expansion of new naval construction.

The importance of the Russian Navy should not, therefore, be exaggerated, but equally its potential should not be under-played. It is necessary for the Western Alliance to speculate on Russian intentions and to determine how and in what situation a particular threat might be mobilized against its interests. The Russians, of course, see a clear need for maritime defence. They have seen the Western powers exercise maritime power all over the world for decades and they experienced a humiliat-ing rebuff over the Cuban incident. As they see it, they are menaced from the sea by the Western strike fleets and above all by Polaris boats that lurk within striking distance of their major cities. It is natural for them, therefore, to make defensive provision. Along with their defensive posture they have also developed, particularly with their ballistic missile submarines, an offensive capability, though since it has predominantly a second-strike capability it can fairly be presented as a deterrent weapon system. As the Russians have steadily moved out from their own coastline, they have begun to operate in seas previ-ously almost the exclusive preserve of the Western powers. They have in the main appeared to be content to mark the ships of the NATO navies rather as a footballer marks his opposite number. As their deployment has become more extensive, so they have come to realize the more subtle influ-ences and effects of sea-power. Effectively controlled, maritime strategy can become a political weapon.

Yet maritime strategy is still seen far too frequently in terms of single-service identities. Too often a maritime strategy is developed that merely fits the size and shape of an existing navy. The different emphasis put on submarines, for instance, is a remarkable feature of the future trend of development between the Warsaw Pact navies and NATO countries. The advent of the nuclear-powered submarine, with its immense flexibility stemming from its unlimited under-surface cruising capacity, has made far too little impact on the overall shape of either the United States Navy or, even more markedly, the British Navy. The British Navy only recently accepted the dual role of both anti-submarine and anti-ship for their nuclear-powered conventional submarines. The allocation of financial research-and-development resources in the United States and British navies to underwater anti-ship and anti-submarine weapons systems has been lamentably low. It is a situation which could have occurred only by advocating policies which owe too much to the past history of the surface ship and which ignore its increasing vulnerability. The balance of naval forces needs to be changed radically. It would be foolish to argue for any navy to operate completely beneath the surface, but the shrouding quality of the sea in an age of satellite surveillance and intercontinental missiles with pinpoint accuracy is one of the strongest military assets that the maritime area possesses. It has been woefully inadequately exploited by Western navies in marked contrast to the situation in the Russian Navy, where an amazing expansion of underwater forces is already occurring and will, if continued, demand a profound change in NATO's current maritime strategy.

Any military situation, particularly a maritime engagement, can all too easily be misinterpreted. At a time when NATO maritime exercises are constantly being shadowed by Russian naval vessels, the possibility of misinterpreting an unintentional or provoking incident is obvious and by no means far-fetched. (This concern motivated talks between the United States and the Soviet Union in 1971 on accidental naval incidents.) It is important, therefore, that politicians should begin by questioning the principles on which retaliatory decision-making is delegated to military commanders and particularly to individual ship captains in any situation short of total war. The current arguments for an instant offensive weapons system relying solely on radar and other electronic aids to be fitted to all surface warships raises the same fundamental issues. The whole basis of fitting surface-to-surface guided weapons to small frigates, in addition to surface-to-air defensive missiles, needs serious questioning. Should such ships use such powerful offensive weapons in circumstances when they are operating alone? Should they respond only in times of declared war? Would one ever envisage operating frigates alone in times of declared war? Or would they not more realistically form part of a task force with the offensive capability being shared with accompanying submarines, air support or big ship missiles?

Some of the most politically and militarily unrealistic scenarios are capable of being produced for naval operational research analysis to justify individual weapons systems. An example of this is the isolated frigate scenario, in which the frigate is supposedly involved in an incident miles away from the reach of shore-based aircraft. The vulnerability of the frigate is then argued as being the justification for a surface-to-surface guided weapon being fitted to all frigates. This is in order to circumvent the so-called 'missile gap' with an instant retaliatory capacity. The scenario borders on the absurd. Political and military reality dictates that no small frigate should ever operate alone in times of military tension. Nor, on the sketchy radar information on which such a ship relies for firing, should an isolated frigate in times of peace lightly contemplate responding before confirmation of an attack.

Any incident must be judged on its own merits, but the belief that an offensive automatic response is expected of every ship's captain needs at least to be challenged. The problem is to define different guidelines for responding in times of peace and in times of war. It is inherent in military strategy, and in the whole ethos of naval strategy of every navy in the world, that the individual ship's captain defends his ship to the last man. The very idea of withdrawing the right to respond to a threatened attack is absolute anathema to any naval officer. Yet the fundamental questions still need to be asked even for conventional weapons, not so much by the servicemen as by the politicians, and by the people from whom the serviceman's authority to wage war comes. It is not enough to argue that, if a mistake is made, you simply apologize. The danger of uncontrollable escalation is too great. We need to question whether we should allow offensive action to be taken instantly, particularly in a maritime environment where the possibility of error is so high. To act offensively in times of peace merely on the basis of a single frigate's electronic warning system is to risk a serious miscalculation, as is shown by recent history.

The Gulf of Tonkin was well known as an area where electronic interference was common, thus making interpretation of patterns on the radar screen immensely difficult. In the absence of any disclosures of the actual content of the intercept messages, it is reasonable to assume that the only strong evidence for the 1964 attack was radar and sonar. Radar would have detected the existence of the PT vessels, but only sonar information could have given rise to evidence on the firing by the North Vietnamese of a 'number of torpedoes'[3] — which were the words used by Secretary of State McNamara in testimony to the Senate Foreign Relations and Armed Services Committee. According to John Finney, even Defense Department officials are now saying that only 'perhaps two but more likely one' torpedo was fired.[4] Others question even this.

Apparently the only visual report of the sighting of a torpedo wake came in affidavits taken after the incident, and so it was only on the sonar reports of the torpedo attack that the actual decision to retaliate was taken. One does not need to be a sonar expert to question whether, with two ships operating at high speed and changing direction constantly while in close proximity, any sonar equipment built primarily to detect submarines would be likely to be able to detect the firing of perhaps two, but more likely one, torpedo.

Whether or not a torpedo was fired must, therefore, in retrospect, be a matter of grave doubt — even now with the benefit of all the evidence from the extensive inquiries that followed the incident. It is unquestionable, therefore, that twelve hours after the incident there was wholly insufficient proven evidence to justify the decision to retaliate against North Vietnam.

Not enough people realize that, in times of peace, to give the captain of an isolated ship or the commander of a tactical missile launcher the right to respond to a supposed attack even with conventional weapons is virtually to delegate authority to the interpretation of electronic information from radar and sonar equipment – information which has already been shown in practical situations from the 1960s to have been woefully inadequate as a basis for any instant retaliatory action. Instead of arousing people's emotions and national pride, politicians should condition their public to understand that it might be better to face a minor territorial incursion or the loss of a naval ship, possibly under humiliating circumstances, than to risk the escalation of a war, at least until the report on the initial situation has been verified.

This problem of relying on electronic information is of particular concern in the area of early warning systems for land-based intercontinental ballistic missile systems (ICBM). These missiles are vulnerable to a first-strike enemy attack. In contrast, the whereabouts of submarine-launched missiles are unknown, so that they are impossible to destroy in any first-strike operation. Land-based missiles have to be fired and off their launching pad within the period from the first radar warning of an attack to the final confirmatory impact; this gap can be as little as four minutes.

No nation should continue to rely on such dangerous weapons systems and it is quite extraordinary that politicians in the Soviet Union, the United States and France should continue to deploy such dangerous systems. China has only just started to develop submarine-launched missiles so that her present deployment of land-based missiles is understandable. The French decision is also somewhat easier to justify, since they have still to develop a viable force of submarine-launched missiles.

But the two super-powers have already achieved a total megatonnage of nuclear warheads capable of being launched from submarines, which makes any additional land-based weapons system wholly superfluous. A major aim of SALT could well be to achieve a total abolition of all land-based inter-continental ballistic missiles. In which case, the world would have some assurance that at least no nuclear response would ever have to rely solely on the interpretation of radar and other electronic warning devices. A political decision to respond would only then ever need to come after confirmation of an actual nuclear explosion.

The Russians' emphasis on building up their numbers of submarine-launched missiles indicates that they see the importance of such a second-strike system. Perhaps by the middle 1970s, when the two super-powers can each be convinced that they have not only a reasonable degree of parity of submarine-launched missiles but also a sufficiency of nuclear warhead megatonnage, they may agree to abandon their dangerous land-based missile systems.

The Americans' decision in 1972 to increase expenditure on their third-generation, deep-diving, slow-moving, long-range missile-carrying submarines, bringing the first into service in 1978, confirmed the future importance of maritime strategic forces. President Nixon also emphasized the importance of conventional maritime power by sailing a large task force into the Indian Ocean during the 1971 Indo-Pakistan war. This initiative did little more than alienate the Indian people even further from an American Administration which had throughout pursued a militantly pro-Pakistan policy. It was nevertheless another indication of the potential political impact of maritime power and could be seen as a warning to the Russians that their maritime build-up in the Indian Ocean would not go unchallenged. It is significant that the advocates of negotiations aimed at achieving balanced maritime forces in the Indian Ocean are now being listened to with greater respect.

Chapter 10. International Maritime Law

Looking at the more serious maritime incidents that have occurred over the last ten years, one cannot fail to be struck by the chaotic nature of so much of the international law as it relates to the sea. In the Arab-Israeli conflict over the Straits of Tiran, the Cuban crisis, and the Gulf of Tonkin and *Pueblo* incidents one sees again and again clearly conflicting evidence as to various national rights: what constitutes an international waterway? what are the boundaries of territorial waters? when is free passage through certain straits an international right and when is it a privilege conferred by the nation that claims a legal right to control access? There is little that is new in these controversies, but their importance lies in their potential for acting as a trigger for military action.

The continental strategy which has tended to dominate strategic thinking, particularly in Europe since 1945, has largely stabilized the latter's boundaries. Even in Berlin, because of the physical presence of the wall, there is a well-defined boundary. In present circumstances, it would be difficult to misconstrue an act of aggression in the continent of Europe. A military intrusion across such well-demarcated territories would clearly be a deliberate action with very little room for disagreement, whether in international opinion or law.

The position is very different at sea, and it is worth recalling some of the treaties from which the present unsatisfactory situation derives what little authority it possesses. The history of the Black Sea Straits also reveals some quite genuine analogies with present-day problems.

The Black Sea Straits, defined by the Montreux Convention as including the Dardanelles, the Sea of Marmara and the Bosphorus, have been fought over and contested for centuries. From 1453 the Ottoman empire, centred at Constantinople, established complete control over the Straits. Then, in 1774, under the Treaty of Kutchuk-Kainardji, control was vested theoretically in the Turkish government, only to be taken from them under the terms of the Armistice of Mudros in October 1918, and exercised by the three Great Powers. On July 24th, 1923, the Treaty of Lausanne, which Russia refused to ratify, was signed, giving freedom of passage for commercial vessels and aircraft for all nations, in both peace and war, except where Turkey was a belligerent, when she had the usual right to proceed against enemy merchantmen and to search neutral vessels. Warships were allowed freedom of passage in peace, subject to an overall limitation on size that no one power might send into the Black Sea a force larger than that of 'the largest fleet maintained by a littoral power in that Sea'.[1]

It was decided that the European and Asiatic shores of the Bosphorus and the Dardanelles, the Greek and Turkish islands commanding the exits of the Dardanelles and those in the Sea of Marmara, with one exception, were to be demilitarized. Turkey was allowed to modify the zone in times of war – provided that she notified the signatories. An International Straits Commission was established, brought into being by the Treaty of Sèvres, and the Presidency of the Commission given permanently to Turkey. The signatory powers were obliged to meet any threat to the freedom of the Straits or to the security of the demilitarized zone by all the means that the Council of the League of Nations might decide for the purpose.

It is interesting that Russia's refusal to sign was on the basis that the Straits should be closed to warships both in peace and in war – though in 1930 two Russian warships passed unnoticed through the Straits. At that time the Russian Navy was a small force, and the Russians were presumably content to remain within the confines of the Black Sea, with no vision of the world-wide maritime presence which was to emerge in the 1960s.

In 1930, Turkey began to emerge as a more formidable power in her own right. In 1932 she was admitted to the League of Nations, putting an end to the strange situation where the Presidency of the Straits Commission, which was a League of Nations institution, was occupied by a non-member state.

Turkey at this time was fostering good relations with the Russians. On May 23rd, 1933, at the Disarmament Conference, Turkey demanded that the demilitarization clauses of the Lausanne Treaty should be abrogated. A similar proposal was again made by Turkey during the July 1933 Greco-Turkish negotiations which gave rise to the Balkan Pact. The militaristic attitude of Italy was a major Turkish preoccupation. Despite the 1928 Italo-Turkish pact, she feared an Italian threat to Anatolia.

In 1936, Turkey wrote to the Secretary-General of the League of Nations renegotiating her claims for a modification of the demilitarized clauses. The League clearly wished to avoid any further pre-emptive national action, such as the Italian annexation of Abyssinia and German reoccupation of the Rhineland, both of which were severe blows to its authority. Turkey's anxiety was genuine enough – the world was once again rearming. She saw that the four-power guarantee which was the backbone of the Lausanne Treaty was now meaningless, since Britain and France were in conflict with Italy and the fourth power, Japan, had withdrawn from the League. Kemal Ataturk was an enlightened leader of the Turkish people, for he realized that a legal solution would be of far more value than a pre-emptive military action, which was clearly within his power. All the signatories of the Lausanne Treaty, with the exception of Italy, met at Montreux to consider the critical Turkish draft, which was pretty favourable to Russia, allowing her fleet to expand, but not allowing a comparable increase in the size of any fleet that could pass into the Black Sea, and actually cutting down their tonnage. This went far beyond the original request concerning the demilitarized zone, and also gave Turkey sole powers of supervision over the Straits.

The British then put forward a revised draft which insisted on the principle that the Straits was an international waterway under the supervision of an international authority. It also proposed that all maritime nations be treated alike, irrespective of whether their territory bordered on the Black Sea. Eventually this draft became the basis of the new convention,[2] which was signed despite the Italian boycott, a clause allowing for an eventual Italian signature being included in the final text.

The main strategic interest in the convention related to Section 2, which stipulated, amongst a lot of detail on tonnage and weapons, an eight-day notification period to Turkey of any intended transit of war vessels through the Straits.

The convention is a quite specific one which did not attempt to codify international law for all straits, or to draw up a definition of an international waterway. It has withstood the passage of time surprisingly well, although tonnage limitations and armament specifications, most of which are worded inappropriately to cover modern weapons systems, have been mainly ignored. The United States and British navies still send vessels into the Black Sea from time to time and make courtesy calls on Turkish ports, as much as anything to demonstrate to the Russians their rights under the convention. These missions occasionally give rise to adverse comment in the Russian press, but the impression is that no one is really concerned, and the Russians presumably see little gain from updating and renegotiating the convention.

The importance of the Black Sea Straits and the Montreux Convention to maritime law is that it upholds the principle acknowledged by most maritime nations, that merchant vessels have the right of passage through the territorial waters of any state, and also concedes the right of that state to question and regulate the passage of such vessels. To this extent all territorial waters are, in effect, international waterways. In the case of canals, such as Suez and Panama, they are frequently classified as internal waterways in which free passage is given by the state as a privilege, not a right. It is important to stress the principle that territorial waters are international, because it is sometimes claimed that gulfs, such as the Gulf of Aqaba, are in a special category – that of closed seas. If one accepts, for the purpose of argument, the twelve-mile territorial water limit that the Arabs claim, one can allege that, since all the Gulf of Aqaba is then covered by territorial water, there are no high seas, and therefore no rights of passage. The absence of the area legally defined as the high sea should not, however, change the rights of free passage, provided the waterway naturally opens on to the high seas; but it is doubtful if international law itself confers any such right of innocent passage. The 1958 Geneva Convention did define international straits as including those 'used for international navigation between one part of the high seas and another part of the high seas or the territorial sea of a foreign state'.[3] The trouble with this ruling is that, though ratified by over thirty countries, including Britain, the United States, Russia and Israel, some countries such as Egypt were not signatories to the convention and therefore do not feel bound by its ruling.

A vexed question is whether warships have the right to pass through territorial waters when there is no state of belligerency between the territorial state and the flag-flying state. The Montreux Convention accepts that the territorial state has greater regulatory power over warships than over merchant vessels but does not have the right to impose a total ban on non-belligerent states.

In the Corfu Channel case of 1949 the International Court ruled that, in the absence of belligerent rights, innocent passage could be claimed by warships through waters that were decreed to be international. As a result, Albania had to pay compensation to Britain for damage sustained by two British warships from mine explosions within Albanian territorial waters. If Albania had warned the British of the existence and position of the mines, they would have been within the law, provided that there was a navigable route, on the basis that they were only regulating the passage of ships through their waters. But the Corfu Channel case ruling on the international status of the waterway is only relevant to that particular case, which quoted as supporting evidence the fact that the channel linked two parts of the open sea and was in current use for the purposes of international navigation.[4]

A special international convention would have to be convened to settle the Straits of Tiran–Gulf of Aqaba question, since the present position is hopelessly confused. Egypt claims that she has the right to prevent Israeli warships from passing through the Straits of Tiran. She claims that she is at war with Israel, and has already used belligerent rights as the justification for preventing Israeli ships from using the Suez canal, which, under the convention of 1888, allowed free passage to both merchant and warships. The validity of this claim is at least defensible, particularly in view of the wording of the Egyptian-Israeli general armistice agreement of February 24th, 1949, which provides that no military or even regular force should pass through 'the waters within three miles of the coastline' of Egypt.[5]

Of course, at the time of the signing of the armistice, Eilat was Egyptian, and had not yet been seized by the Israelis. A much more serious issue, however, is the Egyptian claim that they also have the right to prevent Israeli merchant shipping from using the Gulf of Aqaba, particularly when, from 1956 to 1967, Israeli shipping had been passing freely through the Straits of Tiran. On February 1st, 1957, to reassure the Israelis, the then United States Secretary of State, John Foster Dulles, gave them an aide memoire, which said that the United States 'believes that the Gulf comprehends international waters and that no nation has the right to prevent free and innocent passage in the Gulf and through the straits giving access thereto'.[6] This position was reiterated by President Johnson on May 23rd, 1967,[7] and by the British Prime Minister, Harold Wilson, on May 24th when he said, 'Her Majesty's Government will assert this right on behalf of all British shipping, and is prepared to join with others to secure general recognition of this right.'[8]

This British reaction, which reflected the interventionists' case stemmed from the strong belief – which events proved to be fully justified – that Israel could not and would not tolerate interference with her right to use the port of Eilat, and that unless the maritime nations supported Israel's case on the basis of international maritime law, then Israel would take the law into her own hands. There were fears that a precedent was being established and parallels were drawn with the Baltic Sea and the Black Sea. These arguments were more emotional than factual, but it is worth stressing that the confusion over maritime law could have explosive results. The rights of free passage on the sea involve national pride and emotion, as is well illustrated in the Congressional debate on the Gulf of Tonkin. Senator Humphrey, soon to become the American Vice-President, said,

> Surely the Congress would not condone a pattern of international conduct that would deny the fleet of the US the use of international waters. It is a part of our national history and our national heritage to support freedom of the seas – from the time of George Washington, through the administration of Thomas Jefferson and the incidents with the Barbary pirates, up to this very hour. As a great maritime power, we must insist upon a strict application of international law, in so far as the high seas and international waters are concerned.[9]

The recurrent problems over fishing rights – whether the three-mile or twelve-mile limit applies – are only a small part of a wider question. As more of the Mediterranean powers, such as Algeria, claim a twelve-mile territorial limit, so there is a slow erosion of the seas on which naval warships can sail without risking some form of incident. For the big maritime nations these claims pose considerable problems. If they allow the claim to go unchallenged and do not exercise their rights of free passage, then in time it will be assumed that de facto recognition to the claim has been given. But if they exercise their rights of free passage, it will be alleged by some that they are deliberately provoking an incident. What, for example, would be the attitude of a big maritime nation whose frigate is sunk by fast patrol boats, as in the sinking of the *Eilat* incident, while exercising its right to free passage in the area of a twelve-mile territorial water claim? A long argument would then follow in international law as to whether three or twelve miles was the territorial limit, whether a state of belligerency did or did not exist between the two states, and at best the result would be a compensation award in the International Court, somewhat similar to the Corfu Channel case.

In the meantime, the humiliation caused by the incident would become a major issue at home in the big maritime state. Public opinion, led by a jingoistic press, would demand all manner of retaliatory measures which, albeit at a political price, would almost certainly be resisted by the government of the day. One has only to look back on the emotion aroused by issues like Gibraltar and the Falkland Islands to realize the potential of such a theoretical situation.

The message could not be clearer. It is of paramount importance that the United Nations makes the achievement of a code of international maritime law one of its highest priorities. We are witnessing the emergence of Russia as a world-wide maritime power, in terms of both the number and extent of the operation of her merchant and naval ships. This means that the confusion over maritime law could well be the source not only of minor international incidents, but of the involvement of the super-powers in either an indirect or a direct confrontation. Maritime law can no longer be seen as an obscure academic pursuit. Its present imperfections contain the seed of a major dispute.

Part Four Strategic Decision-Making

Strategic Issues

The problem of confining a discussion oi strategic decision-making to Europe is the risk of endorsing the mistaken belief held by some Europeans that a purely regional European defence strategy can be evolved. There has never been a greater need for viewing the development of any European strategy against the background of world strategic issues. The long-predicted emergence of China as a world power possessing thermonuclear weapons and the will not only to break away from a Sino-Soviet stranglehold but actively to pursue a dialogue with the United States has become a reality. There are also signs that Japan wishes to be more independent of a United States policy of less than total commitment to Formosa and an altogether lower political and military profile in South-East Asia.

The dangers to world security stemming from a recrudescence of American isolationism are obvious and are probably recognized even by some Soviet strategists. The all-pervading question for the medium-sized powers, such as West Germany, France, Britain and Japan, is how to react to the reorientation of American policy brought about by a combination of financial and political pressure. Should these powers accept the trend of American policy as being inevitably towards isolationism and therefore build up their own independent forces so as to forge new super-power alliances? Or should they pursue policies aimed at maintaining as far as possible the existing American-dominated alliances in Europe and South-East Asia?

Even if the medium-sized powers decide to hold to the Alliance concept, accept a junior partnership role and abdicate from any pretensions to super-power status, it is questionable what policies should be pursued in order to achieve a continued American commitment. Opponents of British membership of the EEC fear that the regional economic bias of such a framework will inevitably spill over into a regional defence strategy that progressively erodes the American commitment to the North Atlantic Alliance. Yet it is the very inability of the Europeans to shoulder what the Americans feel is their proper share of the defence burden that feeds the isolationist pressures inside the United States. To continue expecting the Americans to pay the bills is a certain recipe for precipitating sizeable American troop withdrawals. There are grounds for hoping – and no one can predict more than that – that the American commitment to NATO will best be maintained if the American people and their Congress see that, with the emergence of a stronger European identity within NATO, Europe will accept a greater share of its own defence burden. But Europe must be seen to be aiming at interdependence and eschewing independence and the pursuit of super-power status.

This is particularly important if the West is to make progress in pursuing détente and in moving towards a successful European Security Conference. Any West German government pursuing the policies of Ostpolitik in the 1970s is no longer committed to the old sterile formula of the necessity for reunification of the two Germanies before any progress can be made in establishing détente. Yet the policy of détente could be critically weakened if the West German government were to be seen by the Russians to be linked in any way with a European nuclear deterrent specifically divorced from the United States. Advocacy of a purely Anglo-French deterrent divorced from the United States but with no West German involvement is likely to be equally disruptive: for it would probably be impossible, in terms of current domestic politics, for any West German government not to insist on a measure of participation in any proposal for an Anglo-French force. They might be forced to participate, despite knowing that such a policy would severely threaten progress towards establishing better East-West relations.

A strategic policy for Europe cannot therefore divorce itself from the realities of democratic politics. It may well transpire that the policy of disengagement much discussed in Europe in the 1950s could again become the best chance for achieving a stable peace. A meaningful disengagement would need to comprise an area of distinct separation of foreign troops and weapons, and a defined area of thinning out of foreign troops and weapons. The reserve backing of a credible second-strike strategic nuclear force would, in the early stages, be essential both for West German agreement and for the security of Britain and France. Since the area of disengagement would inevitably comprise the two Germanies, it is hard to see either country accepting a total disarmament of its own forces, but these would have to be greatly reduced and frozen at comparable levels. Such an outcome is not an inconceivable objective for the mid-1970s. It is, therefore, too simple to believe that the existence of nuclear weapons is in all circumstances an impediment to progress in the field of détente. The paradox is that their very existence might well provide the framework for an initial agreement on mutual and balanced force reductions and the vigorous pursuit of a policy of disengagement.

The West Germans rightly attach great importance to the strength of the American contribution to the Alliance, and this would be particularly needed in the early stages of disengagement. It is vitally important for the continued strength of NATO that in principle the concept of burden-sharing is accepted by the European members of the Alliance. Many of the people who question the very existence of NATO are also the strongest critics of an independent European deterrent, their overriding priority being the substantial reduction of defence expenditure; they would presumably rely on the gesture of unilateral disarmament and the hope of détente.

But it is perfectly consistent with advocacy of the concept oi the North Atlantic Alliance to press for substantial organizational changes within NATO. Indeed, with or without changes, present levels of American support will not continue. It is necessary, too, for European politicians to stop seeing the unity of Europe in purely regional terms. There is no doubt that the dilemma Europe now faces is full of contradictions. To accept a greater share of the defence burden there needs to be a greater degree of political unity in Europe. Yet the very pursuit of such unity feeds attitudes which cry out for European independence. The harsh facts are easily available if only the politicians would face up to them: super-power status for Europe can be achieved only within a federal state and only after a period of decades in which defence expenditure and defence manpower would have to rise to levels that public opinion would be most unlikely to accept. Super-power status, even if achieved, would not make any significant contribution to world peace that could not be better achieved by a strong Europe within the Atlantic Alliance. To achieve a strong European identity within NATO France will have to return as a full participating member. An agreement will have to evolve on nuclear as well as conventional strategy that makes it possible to envisage NATO as a truly integrated force. A commitment to greater standardization of equipment and logistics will have to be matched by joint European procurement policies and a willingness among member nations to contribute an equivalent percentage of their gross national product to defence. Only if these decisions can be taken and implemented does it make sense to talk of a European as Supreme Allied Commander or would it be safe to lose the existing American domination.

These changes are urgently needed; if they take place, NATO will have assumed a very different identity and it might help to ease the political transition if the Organization were to alter its name. France would then be rejoining not NATO but an alliance with a changed organization and a military structure strongly linked to the United States but not wholly dependent on the United States. The North Atlantic Treaty, to which France has never objected, would remain unchanged.

Chapter 11. The Evolution of NATO's Nuclear Strategy

The signing of the North Atlantic Pact and the establishment of NATO in 1949 also marked the start of the erosion of the West's nuclear monopoly, for in that year the Soviet Union exploded her first atomic bomb. Through the early 1950s the Russians continued to explode nuclear devices, but they lacked an effective delivery system, having neither bombers with an intercontinental range nor missiles. In November 1952, the United States exploded her first thermonuclear device, or hydrogen bomb as it was called. This was quickly followed by the Russians exploding their own thermonuclear device in August 1953. At this time, the nuclear superiority of the West dominated their strategic thinking. The then United States Secretary of State, John Foster Dulles, spoke in 1954 of 'massive retaliation at the time and place of our choosing', and this attitude was reflected in the policy of 'brinkmanship' which Dulles followed throughout the middle 1950s. It led to a reduction in American troops in Europe and an acceptance that the allied conventional force level in Europe would not attempt to match the Soviet Union forces. At times, the balance of the forces was as much as 5 : 1 in favour of the Russians.

Slowly, however, the West began to realize that its nuclear superiority was being challenged by the rapid development of Soviet missile technology, and this was highlighted in 1957 by the Russians putting Sputnik 1 into orbit. In 1957 the British government, still nursing its humiliation from the Suez intervention, put the main emphasis of its future defence policy on aircraft capable of carrying hydrogen bombs. Britain underlined this policy change by unilaterally withdrawing troops from Germany, thereby weakening NATO's conventional forces. A similar action was also taken by France. This change of policy was surprising in that it was introduced at a time when the theory of massive retaliation was being seriously attacked by academic thinkers outside national governments. These writers showed a remarkable unanimity in dismissing the conventional strategy that the West should meet a limited Soviet attack with massive retaliation. They argued, instead, that a limited attack should be met by limited measures, for they saw that no sensible government would actually consider putting its whole population at risk for an initially limited attack, especially if that attack could not be seen by the people as an immediate threat to their homes and lives.

As a direct consequence of its inadequate conventional capability, in 1957 and again in 1958 NATO called for tactical nuclear weapons to be deployed in Europe to make up for the numerical superiority of the Russians' conventional forces. At the same time, it was decided to station American intermediate-range ballistic missiles (IRBMs) in Britain, Italy and Turkey. But NATO's official strategy in the late 1950s still depended on massive retaliation. The one major strategic gain in the 1950s was the increasing awareness among Americans that their national defence could no longer be based on defending their own national boundaries. The old concept of 'Fortress America' vanished with the realization that an aggressor nation could mount an attack as easily from its own country as from outlying bases. But this realization also carried a new and potentially more damaging threat to NATO, for while NATO depended on massive retaliation it meant that an American President might be risking the lives of citizens in Chicago, Washington and New York by responding to a limited incursion of Soviet troops across the Elbe. American doubts about such an automatic commitment only served to arouse suspicions in Europe about the real effectiveness of the United States as a NATO partner; doubts which were not entirely appeased by the argument that the presence of American troops on the ground in Europe would constitute an automatic obligation on an American President to commit his country wholeheartedly to NATO.

In 1957 the problem was dramatically stated by Henry

Kissinger, who in 1968 was to become President Nixon's chief adviser on these matters.

> What if the Red Army attacks in Europe explicitly to disarm West Germany and offers to the United States and the United Kingdom immunity from strategic bombing and a withdrawal to the Oder after achieving its limited objective? Is it clear that France would fight under such circumstances? Or that the United Kingdom would initiate an all-out war which however it ended might mean the end of British civilisation? Or that an American President would trade fifty American cities for Western Europe?[1]

In April 1959, Secretary of State Christian Herter told a Senate Committee that an American President would involve the United States in total nuclear war only if 'the facts showed clearly that we were in danger of devastation ourselves.'[2]

In July 1959, Henry Kissinger wrote 'The defence of Europe cannot be conducted solely from North America, because ... however firm allied unity may be, a nation cannot be counted on to commit suicide in defence of a foreign territory.'[3]

These remarks began to feed European suspicions. General Pierre Gallois,[4] one of the best known of all the proponents of independent national nuclear forces, used the writings of General Maxwell Taylor,[5] who later became Chairman of the Joint Chiefs of Staff under President Kennedy, to illustrate the point that the United States would use nuclear weapons only to assure her national survival. In effect, nuclear weapons would be used only for the United States' own protection and the defence of other nations would be left to the fortunes of conventional war.

After the Suez affair in 1956, there was considerable bitterness in the British and French governments concerning the attitude of the Eisenhower Administration. They considered that the Americans should have supported their intervention and that their refusal to do so had critically undermined their position. This allegation is accurate in relation to the American withdrawal of financial support, but it has also been used to doubt the credibility of the United States commitment to defend their allies. However, Kennet Love's excellent account[6] provides no evidence for the more serious allegations that President Eisenhower had not backed France and Britain when the Russians made veiled threats of a ballistic missile attack. Nor is there any evidence of prevarication when Bulganin proposed to Eisenhower the joint and immediate use of their two countries' naval and air forces under United Nations direction. The evidence shows that Eisenhower made it clear to Bulganin that, if the Russians intervened, he would support France and Britain and that this would mean global war.

The other main argument from Europeans questioning American intentions arises over the Cuban missile crisis. When President Kennedy's special envoy, Dean Acheson, arrived in Paris on October 22nd, 1962, to tell General de Gaulle of the contents of the speech President Kennedy was to deliver, de Gaulle went straight to the point by asking, according to Elie Abel's account, 'May we be clear before you start. Are you consulting or informing me?'[7]

Dean Acheson then confessed that he was there to inform, not consult. 'I am in favour of independent decisions,' said de Gaulle. 'You may tell your President that France will support him. I think that under the circumstances President Kennedy had no other choice. This is his national prerogative and France understands.' After that, de Gaulle argued that in a situation like Cuba Europe could be involved against her will, and his fundamental point was to link the Cuban episode with his own stand against any arrangement which would allow the United States to control or dominate French policies. In his famous press conference on January 14th, 1963, he spoke at length about Cuba, and implied a relationship to Berlin and possibly Turkey.

The Americans, finding themselves exposed to a direct atomic attack from the Caribbean, acted in such a way as to rid themselves of that menace and, if it had been necessary, to crush it without its having occurred either to them or to anyone else that the game would necessarily be played in Europe and without recourse to the direct assistance of the Europeans. Moreover, the means which they immediately decided to employ in order to counter a direct attack, whether it came from Cuba only or was combined with another originating elsewhere, these means were automatically set aside for something other than the defence of Europe, even if Europe had been attacked in its turn.

It is dubious whether this allegation has any substance, since there was no withdrawal of the American forces located in Europe during the period of tension and the full alert of all strategic forces was applied world-wide.

The importance of all these fears is not so much for their validity, which has been somewhat alleviated by the more realistic strategy adopted in the 1960s, as for their persistence. It is necessary to know why they exist to comprehend the genuineness of the fears that were held by many Europeans in the late 1950s and why they are still held in the early 1970s. It would be false to pretend that the anxiety is any less today, particularly when there will certainly be American troop withdrawals from Europe, but it does become less credible when the American forces can be seen to be taking part in a realistic NATO strategy which is identifiably European. The 1960s have seen the emergence of a new strategy for the Western Alliance. It has become fashionable to laugh off the differences between the present strategy of a flexible response and the old trip-wire concept as merely playing with words. It is true that there can be no one strategical concept to cover the whole of NATO, but the decisive shift towards aiming to establish effective balanced conventional forces in order to allow an initial pause in any limited attack cannot be shrugged off as of no consequence. It is an approach which allows more alternatives, but it also presupposes 'a centralised system of command and control and highly invulnerable strategic forces'[8] – a situation which is far from being achieved.

It is, however, a strategy which bears some resemblance to reality. It has not solved all the NATO problems, of which the most immediate is to resolve the place of tactical nuclear weapons systems within the Alliance, but is has given NATO the possibility of dealing with small-scale incursions or accidental conflict without the previous automatic commitment to massive retaliation.

The movement towards a flexible response strategy was instigated by the Kennedy Administration as soon as it took office in 1960 and has been evolved largely through the personal commitment of two extraordinarily capable politicians, Robert McNamara, Secretary of Defense in two separate Administrations from 1960 to 1968, and Denis Healey, the British Secretary of State for Defence from 1964 to 1970. However, it took until the middle 1960s for the policy of the Alliance to be changed so that there was no longer an automatic nuclear response to an attack from substantial forces from across the Iron Curtain. As late as 1964, 80 per cent of the Alliance's air forces were reserved for use after the war had gone nuclear, and were not available to assist a conventional war. By contrast, at the start of the 1970s NATO was committed to dual capability aircraft with the majority committed for conventional defence.

The build-up of the conventional capability has taken time, not helped by France's withdrawal from NATO, or by Canada's reduction of her European-based force levels. Actual force levels in Europe are difficult to compare. There is a tendency for NATO to measure its land army capability by counting divisions. This tends to exaggerate the Warsaw Pact capability, since NATO divisions contain more men and have a greater fighting capability than those of the Warsaw Pact. In 1968, McNamara was able to claim in his annual posture statement that planned NATO forces were adequate to meet its objectives. This, however, was based on a simple counting of heads, ignoring whether the men were in the right place or primarily fighting or logistic personnel. The British, in particular, challenged this interpretation because of the less favourable 'teeth to tail' ratio of NATO forces, and also stressed the tactical superiority of the Russians, since they would have the initiative that comes from starting any aggression.

At a time when negotiations are starting on mutual and balanced force reductions (MBFR) it is especially important that any discussion on relative force levels in Europe should be conducted free of emotional appeals to unrealistic comparisons. The key area is the central region which comprises West Germany and Benelux on the one hand, and East Germany, Poland, Czechoslovakia and Hungary on the other. Figures are sometimes quoted of force levels in NATO's central region of more than sixty Warsaw Pact divisions confronting twenty-three divisions or their equivalent on the NATO side. This leads commentators to refer to a 3 : 1 ratio, but this is an absurd basis for comparison, since NATO divisions are much larger than those of the Warsaw Pact. A typical NATO division force is almost *twice* the size of a Warsaw Pact division and a United States divisional force is *three* times the size of the Warsaw Pact divisions. The most specific American statement of the military balance was given in 1968 by Defense Secretary Mc-Namara, and this assessment is not substantially different in 1972:

> In all regions except Norway, the NATO pact forces are about equal in manpower. NATO has about 900,000 troops deployed in all regions of continental Europe, compared to 960,000 troops for the Warsaw Pact. While manpower comparisons alone are not conclusive measures of military strength, I believe they are reasonable first appropriations of relative ground-force capabilities.
>
> In the case of air forces, our relative capability is far greater than a simple comparison of numbers would indicate. By almost every measure – range, payload, ordnance effectiveness, loiter time, crew training – NATO (especially United States) air forces are far better than the Pact's for non-nuclear war.[9]

Alain Enthoven, a former Under Secretary in the Department of Defense, has written[10] criticizing NATO force-level comparisons on the grounds that NATO plans always for the worst case and attempts to obtain more forces and larger budgets by exaggerating the size of the threat. Also, most of the traditional comparisons significantly ignore actual effectiveness.

After the Czech invasion in 1968 the main burden of strengthening the Alliance was carried by the European members to the extent of being responsible for something like 90 per cent of the improvements. It is clear that this pattern will have to be followed during the 1970s, but there are political and financial limits to increasing the European contribution, just as the same limits have already been reached in the United States. The American commitment to Europe must be seen in McNamara's own words as 'a fundamental expression of vital self-interest as well as a statement of obligations'. Detailed proposals were put forward in 1969 by Alain Enthoven for a major reduction of 100,000 American troops spread over five years which, he argued, need not lead to a reduction in NATO's conventional capability, since the Europeans could make up for such reductions if they had the will. The best solution would be for balanced force reductions to take place simultaneously in both the Warsaw Pact and NATO forces and for this agreement to coincide with American troop reductions. Any troop reductions would need to be planned well in advance and would be necessarily accompanied by a diminution in American domination within NATO. Troop reductions accompanied by a reduction in the American nuclear guarantee for Europe would be very serious. This need not occur and it is arguable that even 100,000 American servicemen in Europe would be a sufficient hostage to assure the nuclear guarantee.

To ensure that no precipitate United States action takes place, it is in Europe's interest not to contest modest American troop reductions but to understand the Congressional pressures that any Administration will be under on this issue. To adopt a posture of public criticism and total resistance will only reinforce the critics of NATO in America, who point to the persistent refusal of the Europeans to live up to their obligations.

The United States government itself has pointed out that Western Europe now represents, after the United States, the greatest aggregation of economic, political and ideological strength in the world. The initial six Common Market countries and Britain have a higher total population, military manpower pool and gross national product than the Soviet Union. The supplying of adequate conventional forces is, and should be, a major European responsibility for the future.

It is important, if one accepts this argument, not to pursue the logic too far. There is a tendency to argue from the importance of conventional forces to the total exclusion of nuclear weapons. It is claimed by some people, despite evidence to the contrary, that a nuclear war is inconceivable. Nuclear war is conceivable. It should be NATO's aim to have sufficient forces to contain an ambiguous frontier conflict for a period prior to the aggressor's intentions becoming clearer, and governments being able to decide on whether to authorize the use of nuclear weapons. The plain facts are, that it would not make sense to rely on all-out conventional defence. As Denis Healey put it, speaking with full knowledge of all NATO intelligence information:

> All Soviet exercises and training assume the use of nuclear weapons from the word 'go' ... If we ever did face an all-out attack, the other side would use nuclear weapons to begin with: there's a great deal of evidence for that both in the exercises they do and in their strategic journals.[11]

NATO's strategy of deterrence has always been firmly based on the credible threat of nuclear escalation, and no one in NATO envisages a long-drawn-out war in Europe like the Second World War. If one accepts that the use of nuclear weapons is the only alternative to surrender in the case of a major attack which is not being held by conventional forces, the central issue for the Alliance is the decision-making process which will control the use of nuclear weapons. One of the extraordinary omissions during the first thirteen years of NATO's existence was the total absense of any serious political discussion on the actual detailed decision procedures necessary to control its nuclear potential.

In 1962, the 'Athens guidelines' were drawn up at a NATO meeting in Athens. These were phrased in what one can only describe as horrifyingly general terms. They covered how decisions would be taken and what consultations would take place, but did not cover how nuclear weapons would be used. Nevertheless, the meeting was still a major advance and it reflected McNamara's belief, stated at Ann Arbor, that the United States wanted and needed a greater degree of Alliance participation. In 1966, the next major advance in consultation was made with the establishment of the Nuclear Planning Group (NPG) within NATO. This group consists of the United States, West Germany, Britain and Italy as permanent members and includes three other rotating members, one from Scandinavia and Canada, one from Belgium and Holland, and one from Greece and Turkey. The NPG is a sub-committee of the Nuclear Defence Affairs Committee (NDAC), which is open to any member of the Alliance, and these countries are all given an opportunity to comment on NPG papers. Everything which is recommended by the NDAC has to be endorsed by the full NATO council or by the Defence Planning Committee. Initially, Iceland, Luxemburg and France did not join the NDAC and Norway did not request membership of the NPG. The NPG ensures that the non-nuclear members of NATO have a voice in the creation of NATO's nuclear strategy. Its foundation has removed much of the pressure for closer involvement that came in the early 1960s from countries like Germany and Italy. It has also meant that the attempt to establish the Multilateral Nuclear Force (MLF) is felt by the very countries who were initially strongly in favour as being no longer worth pursuing.

The task of the NPG was to establish a concrete doctrine governing the initial use of nuclear weapons. For it was felt that if the Alliance had not reached agreement in principle in peacetime on guidelines for the use of nuclear weapons, it would hardly be in a position in a time of crisis to make the necessary rapid decisions. The actual use of nuclear weapons would, under any circumstances, become a question of finely balanced judgment. It would depend on individual circumstances, the strength of the forces actually available and likely to become available and an assessment of when the Alliance's conventional forces could be overwhelmed. The immense difficulty comes in judging the nuclear threshold, particularly if this involves the first use of tactical nuclear weapons, a contingency for which NATO must plan but which it hopes will never arise.

The first major study that the NPG embarked on was to establish political guidelines for the initial use of tactical nuclear weapons. The purpose of the first use of these nuclear weapons is to re-establish the credibility of the deterrent, for it seems a reasonable presumption that the Russians would not start a major conventional attack if they believed that NATO would resort to strategic nuclear weapons. The first use of tactical nuclear weapons by NATO would therefore be largely demonstrative, showing the Russians that NATO would logically escalate, if necessary, up through a range of responses until ultimately it would use strategic weapons.

The critics of the use of tactical nuclear weapons point out that, since they are usually in the hands of front-line units, they are not as easily subject to central command and control as strategic weapons, which do not even need to be sited on European territory. They also question whether politicians can effectively control the escalation of nuclear weapons and whether an initial tactical use must lead inevitably to the early use of strategic weapons. It has always been agreed that decisions on nuclear release can only ever be taken at the political level, and that in effect NATO's decision must always rest with either the President of the United States or the British Prime Minister, whichever is the political leader who actually owns a particular weapons system. The consultation procedure within NATO for the use of tactical weapons is aimed at ensuring that the non-nuclear members of the Alliance can exert influence before the decision is taken. This is of particular importance when the host country's ground troops are most closely involved. The logic of a policy of excluding tactical nuclear weapons is either to retain the policy of automatic massive nuclear retaliation, or to accept – in the absence of an overwhelming conventional defence capability – that certain countries, such as West Germany, are expendable and should sustain massive military and civilian losses before the nuclear powers, whose territory is conveniently physically removed from the most likely battlefields in Europe, choose to intervene.

The importance of the NPG is that countries like West Germany now have the opportunity of ensuring that the NATO guidelines are relevant to their own country. The original draft of the provisional guidelines for the tactical use of nuclear weapons, which was accepted by the NPG at its Washington meeting on November 12th, 1969, was written by the British and German governments. It is this type of collaboration from a country most intimately involved that ensures that German Gaullism is unlikely to return, and that NATO will no longer have to grapple with the claims from non-nuclear countries for direct control of nuclear weapons in Europe. Helmut Schmidt, appointed by Chancellor Willy Brandt as the new Defence Minister in 1969, wrote as long ago as 1961 that

> it is plainly absurd for the Federal Republic, looking over its shoulder at the Soviet Union, to demand strategic mass destruction weapons. For the Federal Republic to be equipped with nuclear missiles capable of devastating Moscow or Leningrad would inevitably provoke the Soviet Union in just the same way as the supply of nuclear missiles to Cuba would provoke the United States.[12]

These were prophetic words written a year before the Cuban missile crisis, but the sentiment is as true for the 1970s as it was for the 1960s. The welcome decision of the West German government to sign the Non-Proliferation Treaty and the policies of Ostpolitik are doing much to improve relations between the Soviet Union and West Germany, and even Berlin in 1971 was the subject of a satisfactory agreement involving access through East Germany. NATO must ensure that the initial use of tactical nuclear weapons is confined to small-yield weapons which would reduce the risk of an automatic escalation to general nuclear war, and this is being studied. The NPG began the 1970s by considering guidelines for responding to the initial use of nuclear weapons by the Warsaw Pact and what action NATO would take if its initial use of tactical weapons had no effect on Russian aggression.

No factual account of the NPG can attempt to evaluate the likely effectiveness of the guidelines that it has produced. The price of democracy is a little untidiness. No one has the right to expect a perfect decision procedure from a democratic organization of fourteen states. It is also right that any guidelines are not based on principles of automatic application. There must be room for flexibility of interpretation. These caveats notwithstanding, and recognizing the considerable advance that the NPG represents, the situation is still very disturbing. The indications are that the procedures are still far from satisfactory: the guidelines are not complete and the pace at which they have been introduced is far too slow, when one considers that for every hour that they are not completed the Alliance is that much more vulnerable and likely to make an ill-considered response. In the past there may have been too much attention focused on the possibility of accidental involvement, but even that danger is not entirely eradicated though the 1971 SALT agreement covering inadvertent firing and improving the American-Soviet 'hot line' via satellite communication should help. As long as three Western countries – France, Britain and the United States – all possess independent national nuclear weapon systems, the problem of ensuring centralized command and control procedures is made immeasurably more difficult. The overriding challenge for NATO in the 1970s is to examine the possibilities of an arrangement whereby its three nuclear members form an integrated strategic and tactical force capable of responding within the limits of agreed NATO guidelines to any aggression from the Warsaw Pact countries.

The Czechoslovak crisis in July 1968[13] should not be interpreted as a military threat to NATO serving only to emphasize the current military danger on NATO's central front The main lesson is a different though no less important one. The crisis showed how effective a force the Warsaw Pact has become. This stems from a highly developed centralized Soviet control over a force whose equipment and weapons are highly standardized. For administrative, operational and logistical purposes the Warsaw Pact forces are now organized and directed on the lines of a Soviet Military District.[14] This allows the Pact to operate swiftly and forcefully, and raises fundamental questions as to how far NATO can continue to rely on a period of political warning prior to any overt military crisis. It also only underlines the urgent need for a centralized command and control of NATO's tactical and strategic forces, for greater standardization and for the return of French forces to NATO. It is argued by some people that there is intrinsic merit in having more than one centre of decision for the first use of nuclear weapons within an alliance, and that the very diversity of decision increases their deterrent value. Denis Healey[15] is himself credited with having argued this theme in late 1964 when the Labour government made the critical decision to retain a national nuclear deterrent. A similar theme is now often extended to justify tolerating the position of France outside NATO. That argument is dangerously mistaken, particularly when applied to strategic rather than tactical weapons. It would be suicidal for Britain or France singly or collectively to resort to the first use of strategic nuclear weapons, and the first use of tactical nuclear weapons should only ever be considered in concert with the United States.

The Soviet Union, since the removal of Khrushchev in October 1964, has decisively changed its strategic policy. Khrushchev relied on minimum deterrence, and aimed to have only such forces as were necessary to deter. This policy has been replaced by a resolve to move from a position of nuclear inferiority, as judged by missile numbers and shown up by Cuba in 1962, to a position of at least nuclear parity in numbers.

The Soviet Union has also shifted away from planning solely for a nuclear war to recognizing at least the possibility of a conventional war with a role for large conventional forces.

Given these policy objectives, a programme of military expansion in the Soviet Union from 1965 to 1975 was inevitable. But the extent of the financial commitment to these objectives has been immense. The percentage of Soviet GNP devoted to defence has been estimated as 8 per cent in 1972. In the 1970s, defence expenditure will rise by 5 per cent per annum in real terms;[16] the military complex already consumes some 25 per cent of total resources. It can be argued that these policy changes will be shown to have been a stabilizing factor; and that only after having removed the danger of a United States first-strike nuclear attack against the Soviet Union could they have afforded to participate in SALT and promote a European Security Conference. Paradoxically, these changes in Soviet Union strategic policy pose a greater threat to the security of the West while reducing the risk of a nuclear holocaust. In the Khrushchev era, the threat was less, but the dangers of an ill-considered response were higher because of the 'all or nothing' doctrine. Under Khrushchev, the choices before the Soviet Union were so limited that planned and deliberate Soviet aggression was inconceivable. Despite his bellicose public image, Khrushchev was a strong believer in tight political control of the military and minimum defence expenditure, but there was inherent in this policy an element of insecurity that came from its acceptance of a measure of inferiority. The new policies not only ensure a greater choice, they allow a wider margin for manœuvre. They are designed to give a survival capacity with an offensive capability. The whole strategy is founded on a degree of realism that carries far greater credibility.

The Warsaw Pact countries have in effect developed a somewhat similar strategic posture to NATO's flexible response. They remain convinced, however, that NATO would use nuclear weapons early, and their own planning has always given a dominant place to the first use of nuclear weapons, a commitment to chemical weapons and a readiness to consider launching missiles on receipt of a warning without waiting for confirmatory impact. They see NATO's nuclear forces as being so dominated by America that they are United States forces in fact if not in theory. The real deterrent value of having Western nuclear powers other than the United States within the Alliance is the extent to which they bring a European influence to bear on any decision but particularly those involving the use of nuclear weapons. It does not stem from the extent to which there are separate centres of decision, which is a destabilizing factor, fragmenting control.

Advocacy of multiple nuclear decision-points even within an Alliance runs completely counter to McNamara's views on the need for centralized operational control and is often merely an attempt to rationalize an existing situation which avoids having to face the difficult problems of integration and multi-national control. Viewed from Russia, a diversity of enemy decision-points in a time of crisis cannot but increase any tendency to opt for a first strike. Whereas the Russians might have confidence that the United States, with her wholly credible second-strike capability, would be likely to pursue a policy of total restraint whatever the provocation, they might not count on such restraint from a more vulnerable British or French government. This is even more the case when, as will be the situation until the middle 1970s, the French strategic nuclear deterrent is maintained by a vulnerable first-strike ballistic missile system situated in the Vaucluse mountains in southern France. It is a sad commentary on the reality of strategic progress that 1971 should mark the re-emergence, for the first time since they were withdrawn in 1963, of land-based strategic ballistic missile systems in Europe which have the range to strike at the Soviet Union.

In the early 1960s it seemed possible that both France and Britain would be priced out of maintaining a nuclear deterrent system. But there are now three allied nuclear powers, all with nuclear forces theoretically designed to counter Soviet military expansion in Europe but with only the British and American nuclear forces subscribing to a common strategy and to joint targeting. The omission of France from a similar arrangement is not only dangerous but absurdly wasteful in terms of the total Western defence effort. If the Western powers are seriously to pursue policies of détente with the East during the 1970s they will have to be prepared to reduce conventional military force-levels in Europe. It will mean at times inevitably conceding some numerical advantage to the Warsaw Pact, and also accepting an increased susceptibility to a surprise attack which arises merely from the geography of Europe when troops are withdrawn from the boundaries of the central front.

Under the right circumstances these risks can be justified, but they will be acceptable only if the West's strategic nuclear guarantee remains invulnerable and credible. It cannot be overstressed that progress towards rapprochement and dis-engagement will come about only if the politicians in Western Europe have confidence in the strategic deterrent forces of the Alliance. To undermine the credibility of these forces over the next two decades will be to ensure the continuance of hostility and fear in Europe and to prejudice any chances of meaningful reductions in national defence expenditure and the establish-ment of peaceful relations between East and West.

Chapter 12. National Deterrents

THE BRITISH DETERRENT

In 1940, Britain's knowledge of the potential for applying nuclear technology to weapon development was in many crucial areas superior to that of the United States. Yet after the two countries had combined their efforts following America's entry into the Second World War, the areas of parity were inevitably replaced through the war years by a growing United States superiority. An early and important stage in the exchange of nuclear information was the Quebec Agreement, signed by Britain and the United States in 1943 and the text made public in 1954. The Agreement stated that 'we will not either of us communicate any information about Tube Alloys to third parties except by mutual consent.' Tube Alloys was the code name for atomic bomb research and development. The Quebec Agreement has never been revoked, but it was to a large extent superseded by President Truman's unilateral decision to pass the 1946 McMahon Act, which severely limited the giving of nuclear information by the United States to Britain. Restricted data under the McMahon Act covered the manufacture or utilization of atomic weapons and the production or use of fissionable material in the production of power. It did, however, give the power to vary the terms of what constituted restricted data from time to time, provided that such changes did not adversely affect defence and security.

In 1950, as a consequence of the McMahon Act, Britain started developing her own isotope separation plant at Capenhurst with the capability for uranium enrichment without the benefit of any American technological knowledge. This was despite the fact that much of the American technology used at their Oak Ridge plant had been developed by British scientists. Even the 1954 relaxations to the McMahon Act did not change the situation, since data relating to the fabrication of atomic weapons were still restricted.

The distinguished French scientist Bertrand Goldschmidt[1] claims that, in 1955, the French started negotiations with Britain in an attempt to have the United Kingdom Atomic Energy Authority build an isotope separation plant using the technology developed at Capenhurst. This initiative was blocked by the United States, invoking Anglo-American agreements which were said to preclude such collaboration because of the military implications. This interpretation has never been officially confirmed, but it seems highly probable, for in June 1955 Britain concluded an agreement with the United States covering cooperation on the civil uses of atomic energy, and this would certainly have made Britain very susceptible to American pressure to forgo any proposals for Anglo-French cooperation. Throughout the 1950s and 1960s Anglo-American nuclear agreements were marked by Britain's undue sensitivity to her dependence on America. Britain sought only short-term gains and failed to take a realistic view of her European responsibilities. She attached an almost mystical importance to the so-called special relationship, which led to a progressive reduction of her independence, particularly over nuclear issues.

The year 1955 was also the year when Britain deliberately absented herself from the crucial Messina Conference which preceded the Treaty of Rome and the establishment of the European Economic Community. It was ironic but perhaps understandable that it should also have been the year when she failed to understand that Anglo-French cooperation within NATO over nuclear technology, first in the field of nuclear propulsion and later in nuclear weapons technology, was the very issue on which the already strained entente cordiale could be revived.

In 1956, Anglo-French relations were shattered by the Suez débâcle. It was symptomatic, however, that the first post-Suez British diplomatic priority was to concentrate on repairing Anglo-American relations. In March 1957, President Eisenhower and the new Prime Minister, Harold Macmillan, met in Bermuda. President Eisenhower, confronted by his old wartime friend – for Harold Macmillan had been particularly close to him in North Africa – was keen to forget the whole Suez incident. In exchange for an agreement to station Thor missiles on British territory under the 'double veto' joint control system, Eisenhower agreed to restore nuclear weapon collaboration. John Foster Dulles, however, only approved the nuclear exchange agreement because it assured Britain's support in the nuclear test ban negotiations. He personally persuaded the Joint Congressional Atomic Energy Committee to agree to the 1958 amendment to the McMahon Act, which permitted the release of information on nuclear weapon technology to any ally who had made substantial progress on nuclear weapons. Dulles made it clear at the time that such an agreement related only to Britain and did not include France. It is a mistake to belive that in 1974 Britain will be free to exchange nuclear information with France.

The French responded to this further evidence of an exclusive Anglo-American nuclear club by a decision to build their own isotope separation plant and a greater commitment to developing their own nuclear weapon capability. The Americans' official position in 1957 and 1958 was, however, far more flexible on the question of European cooperation than might have appeared on the surface. They urgently wanted to put their Thor missiles in continental Europe as well as in Britain, and the Administration was also at this time prepared to give its NATO allies technical details relating to nuclear propulsion for submarines, though it was dubious whether such an offer would ever have been accepted by the Joint Congressional Atomic Energy Committee. Yet no substantial cooperation emerged; Italy and Turkey took the already out-of-date Thor missiles, and the only real consequences were seen later over the Turkish missiles in the midst of the Cuban missile crisis.

A Franco-German initiative followed the Bermuda meeting, which is interesting because of the important personalities directly involved. The implication behind the secret discussions to give West Germany access to nuclear technology could have had the profoundest political consequences and repercussions. Franz-Josef Strauss and Jacques Chaban-Delmas, then Defence Ministers for West Germany and France, entered into negotiations which included Italy for a trilateral agreement, whereby Italy and Germany, in exchange for nuclear information for primarily civil purposes, would contribute to the cost of the French isotope separation plant. These secret negotiations never achieved very much because of the return of General de Gaulle, who unilaterally revoked the military part of the agreement in September 1958. But the fact that the Strauss–Chaban-Delmas agreement ever occurred should be a clear warning to those who oppose any discussion of Anglo-French nuclear collaboration. It is absurd to believe that continental Europe will always be prepared to be the pawn of Britain and the United States in matters relating to nuclear weapons. In the 1970s with France in a far stronger position in nuclear technology, potential circumstances might recur which would encourage such a trilateral agreement. The key personalities involved then are still likely to remain major political figures during the 1970s, and no one should take it for granted that the attitude of a West German government headed by Willy Brandt, with no nuclear aspirations, would remain if the Christian Democrats were returned to power.

General de Gaulle saw the politics of nuclear weapons as an area of fundamental importance. It involved for him the prestige and position of France in the world; it was also a central determinant in his attitude to NATO. Throughout his ten-year period of office, no decision was made on matters in any way relating to nuclear policy which he did not directly approve himself; in most cases French policy was formulated and instigated directly by him, with the Quai d'Orsay and key ambassadors often given no warning of important new policy pronouncements. For de Gaulle, active participation in nuclear strategy was the key aim of his foreign policy.

On September 17th, 1958, with the Algerian situation unresolved, General de Gaulle produced a major state document, a still undisclosed memorandum which was sent to

Britain and the United States, calling for a new three-power organization outside NATO. This body would have responsibility for taking joint decisions on all political matters affecting world security, especially those involving the use of nuclear weapons. The whole background and history of the memorandum has been extremely well documented by John Newhouse in *De Gaulle and the Anglo-Saxons*,[2] and though the actual memorandum has never been published, the detail that Newhouse has collected is substantiated by some of the people most closely involved. The key question was whether de Gaulle really intended to obtain a veto on the world-wide use of American nuclear weapons; but he must have known this to be impossible, and it is more likely that it was just his opening negotiating stance, typically grandiose and ignoring France's weak position, designed to force a more realistic assessment of nuclear strategy and nuclear-sharing, primarily within Europe.

Whatever its intention, the memorandum proved to be a total failure. Anglo-French and Franco-American relations deteriorated sharply and no common ground for negotiations appeared or were even sought, in particular by the French. France under de Gaulle subsequently pursued a national nuclear defence policy that owed little to the realities of her immediate defence problem or of any conceivable immediate threat. For all its defects, the policy proved to have profound long-term consequences in establishing France as a nuclear power in her own right and in re-establishing her military position in the world.

The possibility of the United States providing nuclear propulsion technology for French submarines, as specifically offered by John Foster Dulles to de Gaulle in July 1958, also collapsed with the French decision in March 1959 to refuse to allow their Mediterranean Fleet to be on call to NATO in time of war. The proposal had also been encountering major difficulties with the Joint Congressional Committee on Atomic Energy, who were at this stage only prepared to countenance supplying enriched uranium. Yet the possibility of sharing nuclear propulsion technology never completely vanished; it lurked in the background whenever the question of greater Franco-American cooperation came up. In 1961, Prime Minister Macmillan was actually dissuaded by the United States from raising the issue on a bilateral basis with the French. President Eisenhower clearly felt inhibited by Congress and it is likely that, if left to himself, he would have been prepared to have offered a far greater degree of nuclear collaboration to the French in the 1950s. Cooperation over submarine propulsion was once again revived in the first few years of the Kennedy Administration, but it made little progress.

The new Administration also raised the possibility of concluding some form of joint targeting of the growing French nuclear capability, and this was even tentatively discussed by officials. American anxiety over nuclear proliferation was combined with intense concern at the possibility of any allied nuclear deterrent being totally outside the agreed command and control structure for European defence. At the end of 1962, McNamara had asked the French Defence Minister, Pierre Messmer, to send experts to America to discuss arms sales. General G. Lavaud arrived in America with a list of highly sensitive items covering nuclear submarines and nuclear weapon technology. In April 1962, President Kennedy was faced by the need to make a personal decision, for his Administration was split on what should be their overall attitude to France, and particularly to de Gaulle. Most of his own appointees were fascinated by de Gaulle and were in favour of making what they considered as little more than a gesture to the French by allowing the proposed sales to go through. President Kennedy, however, eventually decided to accept the more disciplined approach advocated by some State Department officials and rejected the arms sale. He clearly believed that such a gesture would have no lasting effect on de Gaulle sufficient to justify doing anything to encourage nuclear proliferation. Yet, while rejecting General Lavaud's shopping list, the Department of Defense, fully backed by McNamara, astonishingly agreed to sell a squadron of jet tankers which

had the direct effect of extending the in-flight range of de
Gaulle's Mirage IV bombers and, consequently, of enhancing
the capability of the French nuclear deterrent.

This action certainly did not appear to match Secretary
McNamara's known view on independent nuclear weapons and
his strong belief in the need for centralized control of nuclear
weapons and indivisibility of nuclear targeting. On June 16th,
1962, McNamara gave the argument behind his well publicized assertion that 'limited nuclear capabilities, operating
independently, are dangerous, expensive, prone to obsolescence
and lacking in credibility as a deterrent.'[3]

He asserted that

> relatively weak national nuclear forces with enemy cities as
> their targets are not likely to perform even the function of
> deterrence. If they are small and perhaps vulnerable on
> the ground or in the air, or inaccurate, a major antagonist
> can take a variety of measures to counter them. Indeed, if
> a major antagonist came to believe there was a substantial
> likelihood of it being used independently, this force would
> be inviting a preemptive first strike against it. In the event
> of war, the use of such a force against the cities of a major
> nuclear power would be tantamount to suicide, whereas
> its employment against significant military targets would
> have a negligible effect on the outcome of the conflict.
> Meanwhile, the creation of a single additional national
> nuclear force encourages the proliferation of nuclear
> power with all of its attendant dangers.

With this attitude so firmly stated, it is amazing that,
within six months, McNamara should have been an active
participant at the very meeting which would completely
undermine this stated United States position on national
nuclear deterrents.

On December 19th, 1962, at Nassau in the Bahamas, the
British Prime Minister, Harold Macmillan, met President
Kennedy to discuss world affairs. It was the sixth such meeting
to take place in two years and there was already a strong bond

of friendship between the two men. President Kennedy had respected the way in which Macmillan had supported him a few months before during the Cuban missile crisis, and there was considerable mutual respect. They were superficially a strangely contrasted pair. Yet Macmillan's Edwardian image was a highly deceptive one. He was, despite his age, a tough, agile politician, who had welded his party together following the Suez débâcle in an amazing manner and was by then the dominant figure in English politics. A strongly committed European, he had just visited President de Gaulle at Rambouillet to discuss the Common Market, and he was now painfully aware that the Common Market talks were doomed. It was, therefore, an important meeting for Macmillan and it badly needed to be seen as a success at home. He was accompanied by his Foreign Secretary, Lord Home, and the Minister of Defence, Peter Thorneycroft. President Kennedy was accompanied by his Secretary of Defense, Robert McNamara, but Dean Rusk surprisingly did not feel that his presence was essential, and so George Ball, the Under Secretary of State, and a passionately committed European, was present instead. George Ball had already publicly discussed the possibility of a genuine multilateral medium-range ballistic missile force, fully coordinated with the other relevant forces of NATO, in a speech to NATO parliamentarians in Paris on November 16th, but he was far less enthusiastic about a purely British deterrent.

In retrospect, it is tempting to wonder whether Dean Rusk's presence would have made the President hesitate before accepting Macmillan's plea for a national deterrent and contemplate rather more deeply the long-term consequences for Europe before committing the United States to the Polaris agreement. President Kennedy was certainly aware of the problem of nuclear proliferation. In a television interview on December 18th, just before the Nassau meeting, he said

If the French decide they want to become a nuclear power themselves, that is their decision. The question is whether the United States should join in helping to make France a nuclear power, then Italy, then West Germany, then Belgium. How does that produce security when you have ten, twenty, thirty nuclear powers who may fire their weapons off under different conditions?[4]

It was clear from the outset that the central issue would revolve around the proposed cancellation of Skybolt. But though the possibility of the United States offering the Polaris missile was to some extent anticipated by the British, the United States had not done any extensive analyses of the long-term consequences and came to Nassau singularly ill-prepared, particularly in relation to the ramifications of any such agreement on NATO and more especially France. The President was by then quite determined to cancel the Skybolt missile. He saw that it was not going to meet its planned in-service date of 1966 and that the cost estimates were continuing to escalate. This decision had serious implications for Britain, for when the original Skybolt agreement was signed in 1960 it was envisaged as extending and improving the effective life of Britain's nuclear V bomber force, which represented all that there was of the British strategic nuclear deterrent. President Kennedy held out the prospect at the start of the discussion of the joint development of Skybolt with each country bearing an equal share of the future development costs, but he made it clear that it would be up to Britain to bear the full cost of production. This would have been an extremely expensive solution.

In view of the doubts about the actual weapons system, as well as the risk of escalating costs and further delays, the British wisely decided not to continue with Skybolt. Macmillan then argued that the United States had a moral obligation in view of the cancellation of Skybolt to give Britain access to an alternative nuclear weapon delivery system. It was always acknowledged that Britain had no need of American nuclear devices, only the question of a delivery system was at issue. This meant that the most sensitive problems of nuclear-sharing were not involved. Macmillan was strongly against phasing out the V bomber force over the next few years without any prospect of a replacement. He believed that it was necessary for Britain to retain her independent nuclear deterrent and was not attracted to the argument that the money saved by opting out of nuclear weapons could be better used in building up her conventional force.

Secretary of Defense McNamara was in a difficult position, for he had already declared himself strongly opposed to nuclear weapons being held by the smaller powers, such as Britain and France, but he did see some merit in trying to integrate the British and American strategic forces by assigning them to NATO. On December 21st, it was finally agreed that Polaris forces would be assigned as part of a NATO nuclear force and targeted in accordance with NATO nuclear plans. The intention of the agreement was to develop a multilateral nuclear force in the closest consultation with other NATO allies. It was expressed in the joint communiqué that the whole issue 'created an opportunity for the development of new and closer arrangements for the organisation and control of strategic western defence and that such arrangements in turn could make a major contribution to political cohesion among the nations of the alliance'.[5]

It was decided that the United States would make Polaris missiles available on a continuing basis for the British submarines, but that Britain would construct the submarines and also provide the nuclear warheads. Macmillan recognized that the first Polaris boat could not be operational until 1968 at the earliest, by which time Britain's existing airborne deterrent would be obsolete. But for him it was simply a question of whether or not Britain should opt out of nuclear weapons. To obtain Polaris missiles was for Britain an opportunity of purchasing at a relatively low price a proven weapons system whose initial research-and-development costs had all been borne by the United States.

There is little doubt that, though the French position was only briefly discussed at Nassau, the offer to supply France with Polaris missiles was made by Kennedy in good faith, and he also widened the offer privately to include sharing weapons technology. But only the most optimistic Europeans in the State Department thought that there was any real chance of de Gaulle accepting. Psychologically, France could not become party to an agreement drafted in her absence by the Americans and British. But by this time, the United States Administration had become so committed to broadening the arrangements for nuclear control that they were adamantly opposed to concluding a bilateral agreement solely with the British. In the event, General de Gaulle's rejection did not come until his January 14th press conference. Prior to this, on December 28th, the West German government had welcomed the Nassau agreement, stating that in its view the agreement brought a multilateral nuclear force one step nearer. The West Germans, however, came out unequivocally against an American, British, French 'nuclear directorate' in NATO, stating that they were not prepared to accept NATO powers divided into classes, one with and the other without nuclear weapons. In fact, the possibility of a tri-directorate had been specifically broached to the French by the Americans and British in an attempt to make the Nassau proposals seem more attractive; but even this initiative had been rejected by de Gaulle. As so often in the past, insufficient emphasis had been given to the manner in which collaboration was presented to de Gaulle. If the initiative had been truly European, led by France, then it might have been different. As it was, any French involvement in Nassau would look to the world too like an afterthought, as if France was somehow not central to the whole issue.

There is some evidence that there was considerable confusion between the United States and Britain over the exact meaning of what was agreed at Nassau, and to some extent this confusion is reflected in the terminology of the communiqué. The British thought that what was agreed was greater coordination and the assignation to NATO of existing national nuclear forces, whereas the Americans believed that a multilateral force was to be formed as a new force, owned and jointly controlled by both the nuclear and the non-nuclear powers in NATO. Prime Minister Macmillan, in the House of Commons on January

31st, went out of his way to stress the national command structure of the proposed British Polaris, so weakening the importance of the commitment to assign it to NATO. Yet President Kennedy was himself only too well aware of what he had conceded, for he said shortly after Nassau: 'The British will have their deterrent. It will be independent in moments of great national peril, which is really the only time you consider using nuclear weapons anyway.'[6]

The multilateral force (MLF) was not a new concept; it was first formally put forward by Christian Herter, then Secretary of State in the Eisenhower Administration, at a NATO ministerial meeting in December 1960, but the only enthusiasts at that time were Germany and Italy. The new Kennedy Administration, under Defense Secretary McNamara, had initially concentrated on developing the flexible response strategy and ensuring centralization of decision-making in the hope that this would make for a more effectively controlled response. This was the strategy announced to the NATO council by McNamara in Athens. Then in Ottawa on May 12th 1962, President Kennedy committed five American Polaris vessels to NATO, subject to agreed guidelines on their control and use.

Though he urged the European powers to meet their conventional force-level target figures first, he did also mention the possibility of establishing a sea-borne missile force, genuinely multilateral in ownership and control. This tentative posture became increasingly firm as the months passed, and by March 1963 it was possible for the Administration to put forward detailed proposals for a multilateral force of a fleet of twenty-five mixed-manned surface ships armed with Polaris missiles. The first proposal was for nuclear submarines with Polaris missiles, which would have been a much more effective force, but Congress was adamantly opposed to imparting any of America's nuclear technology to European members of a mixed-manned force. (It is, for example, still the rule today that no British personnel can go to the reactor section of an American Polaris boat.) It was then argued that the proposed surface fleet was potentially far too vulnerable to detection and attack for it to be equipped with expensive Polaris missiles.

Slowly the enthusiasm for the multilateral force withered away as the detailed problems of how to organize control procedures became more and more complex. The Soviet Union's opposition to the concept of the multilateral force was deep-seated, based on a fear of nuclear technology being made available to the Germans, leading either to a German national nuclear deterrent or to collaboration with the French. This was a prospect that seemed real enough following the signing of the Franco-German pact in January 1963, and was greatly enhanced by the well-advertised German support for the MLF concept. To complete the picture Herr Strauss, then out of office, was also campaigning for policies which looked supremely like German Gaullism. This left Chancellor Erhard and his government colleagues with little choice but to pursue with considerable tenacity the concept of an MLF agreement. In Britain the Labour Party in opposition was particularly anxious about the prospect of a 'German finger on the nuclear trigger', and there was little enthusiasm for the MLF in the British services.

The problems were easy to identify, but the will to come to grips with developing adequate control mechanisms, for either an MLF or a multinational defence force, was sadly lacking. Eventually the MLF proposal encountered a succession of political and military difficulties. General de Gaulle was always opposed and used the Common Market tariff negotiations to exert pressure on Erhard. Thus the MLF proposal lost all its initial impetus and was quietly dropped. In November 1964, Britain produced a half-serious proposal for an Atlantic Nuclear Force, but it was essentially a political initiative aimed at destroying the MLF. Again the central problem was the control mechanism, and this was never effectively tackled. Discussions on majority voting, multiple vetoes and double-key arrangements always foundered on the problem of persuading national governments and national parliaments to give up control over what they considered to be a key area of policy. Some countries were very reluctant to accept any American veto, preferring the force to be entirely European.

In Britain, during the October 1964 election, the Conservative government deliberately stressed the independent nature of the nuclear deterrent, while the Labour opposition scoffed at the whole concept of nuclear independence and pledged themselves to 'internationalize the deterrent', and to renegotiate the Nassau agreement. The election over, however, the new Labour government proceeded to continue building the Polaris submarines. They cancelled the fifth submarine on financial grounds and could easily have cancelled the fourth, on which the only expenditure incurred related to 'long lead' equipment items. This would have left three submarines – a suitable number to ensure that the deterrent was never seen as independent but only as a contribution to NATO. But they accepted the advice of their military advisers on the need to retain four submarines in order to have one submarine on patrol at all times, and so lost a unique opportunity to kill once and for all the whole concept of a separate British national deterrent.

Considerable political controversy in the early years of the new Labour government's life revolved around the refusal to live up to their electoral pledge to renegotiate the Nassau agreement, and in the course of the argument various interpretations were put on the existing status of the four British Polaris submarines. However, the position is factually quite clear. The British Polaris force is regularly and permanently assigned to NATO and plays its full part in NATO's operational planning and targeting arrangements. In circumstances which are admittedly hard to conceive ever happening, a British Prime Minister could exercise full control over the targeting and firing of the British Polaris missiles. It is, therefore, theoretically still a national deterrent, but it is primarily, and in effect exclusively, committed to a multinational strategy.

For the reasons already stated relating to the refit cycle of the Polaris submarine, is is argued that there must be four submarines in operation, and that this is the minimum necessary to ensure a credible national deterrent. It is interesting that the French, having at one time planned to build five submarines, may now build only four mainly because of financial pressures. It needs to be stressed, however, that in view of the likely delays over refitting, even four submarines may not prove a truly viable deterrent force in their own right. The effectiveness of any deterrent would be markedly increased by every additional submarine. Yet one Polaris submarine, actually on patrol, is still by any standards a formidable unit, capable – with its sixteen missiles – of inflicting a heavy toll on any aggressor nation and able to fire from its submerged position in any part of the ocean with a quite extraordinarily high degree of accuracy. Unless and until the Soviet Union develops a comprehensive anti-ballistic missile (ABM) system around its major cities, there is no reason to believe that the A3 missiles on British Polaris submarines – with some modification – will not be capable of adequate penetration for the next few years; so the question of developing a second-generation missile system is not an immediately pressing issue. The future of the British Polaris force need not become of central importance before the middle 1970s. It is in the context of a second-generation force that the controversial issue of Anglo-French nuclear collaboration becomes an option worth serious discussion. The major problem in any such collaboration would be one of integration within the existing NATO strategic defence system. To understand why this poses such severe problems one must study the evolution of the French deterrent.

THE FRENCH DETERRENT

It is a mistake to see France's decision to develop her own nuclear weapon system simply in terms of General de Gaulle. The decision goes back to the Pleven government in 1951, although a firm decision to initiate the first development pro-gramme was not taken until 1953. Development of a nuclear weapon system has continued ever since. The only period when there was any significant wavering was under the Socialist

Prime Minister Guy Mollet, who was trying to persuade his own left wing to support signature of the Euratom Treaty and had to contend with powerful dissenters within his party against France developing nuclear weapons. Authorization for the first French atomic bomb test, which took place in February 1960, was given by Prime Minister F. Gaillard in April 1958. Thus the crucial decision had been taken even before General de Gaulle's return to power.

As already stressed, in the late 1950s France made several high-level initiatives to the United States and Britain, as well as the famous de Gaulle memorandum. Their object was to develop an arrangement where nuclear technology could be made available to France, and where France would not be overlooked in important matters of mutual defence interest. The Eisenhower, and later the Kennedy, Administration was particularly concerned about the possibility of the spread of nuclear weapons and was most reluctant to impart any of its knowledge relating to nuclear weapons. This was also an extremely difficult issue for any Administration, for over the years Congress had laid down very strict criteria regarding the dissemination of nuclear knowledge. Even had Britain been willing to share her knowledge, she was bound by treaty obligations to agree first with the United States the basis of any such interchange of information. But in 1959, the United States did agree to supply France with highly enriched uranium[7] over a period of ten years. In fact, only half was delivered and in 1964 the United States refused further supplies on the grounds that, although the French had initially proposed using the uranium for their range of hunter-killer submarines, they were now proposing to use it for their offensive intercontinental missile-carrying submarines.

The first major statement explaining why France should develop her own nuclear weapons was made by General de Gaulle in his address to the École Militaire on November 3rd, 1959. The speech came after a series of French decisions which had had an important impact on NATO. In 1958, France refused to accept NATO rocket bases on French territory, as they would not be under French control. She had put up great resistance to the idea of developing a unified air defence system for Europe, which she thought would be arranged with its chief axis on London. In March 1959, France withdrew her Mediterranean Fleet from NATO and General de Gaulle declared his objection to the whole NATO concept of integration, which in his view could deprive a government of its essential role and responsibilities in the domain of its own defence. France acutely felt the special position of the British Mediterranean Fleet and the fact that the American Sixth Fleet was not subject to NATO. France also felt that she had two distinct missions: keeping the Mediterranean open, and maintaining her traditional links between the northern and southern shores of the Mediterranean. In 1959, the French refused to allow the stockpiling on French territory of nuclear weapons from American aircraft stationed there under NATO command, which resulted in the United States removing fighter and fighter-bomber squadrons from France. Again the French government pointed out that the British had been granted joint responsibility for the use of atomic warheads situated on British territory, but that no such privilege had been offered to France.

General de Gaulle argued to the staff college students that France must be self-sufficient and independent in her own defence. It was a declaration of a deeply held faith founded on his own experience and an interpretation of French history. 'As France can be destroyed from any corner of the world, we also must be able to reach any corner of the world. France must be able to provide herself with an atomic striking force.'[8]

Again, on November 10th, in a press conference, de Gaulle stated that France would be doing a service to the equilibrium of the world by equipping herself with nuclear weapons. It was the view of French Gaullists that no country could rely on another country's readiness to involve itself in nuclear destruction merely to defend an ally or honour some formal treaty or obligation. The 1959 defence budget showed an allocation of some £30 million, double the previous year's amount, for the development of the nuclear programme, or *force de frappe* as it was now called. A further heavy commitment was also made for thirty Mirage IV jet bombers to carry the nuclear weapon.

In November 1957, France resisted strong pressure in the United Nations, suffering an adverse vote when she held to her intention to test nuclear weapons in the Sahara and refused to comply with any test ban agreement that might be reached in Geneva. In February 1958, in the Sahara, the French successfully exploded their first nuclear bomb at the very time that the other three nuclear powers – the United States, Russia and Britain – were trying to reach an agreement outlawing nuclear testing. By 1960 General Buchalet, military director of the French Atomic Energy Commissariat and General Ailleret, the head of the Special Weapons Division, were openly advocating American help to speed up their development of nuclear weapons. Since it was clear that France was now a nuclear power and determined to go ahead with or without American aid, some American commentators began to ask whether it was a sensible use of resources to stretch the French military budget so that France would have to reduce her NATO commitments. It was argued that it would be sensible to give the French certain nuclear arms in return for promises to use those weapons as NATO required. Yet top American politicians were still at that time saying that the United States did not regard two nuclear explosions as qualification for French admission to the 'nuclear club'.

In July 1959, the French government put forward estimates for spending approximately £450 million on the development of the nuclear striking force for the next five years. Prime Minister Debré told the National Assembly Finance Committee on July 24th that political power among nations was coming more and more to be judged according to whether they had the bomb and the missiles. Those who had, had the right to speak, claimed Debré, and those who had not were only 'satellites'.

General Lavaud, Chief of the Army General Staff, published

an article in August in which he argued the surprising thesis that, though the French deterrent could not inflict as much damage on Russia as the American deterrent could, it would still be powerful enough to make the Russians pay a certain price. Quite apart from the near improbability of Russia launching an attack solely against France, the argument seemed to be that, though the super-powers had to have highly sophisticated weapons, a smaller nation such as France could get away with only a small deterrent. This was the doctrine of proportional deterrence. In September 1960, Prime Minister Debré widened the argument and quoted France's special African responsibilities – which, he said, America did not understand – as one reason for developing a national nuclear deterrent. He also argued that France could not rely on America coming to her aid and certainly the ability to invoke 1940 was a powerful if unspoken argument. Few had forgotten the reluctance of the Americans to become involved at that stage, and some of the more sophisticated commentators could also quote the British refusal to commit precious fighter aircraft to cover the land battles raging over French territory.

It is interesting to note that, despite all these arguments, the Military Bill before the French National Assembly, containing the large financial allocation for nuclear weapons, had a stormy passage, the voting being 42 to 33, with 3 abstentions in the Defence Committee, and 28 for and 28 against in the Foreign Affairs Committee. An amendment proposing that the government put to its NATO allies the question of a nuclear striking force in integrated form was actually carried, though of course no action followed. The Senate initially rejected the bill by 186 to 83. Further opposition ensued and it finally became law after three censure debates on December 6th. This was controversial legislation even by French standards.

In retrospect, the United States and Britain may have lost a unique opportunity, for even at this late stage an offer to collaborate and save research-and-development costs and maintain conventional force levels would have been very tempting to the French people and even to many Gaullists within the French government. It would have been necessary to understand General de Gaulle's wish for independence and to propose substantial changes in NATO's structure for strengthening European control, but some form of agreement might have been reached. As it was, Debré could easily dismiss the arguments for a European force from within his own party, by pointing out that West German involvement was banned by WEU treaty and that the other European countries had neither the will nor the resources to produce nuclear weapons. Only Britain was a possible partner, but she was uncooperative and determined to pursue her own independent nuclear deterrent. Once again, Britain's appalling insularity in matters of fundamental European interest ensured substantial difficulties for the future. Inside Britain the major mistake was to believe that the French position could be attributed entirely to the personality of de Gaulle. There was far too little recognition of the genuine nature of many of the French doubts about NATO and of its over-dependence on the United States. In fairness, Britain and the United States did make repeated efforts to reach a rational agreement on nuclear matters, but de Gaulle's objectives were not wider European objectives. He was motivated throughout this time by his own idiosyncratic view of France which made any meaningful dialogue extremely difficult to achieve.

The theory behind the French nuclear deterrent lay in a reflex second-strike force, whose purpose was to deter a strategic attack. But it was argued that France as the lesser power would risk annihilation if she did in fact respond with a retaliatory strike. It was also seriously questioned, even within the French armed services, whether such a reflex force would ever penetrate enemy defences and actually reach its target. This criticism became progressively more relevant as Soviet ground-to-air missile technology became more advanced. By the middle 1960s French airborne nuclear deterrents were rendered largely obsolescent.

A further heavy financial commitment was undertaken with the French government's decision to build a gaseous diffusion plant at Pierrelatte in the Rhône valley. The plant was necessary for the manufacture of thermonuclear bombs, though it could also supply fuel for nuclear-powered generating plants. It was again an example of heavy national investment, paid for by reducing the conventional arms defence budget, when facilities already existed in Britain and in the United States which could have been utilized, given the political will, at a fraction of the cost.

In the second five-year defence plan, from 1965–9, it was envisaged that the manned aircraft capable of in-flight refuelling and widely distributed over the country would make way for ballistic missiles designed to be launched from air, sea or land platforms, and that the fission bomb would be replaced by thermonuclear bombs. It was clear that the French were developing various types of nuclear weapons and a varied delivery system, including short-range tactical weapons for battlefield and anti-aircraft use and longer-range weapons systems for strategic deterrence. In January 1964 it was announced that, should the need arise, the President of France, General de Gaulle, would give the order directly to the air force general commanding the *force de frappe* and it was made clear that France now possessed a limited number of Mirage IV bombers equipped with atomic bombs. Scepticism about the effectiveness of this force was very marked in the French press. It was attacked as a status weapon and its strategic justification was dismissed as mere bombast. It was felt that in order to exercise any true deterrence it would need to be able to maintain a fleet of bombers constantly in the air, like the American Strategic Air Command, and yet everyone knew that there were not enough Mirage bombers to back up such an extensive flying commitment, and that only half the eventual fleet of sixty-two planes would ever be available at any one time.

It is interesting that in July 1962, well before Britain negotiated the December Nassau agreement, the French had announced their determination to build a fleet of five missile-carrying nuclear submarines, with megaton warheads which could be trained on Russian cities. The first was to be ready in 1970, but was delayed in the event until 1971.

On January 14th, 1963, General de Gaulle made it clear in his formal press conference that not only would France block British entry into the Common Market but she would not contribute her nuclear arms, when she had them, to the proposed NATO multilateral nuclear force; nor was she interested in the American proposal to sell France Polaris rockets. At the time, he said, France did not have the submarines or the warhead that the rocket presupposed, and by the time she had developed these, Polaris might be out of date and she would have manufactured a suitable missile for herself. De Gaulle believed that the right of withdrawal from a multilateral force would involve too many complications in a crisis, coming at the very moment when the force would be most needed. He was also determined to block West German participation in a multilateral nuclear force, particularly at a time when France's own nuclear force was in its infancy.

In 1964, France also had difficulty in obtaining certain electronic equipment from the United States for her Mirage IV fleet, which did not help American-French relationships, already cool because of the French decision to recognize Communist China. In 1965 the United States became seriously concerned that the French might leave NATO, and it was widely reported that President Johnson had specifically asked senior Cabinet ministers to ensure that French sensibilities were recognized. The Americans offered to coordinate targeting between Strategic Air Command and the French *force de frappe*, but the gulf was becoming wider. General de Gaulle was always bitterly critical of the so-called McNamara doctrine of a 'flexible response' to any Soviet attack on the NATO central front, and was in no mood to collaborate until his own doctrine of immediate and massive nuclear retaliation was adopted again as the NATO strategy. All this time France had refused to participate in the eighteen-nation disarmament conference which opened in Geneva on March 15th, 1962, and, with China, had refused to sign the Test Ban Treaty in August 1963. Anxiety over French attitudes to the Test Ban Treaty led to a further attempt in the summer of 1963 by the United States and

Britain to persuade de Gaulle to accept nuclear weapons information from them in return for signing the treaty. It was a vain attempt, but effectively answered the criticism that failure to achieve nuclear collaboration was solely due to the British and the Americans. The more one analyses the collaborative initiatives of 1958 to 1963, the more one is led to conclude that de Gaulle did not really want any agreement. Agreement would have always been too fettered to comply with his vision of a free France at the centre of a Europe stretching from the 'Atlantic to the Urals'.

On February 21st, 1966, General de Gaulle announced that he would withdraw all remaining French forces from NATO. In an aide memoire to her allies on March 28th and 29th, 1966, France formally announced the intention of withdrawing her forces from NATO on July 1st, 1966, and set a deadline of April 1st, 1967 for the removal of all allied commands and American and other foreign forces from French soil. This meant the complete transfer of the SHAPE headquarters from outside Paris to Brussels. It was the policy of integration within NATO which was such anathema to de Gaulle. The French never broke all their formal contacts with NATO and still claimed to be members of the Alliance. It was agreed that French troops would remain in West Germany and collaborate with NATO forces in any war situation which might occur as defined in Article V of the North Atlantic Treaty, but French strategic planning was now totally separate.

In June 1968, increasing economic difficulties and severe internal problems eventually forced the French government to cut defence spending. It was clear, even to the most committed Gaullists, that they would have to cut back on the thermo-nuclear budget. Yet on August 24th the first thermonuclear explosion was successfully carried out. In retrospect, the massive financial cost of the nuclear programme had been achieved only by ruthlessly giving it the highest priority in the overall national expenditure programme, and it had been done at a time when there were other urgent calls on the budget. Another serious consequence of the nuclear programme was that it had been achieved at the expense of France's conventional defence forces. In October 1968, with France still facing severe financial problems, the decision was made to proceed with the development of intercontinental ballistic missiles. This ensured that France would eventually have a complete armoury of missiles, but it was to be done at a crippling cost in terms of internal unrest from dissatisfaction at the pace of social reform and against a background of crisis over the French franc. The cancellation of the nuclear test programme for 1969 was a rare but significant sign of how severe the financial burden of the nuclear programme had become.

There is some evidence that towards the end of de Gaulle's presidency his defence policy changed. The invasion of Czechoslovakia showed that the Russians were still prepared to impose their will on Warsaw Pact countries and it was obvious that de Gaulle's dream of a united Europe, which included the Eastern bloc, was a long way off. Nor had the French decision to leave NATO led to any weakening of the Warsaw Pact unity, and countries like Rumania had still remained members. De Gaulle was also concerned by a variety of American policies, particularly for their possible impact on NATO. He saw the Non-Proliferation Treaty as a threat to the development of an eventual European nuclear force. The proposed Strategic Arms Limitation Talks were, he felt, too closely confined to the two super-powers and, taken with the Congressional pressure for troop withdrawals from Europe, likely to lead to decisions about European security being made with insufficient European involvement.

In the 1970s these trends have become even more obvious. The importance of the American troop reductions does not lie in endless arguments about the actual numbers of troops to be withdrawn, but in the fact that to many Europeans any American troop reductions will be seen as the prelude to total withdrawal. These Europeans see the arguments that lie behind reducing American force levels as basically reflecting a growing belief in America that the defence of Western Europe is not a vital national interest. Such a change in American priorities, if it were true, would completely undermine the credibility of the existing American nuclear guarantee. It is important for those people who do not believe that it is in Europe's interest to develop militarily into a super-power with its own deterrent to ensure that the American commitment to the defence of Western Europe remains firm for the future.

There is a danger that some people within the movement for European unity may be carried away in their zeal to believe that there is some inherent virtue in a European nationalism that would justify opting out of the Atlantic Alliance. The danger of Gaullism is its belief that Europe can only re-establish its identity after severing the American connection.

Many strong believers in European unity believe that the greatest contribution Britain can make to Europe is to ensure the survival of the concept behind the North Atlantic Treaty. The goal of European unity and Britain's entry to the EEC is fully compatible with the maintenance of existing defence alliances that will ensure that the narrowness of European Gaullism is replaced by a more balanced and realistic view of the politics of power in a nuclear age. Henry Kissinger, arguing for Europe to retain some capacity for independent action in the political and military sphere, wrote in 1964: 'Paradoxically, the unity of the Atlantic area can be encouraged by a structure which, in granting reasonable autonomy, reduces the desire for it.'[9] It is worth examining what structure can provide a measure of European autonomy without weakening the unity of the Alliance.

Chapter 13. European Defence

A European defence force is not a new concept and it is easy to forget how near continental Europe came to establishing such a force in the 1950s. The invasion of South Korea on June 25th, 1950, was perhaps the most important single factor in promoting the cause of European defence, since it resulted in considerable pressure from the United States for West German rearmament. President Truman openly advocated in September 1950 that Europe should increase its land forces and suggested ten West German divisions. The American Secretary of State, Dean Acheson, also made it clear in that same month that the United States envisaged the development of an autonomous German army. A German army was rejected by the French Prime Minister, Robert Schuman. But France, Britain and the United States did agree to treat any attack against the Federal Republic or Berlin as an attack against themselves. Such an agreement lacked credibility, for there were no real proposals on how the commitment could be supported on the ground with sufficient troops. Eventually, pressure from prominent Europeans, which had been building up for some time, led to specific proposals. On August 11th, 1950, at the Council of Europe, Winston Churchill, following the lead of Paul Reynaud, formally proposed a motion – which was carried – calling for the formation of a European army under a European minister of defence. In October the French Premier, René Pleven, argued in the National Assembly that, though Germany was not a party to the Atlantic Pact, she benefited from the system of security and it was right that she should share in preparing for the defence of Europe. He stipulated three essential elements: first, the ratification of the Schuman Plan for placing all coal and steel production of France and Germany under a common high authority, which would be open to other European countries; second, the appointment of a

European defence minister; and, third, the establishment of a political body to supervise the defence minister's actions. The French National Assembly subsequently approved the Pleven Plan by 348 votes to 224, and in the mood of optimism which followed it seemed that a European defence force would be established.

The difficulties inherent in the Pleven Plan for creating a European Defence Community (EDC) soon became obvious. First, it was necessary to establish some common ground between the newly established American-dominated NATO and the proposed community. Second, a defence community faced the problem of West Germany in relation to the occupying powers and the fundamental changes in the Occupation Statute which would be necessary in order for West Germany to be able to participate. Finally, before the EDC could be established, the all-important question had to be answered of how to develop financial and political control mechanisms which would effectively integrate a grouping of national armies. The early 1950s was a time when the idealism lying behind the concept of a united Europe was openly and frankly stated. European integration was not subjected to the narrow critical scrutiny and scepticism of the 1960s. The concept of a united Europe was seen not just from a limited national viewpoint, where short-term economic consequences predominated, but as a wider vision. At the conference held in Paris on February 15th, 1951, the climate was such that Robert Schuman reminded the conference that nations once deeply divided were meeting round the same table, forgetting their past struggles in an 'attempt to substitute for the very instrument of these struggles – national armies – a common army that will be able to act only in defence of their common civilization'.[1] These were fine sentiments, particularly coming from the French, who still had bitter memories of the war, but it was ironically the French National Assembly which in effect rejected the EDC treaty when it eventually came up for ratification on August 30th, 1954.

The EDC did not initially arouse profound resentment, but

slowly in Germany and in France the critics gained in strength. In France, where there were genuine fears of German rearmament, the opposition was particularly bitter. Some prominent Europeans opposed the EDC on the grounds that military integration should not precede political integration, and there was also disappointment that the EDC did not embrace the whole of Europe and particularly Britain. On June 5th, 1954, General de Gaulle gave one of his rare but influential press conferences and bitterly attacked the EDC concept. Even in retirement he was still a crucial influence on the Gaullist party, and on a significant section of French opinion. Michel Debré, speaking in the National Assembly in 1953 had voiced the Gaullist arguments against the EDC treaty, which were to become the dominant theme of French foreign policy throughout the 1960s. 'It is necessary to tell all the theologians of little Europe point blank: Europe is not a nation; it is an aggregate of nations. Europe is not a state; it is a grouping of states. To create Europe, this reality must be taken into account.'[2]

The French rejection of the European Defence Community was the start of a persistent and continued refusal by France to accept any significant steps towards European integration which might challenge her own position. Rejection of the EDC led to the now widespread view that any future progress in the defence field cannot succeed until there has been a much greater degree of political integration.

This theory has been challenged, a notable instance being at Macmillan's June 1962 meeting with de Gaulle at the Chateau de Champs, when he clearly indicated that, after entry to the EEC, Britain would Europeanize her defence to the extent of even a European army and a European deterrent. On any rational basis it is inconceivable that, in the long term, defence will be excluded from the movement towards European integration, but whether defence integration can precede political integration is more doubtful.

Potentially a most important public statement on a possible evolution of European defence through the 1970s came from Edward Heath in his Godkin lecture at Harvard in 1967.

Speaking with the greater freedom of a leader of the opposition, though he seemed unaware of the extent to which Britain is dependent on American nuclear technology, he said that logic pointed to an eventual European defence system that would begin with conventional forces and common procurement policies. He went on to say, 'In my view it might also include a nuclear force based on the existing British and French forces which could be held in trusteeship for Europe as a whole.'[3] This was a reference to the Non-Proliferation Treaty not barring succession by a new Federated European state to the nuclear status of one of its former components.

This passage was widely criticized at the time. It was felt to involve nuclear collaboration outside NATO and also to be in conflict with the Non-Proliferation Treaty. Some commentators also thought that it was meant to imply a link with the Common Market negotiations. The emphasis on the Anglo-French deterrent was too reminiscent of Macmillan's previous offer in 1962, with which Heath – the chief British negotiator with the EEC – must have been familiar. It is highly questionable how attractive a proposition to the French the sharing of Britain's existing nuclear technology really is, particularly since so much of it stems from Anglo-American agreements. In 1958 and 1962 it could, if it formed part of a trilateral agreement with the United States, have led to substantial savings in time and expense, but it is dubious at best whether it would ever have acted, even in 1962, as an incentive for the French to accept British entry into the European Economic Community. In an introduction written to his lectures in 1969, Heath justified his earlier comments by saying that his proposals would not involve a breach of the Non-Proliferation Treaty and would positively provide a means for healing the breach between France and her NATO allies. He also specifically denied that the proposal was in some way a condition of British membership to the EEC. It was significant that when he became Prime Minister, Heath did not attempt to start negotiations on an Anglo-French deterrent prior to the EEC negotiations, and denied linking the British application in his talks with President Pompidou in May 1971 with an Anglo-French nuclear deterrent. The government's basic position in its early years of office showed little change from that of the previous Labour government, who had consistently argued that any such arrangement could be discussed only within the NATO framework. As Prime Minister, Wilson had scrupulously avoided any attempt to link nuclear weapon collaboration with the 1967 EEC application. However, he had laid great stress on the benefits for the existing members of the EEC of having access to British technology, particularly in the field of nuclear energy technology. Under the Labour government, Britain had shown that she was less dependent on the strict interpretation of existing Anglo-American agreements when, with Holland and West Germany, she formed a consortium in 1969 to exploit the new gas centrifuge technology for uranium enrichment, though this was strictly confined to civil applications and specifically excluded any military use by the two other non-nuclear powers.

Whether collaboration with the French over nuclear weapons would be in contravention of the Non-Proliferation Treaty is a contentious issue. In 1971 the Conservative government held that nothing in Articles I or II, which are the crucial articles in the Non-Proliferation Treaty,[4] was incompatible with Anglo-French nuclear collaboration, provided no actual nuclear warheads or other nuclear explosive devices or control over such weapons or devices were transferred. It is relevant that Article I omits any reference to delivery systems or to an exchange of technological nuclear information. The treaty was drafted specifically to prevent the proliferation of nuclear weapons to non-nuclear states, and there is no wording prohibiting joint targeting. The treaty contains nothing to prevent vertical integration amongst existing nuclear states, whether they are signatories to the treaty, as is the case for the United States and Britain, or whether they have refused to sign, as have the French. Nor is there any real evidence that it was ever the intention of the signatories that the treaty should be drafted to prevent vertical integration. Indeed, it would have been folly to have so drafted the treaty, for it cannot, on non-proliferation grounds, be in anyone's interest to prevent the integration of the American, French and British independent national nuclear deterrents into one allied deterrent.

The British Labour government were deeply committed in 1968 to pushing through the Non-Proliferation Treaty, and yet there are no grounds for believing that their interpretation of the wording of the treaty was any different from that of their successors. A much more difficult problem affecting any proposed Anglo-French collaboration is the existing Anglo-American agreements, which cover nuclear weapons. These are open to varying interpretations, but the one inescapable conclusion is that, irrespective of the exact legal interpretation, it would be wholly against the spirit of these agreements for Britain to share information, whether on nuclear warheads or delivery systems, with the French or any other nation, without the United States' agreement. It is therefore clear that, short of putting the vital Polaris cooperation in jeopardy, no Anglo-French discussions can occur without at the very minimum the United States giving approval to the discussions, and it would be preferable for the discussions to be trilateral.

The Nuclear Planning Group within NATO would provide a convenient forum for such discussions, but the problem of insisting that any discussions must occur only within NATO is that it necessitates the French returning within NATO at the outset. Though this must be the eventual aim, it is conceivable that in order for the initial talks to commence, a new non-NATO forum might have to be found. The Western European Union can undoubtedly be developed as a forum for conventional defence discussions, but the exclusion of the United States makes it hard to use this as a forum for nuclear discussions. As long as France continues to remain outside NATO, any rational European defence strategy is almost impossible to achieve. The case for radical change in NATO is now overwhelming. The mystical belief that 'after de Gaulle' the French would come back into NATO is becoming less and less credible. It is now time the Western Alliance gave up its comfortable sounding ritualistic obeisance to NATO, stimulated by the twenty-first anniversary celebrations, and faced up to the organization's serious deficiencies. NATO's nuclear strategy has still to be fully developed and the absence of France clearly distorts the fundamental power structure on which NATO must be based for the 1970s and beyond.

Over the years the new generation of European political leaders has built up a profound and healthy scepticism of grand political designs. Particularly in defence, a pragmatic evolutionary approach has tended to dominate political thinking. Though few doubt the need for greater integration, the tendency has been to argue that, until governments are more used to working together and until they build up a fund of mutual trust, then no major political breakthrough is possible. This approach has much to recommend it and, by applying its principles through the unofficial Euro Group, where the European members of NATO meet for informal discussion, substantial progress has been made. The European Defence Improvement Programme and major joint procurement projects such as the Multi-Role Combat Aircraft are important new initiatives which should not be underrated. But the nuclear problem remains unsolved and its importance cannot be overestimated. There is and has been throughout the 1960s an urgent need to develop an integrated command and control structure for the Western Alliance's nuclear weapons in Europe. This issue must now be faced either within the existing NATO framework or in a forum outside. If no agreement is possible within the existing structure, then politicians must be prepared to change NATO's structure. The fundamental question is what form such an agreement should take. The arguments of the early 1960s against the growth of national deterrents were based on the fear of proliferation and the dangers inherent in such weak and obsolescent systems. In fact, though France and Britain have developed and extended their strategic deterrent systems throughout the 1960s, this has not led to any other nations developing nuclear weapons. China, the only other nuclear power, exploded her first nuclear bomb in 1964, but the decision to develop major nuclear weapons had been made in the 1950s.

The other major argument in the early 1960s was based on the McNamara dictum that national nuclear deterrents held by countries without the resources and knowledge of the superpowers were dangerous. Again, this argument, though true, is largely irrelevant, given that no one now believes that France or China will forgo their national deterrents; even Britain under a Labour government chose to retain and build up her own independent deterrent. Any new agreement for the 1970s will therefore have to be framed against the background of what has actually happened in the 1960s; the dialogue on nuclear matters which has been nascent for some years is certain to be revived in the middle 1970s.

In any assessment of the possibility of a specifically European deterrent, or consideration of the existing British and French nuclear forces, the dominating factor is the make-up of the United States strategic forces.

In November 1960 the *George Washington* left port for the first Polaris operational patrol, and it has been the Polaris weapon system that has provided the major contribution to the allied deterrent system throughout the 1960s, just as it is likely to dominate the 1970s.

The United States Navy now has forty-one fleet ballistic missile submarines, each of which is capable of launching sixteen A3 Polaris missiles. The force operates in the North Atlantic, the Mediterranean and the Pacific, and is capable of providing continuous coverage of the key targets in Russia and China. A Polaris submarine has some of its missiles on a few minutes' notice to fire throughout the operational part of the patrol. It gives the United States an invincible second-strike potential, and at present there is no likelihood of any technological discovery making the faster and deeper new submarines vulnerable even in the 1980s.

The United States Administration in 1968 decided to equip thirty-one of their Polaris submarines with a sophisticated second-generation weapon system, the Poseidon missile. In

April 1971 the first of the converted fleet ballistic missile submarines entered service equipped with Poseidon missiles. The Poseidon missile is larger and more accurate than the Polaris missile. It has a Multiple Independently Targetable Re-entry Vehicle (MIRV), the capability of which permits guided delivery of a number of nuclear warheads to separate targets and gives it a much enhanced capability to penetrate any ABM defence network.

The number of warheads that Poseidon will be able to carry is a classified secret. However, ten has been suggested in the first generation,[5] and, as the technology improves, a larger number in subsequent generations. On the basis of thirty-one Poseidon submarines, each with sixteen missiles and with each missile having ten warheads, the United States will eventually be able to deploy – with Poseidon alone – a greater force than the whole of their present strategic forces.

The importance of the Poseidon missile system is its second-strike or retaliatory capability. The arguments which centre on the need to develop further a first-strike or pre-emptive capability are singularly unconvincing. The development of such a capability might have had meaning before the Soviet Union developed her own submarine-launching missile system, but in 1971 she had over 350 submarine missiles, and this number is increasing so rapidly that by the mid-1970s the Russians should have more than the present number of American submarine-launched missiles. Whether the Russians will by then have deployed a MIRV capability is not of overriding importance, since they will still possess a sufficient second-strike capability to make it even more unrealistic than it is at the moment for the NATO powers to contemplate using a first-strike nuclear force. Robert McNamara's often quoted saying that 'The threat of an incredible action is not an effective deterrent' has a superficial attraction, but fortunately it is not really true. In effect, any nuclear response is incredible; yet the fact that such a possibility cannot be ignored is the basis for most sensible modern strategic thought. The other American strategic forces are currently made up of 1,000 Minuteman fixed land-based intercontinental ballistic missiles, fifty-four of the older Titan missiles and over 500 bomber aircraft, all carrying a nuclear payload. Land-based missiles have a second-strike capability only if the missile site is sufficiently hardened by concrete and other means to sustain a nuclear attack or if they are protected by an ABM system. The replacement of Minuteman 1 missiles with Minuteman 3 missiles, each with three independently targeted warheads, continues; by 1975 there will be over 500 Minuteman 3 missiles, doubling the number of targets which can be hit.

The Russians have some 1,510 ICBMs and some 700 IRBMs, and medium-range missiles, markedly redressing the imbalance of the 1960s. All the evidence points to a continued expansion of missiles and warheads.

The greatest tragedy has been the lost opportunity for a substantial measure of arms limitation which occurred when first the Johnson and then the Nixon Administration prevaricated over proposing a MIRV testing moratorium. This was the one really effective initiative in the late 1960s that was open to a United States Administration seriously hoping to halt the arms race. When the SALT talks actually began, the United States had almost completed their MIRV testing programme and so the one chance for taking a major step to halt the quantum leap that MIRV deployment involved was lost. It is now barely conceivable that the Russians could agree to a ban on MIRV testing, for they know that the Americans could circumvent such a ban by fitting MIRVs to their existing missiles without futher testing and with a fair measure of confidence in their effectiveness. History will show the reluctance to push a MIRV moratorium to have been a massive error of judgment. Admittedly, all weapon moratoriums have their dangers, but even with the Russians' persistent refusal to consider on-site testing, there were reasonable grounds for believing that modern detection devices would have been able to pick up the testing of MIRVs, even allowing for Multiple Re-entry Vehicles (MRVs) and the deliberate use of decoys, which might also have been banned. It was a tragedy, too, that throughout this period the main public debate in America focused on ABM deployment, which in terms of world security was far less important. The Congressional critics of ABMs should have realized that, without MIRVs, ABM deployment would have been much harder to justify.

All through this period, despite a Labour government pledged to work for disarmament, Britain never made any public statement giving unequivocal support for a MIRV moratorium. Disarmament cannot be separated from defence. It is only with the technical knowledge and backing that is available to politicians inside defence ministries that nuclear disarmament proposals can carry any credibility. Throughout the critical period in which a MIRV moratorium was considered, responsibility for disarmament was held by a minister inside the British Foreign Office with wholly inadequate access to the specialized technical knowledge available inside the Ministry of Defence. Although responsibility for the Atomic Weapon Research Establishment at Aldermaston was nominally shared between the Ministry of Technology and the Ministry of Defence, this had little practical effect, and control in 1971 was wholly assumed by the Ministry of Defence. In 1968 there were powerful voices inside the United States advocating a MIRV moratorium, and they would have been greatly strengthened by technical support for their arguments coming from British scientists and defence experts. Britain, however, chose only to make private representations, and did not pursue these with vigour for fear of causing offence.

As a result, Britain must take some share of the responsibility for the continued arms race that has been sparked off by MIRV deployment. Between 1967 and 1969 there was no public discussion and very little political discussion inside the British government. Doubts were expressed, but the absurd cloak of secrecy peculiar to Britain that so bedevils nuclear matters once again triumphed. Believing that access to American information would cease if Britain were to criticize publicly, British politicians stayed silent. Even if British experts had all accepted the view that a MIRV moratorium was technically impossible to police, the wider cause of disarmament should still have prompted Britain to speak out in favour of a detailed discussion of the implication of a total MIRV ban.

A major role for Britain in NATO stems from the fact that, even though no longer a super-power, she possesses a knowledge of defence and nuclear matters unequalled by any other West European country. This knowledge carries with it the responsibility to voice friendly criticism to the United States. In any alliance there are issues of such profound importance that the course of true friendship is to criticize, even to the extent of publicly voicing concern.

Britain had a duty to advocate a moratorium as the initial step towards a total ban on MIRV development when the technical arguments against a moratorium were so unconvincing The decision to stay silent was a major error of policy of far greater long-term importance than the decision not to criticize overtly American involvement in Vietnam. Yet it is a miserable commentary on the way defence issues are discussed that few people in Britain or the United States even know that the possibility existed of achieving a MIRV moratorium, let alone the significance of failing to achieve it.

It is because of the imbalance of MIRV technology, with the United States having such a clear lead, that for the next few years any limitation of strategic arms is unlikely to lead to a reduction in warheads. The Russians will almost certainly be unwilling to accept a freeze on existing numbers of missiles and aircraft, unless accompanied by a total MIRV deployment ban or by the inclusion of MIRVs in the total number of missiles. Since this would involve on-the-ground inspection, which the Russians have never accepted, it is unlikely to be achieved. The Russians know that the Americans are introducing a new Short Range Attack Missile (SRAM) for their B-52 bombers and are planning a new B-1 bomber. They also know that they are behind in applying MIRV technology and so a freeze would be likely to ensure a widening of the missile gap for some years to come.

The central immediate issue for SALT is whether it can

produce a ban on further ABMs which, if deployment goes ahead as planned in both countries, will result in a massive drain on financial resources. The Soviet Union already has deployed around Moscow sixty-four ABMs for its Galosh system, and the United States is working on the construction of the Safeguard system around three Minuteman sites, the first of which will be ready in 1974; they also at one time requested funds for a further system, to be deployed around Washington. The United States had by 1970 become very concerned about the large Russian SS9 missile and especially the new underground sites which had been detected; the SS9 has three warheads which, though not at present independently controlled, are thought to be able to land in a pattern which could effectively knock out a Minuteman site, even when hardened by the addition of extensive reinforced concrete around the launching base. It is this concern that formed the major argument for deployment of an ABM system, but the whole justification depended on the doubtful assumption that the Russians were intending to develop the SS9 as a first-strike weapon system and largely ignored the existence of the Polaris and Poseidon system. It seems extraordinary that Congress could decide actually to slow down the conversion rate of Polaris submarines to be fitted with Poseidon, which is a system with a proven second-strike capability, and at the same time accept, albeit after tremendous opposition, the case for an ABM system. Even if they proved technically successful, which is dubious in view of the potential of MIRV technology, ABMs would only confer on Minuteman missiles a second-strike capability. This would be achieved at a tremendous financial cost and risk to the civilian population who would then become the natural first-strike target. The real argument should centre on whether Minuteman missiles are required at all, and this question should be considered without taking too much notice of single-service lobbying.

These facts show that the 1970s will present a completely new dimension of increase in nuclear weapons, and it is this background which must be constantly borne in mind when discussing the relatively small strategic force of the French and British. The two countries are particularly concerned about the outcome of SALT. The lack of any agreement to halt further ABM deployment could have a serious effect on the viability of the French and British deterrents. Their effectiveness to penetrate Soviet territory would be seriously weakened by thick ABM deployment. Such deployment would raise well before the end of the 1970s the whole question of the obsolescence of the existing deterrent systems. Whether a second-generation missile would be justified would then become a serious issue, and rapid decisions would have to be taken.

The possibility of a comprehensive ban on ABM deployment clearly does exist and there are some limited grounds for optimism, but it is likely to be some time before any major breakthrough occurs. The Russians appear to be seriously interested in limiting ABM deployment to safeguard military command and control centres. Unfortunately, though, they have extensive ICBM missile sites collocated with their command centres; this is not true for the United States, whose missile sites are spread all over the country. Russian command and control centres are also closely correlated with major industrial centres, which is again not the case in the United States. The agreement to link discussion of ABMs with offensive weapon systems announced in mid-1971 represented a limited advance, but no substantive agreement had been reached at that stage. It may, however, be possible to reach some limited agreement on ABM deployment in 1972 and to build on this, so as eventually to move towards a phased reduction of medium-range nuclear missiles in Warsaw Pact territory and their counterparts in NATO's continental Europe territory. In the circumstances of a major agreement by 1975 between the super-powers on strategic arms limitation and a separate agreement on multilateral force reductions, the existing French and British strategic nuclear forces might theoretically need to be justified anew. However, it is unrealistic to plan on such optimistic assumptions.

It may be that the pessimism over SALT leading to a really

effective limitation on ABM deployment will prove to have been misplaced. In which case, some argue, the need for a 'hardening' programme to increase the penetration of the A3 missile will not be vital. But the British government seems to have taken the pessimistic view, for it appears that in late 1970 it decided to embark on a 'hardening' programme. This means that for the third time in the last ten years – 1962, 1964 and 1970 – a British government has deliberately rejected an opportunity to withdraw from the future development of a viable nuclear deterrent system.

Despite protestations to the contrary, there is little evidence for believing that a Labour government would have chosen differently, though it is worth noting that in 1967, prior to discussing entry to the EEC with de Gaulle, Labour did decide not to purchase Poseidon. But a decision then would anyhow have been premature militarily. The continuation of an effective British nuclear deterrent in the 1980s can be developed by refitting existing submarines and using a second-generation missile system such as Poseidon. The financial investment for Britain alone, or even in collaboration with France, is far too great to develop the slow-moving, deep-diving submarines which the Americans are planning and which will be able to fire long-range missiles with large warheads. It is also unrealistic for Europe to plan on having access to such American technology in its early development, for it would represent in effect the third generation of United States naval underwater missile systems, and, not unreasonably, would initially be strictly confined to the United States.

It is worth remembering that an effective deterrent system is vastly improved by having access to expensive radar early warning systems, sophisticated communication networks and surveillance technology. It is this American technology which ensures that the British nuclear force remains a viable entity. The intelligence information and technology is made available to Britain under bilateral agreements and has been of immense value. The practice of the agreements goes far beyond any strict legal interpretation of their wording. The integration of the British Polaris fleet with that of the United States Navy has also reached a level that makes it hard to foresee all the consequences if the present level of technical and logistic help were to cease. The spirit is clearly that of a continuing relationship and this is reflected in the wording on future developments in the 1963 Polaris rules agreement. There is no doubt that if Britain wished to purchase Poseidon missiles, this would fall within the framework of the Polaris sales agreement.

The French missile-firing nuclear submarine force is not, in marked contrast to the British, a viable system at present. Until the middle 1970s at least, France will be without a credible second-strike deterrent force. The first submarine, *Redoutable*, entered service only at the end of 1971; the third submarine is unlikely to enter service until late 1974 at the earliest. This means that the French will not be able to rely on having one submarine on patrol at all times until 1975. The fourth and possibly the last of the original order for five submarines will not enter service before 1977; so, even after 1975, the French will be hard pressed to keep two submarines on patrol for a major part of the year and, like Britain today, will be vulnerable to the slightest accident or delay in submarine refitting.

The French missile system is also far less effective than the British. The French missile has a shorter range than the Polaris A3 missile – 1,200 miles as against 2,500. The French nuclear warhead is only 500 kilotons as opposed to Britain's 600-kiloton warhead and France will not have developed multiple warhead techniques until the 1980s.[6] It is perhaps not surprising that France, through relying almost exclusively on her own research-and-development effort, spent an estimated $11,965,000 on strategic nuclear weapons from 1960 to 1971, whereas Britain spent only $4,900,000.[7] The discrepancy between the two countries' spending is widening appreciably. In 1975 it is estimated on current plans that Britain will be spending only some 2 per cent of her defence budget on maintaining the strategic deterrent, while France will be spending approximately 20 per cent of hers.[8] This particular allocation of defence expenditure will mean an even greater reduction in the effectiveness of France's conventional forces. These economic pressures on France could be the most powerful factor inducing a complete reappraisal of French strategy and attitudes towards European defence collaboration. A simple view of Anglo-French nuclear collaboration is based on the premise that Britain has at least a five-year lead on France in nuclear warhead technology and also greater experience in the design and operation of nuclear-powered submarines with their specialized navigational systems. Whereas, unlike Britain, France has her own natural sources of uranium and her own supply of tritium, an important fusionable material produced by a special reactor, France also has a lead over Britain in missile technology.

It is argued that an Anglo-French nuclear deterrent could be established now by merging the existing forces and developing a second-generation weapons system without relying on American technology. But these arguments either ignore or pay scant regard to one central fact: that, in all the crucial areas of nuclear technology, American knowledge and experience not only is far superior to that existing in France and Britain today but is constantly advancing to match one of the most rapidly changing areas of scientific knowledge. To advocate embarking on a course of technological independence is to accept a crippling financial burden with no guarantee of maintaining a viable deterrent system. It is a course of potential danger to the security of Europe and should only ever be contemplated if forced on Europe by an uncooperative and isolationist United States. It is perhaps some small comfort to know that in such a dangerous situation Europe has the capability to develop its own deterrent system. But it is only a small comfort, because the raison d'être for maintaining the American commitment to Europe is not technical but strategic. The deterrent strategy of the Western Alliance depends on the Warsaw Pact countries believing that, should they launch a conventional attack in Europe which leads after a few days to the collapse of Western defences, an American President would be prepared to authorize the use of tactical nuclear weapons as an indication of his intention to use strategic nuclear weapons if the advance continued.

For such a strategy to have any credibility it is necessary for the West to have the capability to retaliate to any first use of nuclear weapons by the Warsaw Pact with a devastating second strike. It is not enough simply to be able to damage Warsaw Pact territory. The facts already given all show that in the West only the United States has sufficient forces to give a certainty of total devastation to any aggressor. No conceivable European deterrent would be of sufficient size or strength to offer the certainty of devastation. A force of eight or ten missile-firing submarines would at best only be able to severely damage an aggressor's territory, and any significant improvement in ABM technology which was not matched by improvements in missile penetration would reduce the deterrent effect even further. It is an illusion – or, as some French commentators aptly call it, a 'mirage' – to believe that Europe can separately develop a viable deterrent force. Nor is it of itself desirable. It would, as has been stressed earlier, become necessary only at a stage where the credibility of the American nuclear guarantee is so weakened that Europe feels it cannot rely on an American nuclear commitment. In this case, Europe collectively might decide dramatically to expand its own nuclear forces and Britain might no longer be able to rely on having access to American equipment, technology or back-up for her own nuclear forces.

But this is a situation very far removed from that which exists today. If the United States did adopt isolationist policies, Western Europe might well prefer to adopt a non-aligned posture or renounce nuclear weapons altogether. It would certainly then be an option worth considering. The overwhelming priority now for the Western Alliance in Europe is to plan for the development in the 1970s of an operationally integrated command and control system for nuclear weapons. This would end the present uneasy situation of what in the last analysis continues to be three independent strategic nuclear deterrent systems for the defence of Europe. It is also vital to develop control systems in relation to existing tactical weapons, whose importance has been consistently underestimated. The scepticism of the early 1960s on the real value of tactical nuclear weapons which was initially held by many in NATO, has been replaced by the official recognition within NATO that the present 7,000 tactical nuclear weapons in Europe are the crucial next line of defence after conventional defence forces have failed to withstand a conventional attack. Whatever outside critics may say, these weapons are at present considered to be an indispensable element in NATO's deterrent against attack. They can be delivered by a variety of means – aircraft, howitzers, atomic demolition munitions. They can be used in the air, at sea or on land. The control of tactical nuclear weapons and their use within as far as possible an integrated strategy is for France and NATO of the utmost importance.

It is necessary to state the practical limitations with which any integrated command structure will have to comply. It is at present inconceivable that any nuclear nation will give to any other nation, or group of nations, the right to fire its own deterrent system without full national endorsement. This means that any mixed-manning solutions or totally unified control systems with authority vested in one individual are unrealistic for the foreseeable future. Valid non-proliferation arguments exclude nuclear weapon technology being transferred to any non-nuclear power, so that the possession of nuclear weapons cannot and should not be widened to West Germany or any other European ally.

It needs to be recognized from the outset that the present structure of NATO is not the vehicle for any new integrated command and control system to which France is likely to agree. Change within NATO should be the aim; yet it is not enough for changes to be made to NATO's structure merely to satisfy the French; it is vital that at least Britain and West Germany understand and to some extent reciprocate some of the French criticisms of NATO. This issue was never tackled by the British Labour government's proposed Atlantic nuclear force (ANF).

The American dominance of NATO was, in 1964, the central theme of Gaullist criticism and still remains so today after de Gaulle's death. Though such criticism is often only couched in terms of objecting to integration in the name of national sovereignty, the central objection is that any abdication of sovereignty is solely to the United States. It is the lack of a European identity to NATO, the lack of a better balance between Europe and the United States, which still remains the all-important issue for the French. Unless fundamental changes in NATO's structure can be achieved so as to reflect a greater European balance, then little progress will be made towards meaningful integration. This is essentially a political decision. To advocate such a switch in NATO's identity is emphatically not to argue for a 'third force', for this is a concept that would involve pursuing a policy of separation from the United States. Separation would gravely weaken the effectiveness of the Western Alliance not only in Europe, but world-wide. No one can exclude separation being forced on a reluctant Europe at some future date. But actually to aim for a third force independent of the United States is to pursue a dangerously destabilizing concept based on the belief that Europe should act as an independent military power or as some form of moral arbiter between the two super-powers. Apart from the strategic policy objections, this fanciful role is based on a total misreading of the resources that are, in practical terms, available in Europe for developing such a force.

In 1964, Britain was spending about 7 per cent of her gross national product (GNP) on defence, and by 1970 this had come down to 5·7 per cent. She was not alone in reducing the share of GNP going to defence. In 1952, Britain's European allies spent about 7·5 per cent of their collective GNP on defence. By 1959, this proportion had shrunk to about 5·5 per cent, and in 1970 it was 4·2 per cent. (West Germany in 1970 spent 3·7 per cent of her GNP on defence, though the total expenditure was greater than Britain's, and France spent 4·7 per cent of GNP.) It is unrealistic to assume, whether for economic or political reasons, that a much greater percentage of national wealth than is being spent at present will be spent on defence in the next decade by NATO countries. Europe's defence effort can be stretched to offset the effect of limited American troop reductions, yet within the available resources there will be no substantial funds for developing totally independent nuclear weapon systems of the sophistication necessary to ensure a viable strategic deterrent force in the 1980s. Even if the development of a third force were desirable, which it currently is not, such a force is for financial reasons alone unattainable in anything less than a ten-year time-scale, and only after considerable expenditure sacrifices in areas of domestic policy.

Defence budgets in all countries are already under severe pressure, for the cost of sophisticated defence equipment is tending to increase at a faster rate than GNP, simply because of the ever-increasing complexity of successive generations of equipment which are necessary to meet an increasingly sophisticated threat. The capital cost of an armoured regiment, for example, equipped with Chieftain tanks is 80 per cent higher than that of one equipped with Centurion tanks, even after all price increases due to inflation have been excluded. On the same basis, the cost of building a frigate is today about 75 per cent higher than it was in the late 1950s.

These financial pressures have already forced Western European countries into closer collaboration in the defence field, particularly over procurement policies. The Multi-Role Combat Aircraft (MRCA), which is a joint development between Britain, Germany and Italy, makes both industrial and military sense because of its guaranteed market. The military advantages will come from the existence of a single aircraft type in three of the largest European air forces. In recent years, the NATO Commander-in-Chief of Central Europe has had fifteen different military aircraft under his command, and it is obvious that such a mix carries severe logistic and operational penalties. With the exception of the variable geometry aircraft (AFVG), it is interesting how successful Anglo-French collaboration has been. The joint helicopter projects and the development of the Jaguar aircraft have all largely been unaffected by the French decisions over NATO.

The advocates of a cautious pragmatic evolutionary approach to European defence use the facts of the growing collaboration in European defence matters to argue against any fundamental structural changes in NATO. They tend to believe that nuclear sharing is such an emotional issue that any attempt to resurrect the question will merely revive the old divisive arguments that dominated the late 1950s and early 1960s.

This steady, cautious approach has dominated Western European diplomacy since the collapse of the ANF concept in 1965. Since then, substantial progress within NATO has been made in the Nuclear Planning Group, but the serious problems remain. The non-participation of France in NATO continues, while the dominance of the United States in nuclear matters has increased, as witness SALT. The certainty of American troop withdrawals is beginning to be accepted throughout NATO and the opportunity for reassessment such withdrawals will give should not be missed. Any American Administration at the point of deciding on troop reductions from Europe will be receptive to the need not only to adopt a less dominant role in NATO but also to cover their withdrawal by some practical offer of technological aid. It will be for the European countries to decide the extent to which they will have to restore troop levels, but hopefully they will not be mesmerized by maintaining a strict man-for-man balance. Any reduction in American ground forces on the central front is bound to raise serious questions. Past precedents indicate that, despite the ambivalence of American policy, there are some grounds for believing that any Administration at the point of reducing its force levels might reluctantly agree to discuss the possibility of making information on its nuclear technology available to Britain and France in respect of the Poseidon delivery system and even in helping over the development of a MIRV capability. It is a simple technical fact that without such technology both the British and the French deterrent systems risk becoming obsolete in the 1980s even if ABM limitation is agreed. The key issue which both countries will have to face in the next few years is whether they wish to retain deterrent forces in the 1980s; and if they intend to do so, some important decisions will have to be taken before 1975. It is as well to discuss the issues in the early 1970s, even if the decisions are not immediately necessary.

It is easy to see the whole nuclear argument as irrelevant, and certainly many sensible Europeans have always found discussions over their own nuclear weapon systems somewhat unreal. It is easy to argue that Europe's nuclear potential is so insignificant that it would be better for Europe to opt out of the whole business, yet experience suggests that a nuclear strategy cannot be ignored. In the last analysis even politicians on the left in both France and Britain have always reluctantly accepted the view that there is a need for the possession of nuclear deterrent forces. When confronted with the stark choice of relying solely on the United States deterrent systems, they have always chosen to pay the economic price for some degree of nuclear insurance through a measure of independence. The case for both countries possessing nuclear weapons does not in reality rest on the likelihood of either country ever contemplating firing its own deterrent independently and in defiance of the United States. It is almost impossible to envisage such a situation. But it is possible to foresee a situation where an isolationist American Administration would find it far easier to keep the United States outside any military conflict in Europe if its allies did not possess any nuclear deterrent forces. The mere possession of nuclear deterrent forces does ensure that, in any period of tension involving other nuclear nations, the super-powers cannot simply ignore the existence of those nuclear nations. The possession of nuclear forces, however small in relation to the American forces, does tend to bind the Western Alliance nuclear countries together. Some critics decry this catalytic effect, but in a situation where Britain or France were to contemplate using their tactical nuclear weapons alone, the Americans would be faced with the necessity of dissociating themselves from such an action. This would be an extreme step ensuring the complete breakdown of the Alliance.

It is probable that Britain's possession of nuclear weapons was originally an added stimulus for France to develop her own capability. Now that France has achieved nuclear status, it is hard to conceive of Britain voluntarily abdicating from being a nuclear power. In a very real sense the politics of Europe alone force the two countries to remain nuclear powers. It is probable that both countries will therefore choose to retain viable deterrent forces for the 1980s, provided that these can be achieved within cost limits that will not impose savage cuts in domestic expenditure.

Realism dictates that the only way in which a credible Allied deterrent force can be established is for Britain, France and the United States to combine. A continuation of the present situation throughout the 1970s is unsatisfactory for all countries. The McNamara warning about the dangers of an obsolescent nuclear deterrent force are as real today as they were in 1962. The absence of any form of integrated command and control system covering all three deterrents, particularly in relation to the French deterrent, is as worrying now as when French hostility to NATO first manifested itself.

Inasmuch as the Americans hold the key to ensuring a credible Allied force, it is worth examining on what terms they might be persuaded to share information on their nuclear technology. In the past there have been signs that under certain circumstances President Kennedy was prepared to offer technological support and forgo any demand for an American veto on the firing of a French deterrent system, provided that it was targeted within NATO in a similar manner to the British. This would be the simplest and best agreement to negotiate, for it would give the French the same semblance of independence as Britain has today while ensuring that in reality France would no longer be operating independently.

Alternatively, the United States might complicate the issue by insisting that the decision to fire should be made on a multi-national basis within Europe. It would be essential for the

Americans to insist that the price for their technology, if France stayed outside NATO, should be a control mechanism dependent on a European NATO nation's agreement: in effect, to demand as a minimum British and French agreement by means of a double-key firing mechanism. In the past, West Germany, particularly under a Christian Democrat government, has shown great hostility to the concept of a tri-directorate excluding West Germany – a concern which has been viewed sympathetically by the United States. In view of West Germany's exposed position, this is an understandable objection. To remove it, a third alternative would be some mechanism involving the large European countries – Italy, Britain, France and West Germany – in a European Nuclear Planning Group. It has to be faced that West Germany is now in every sense a full member of the Alliance and has rights as well as responsibilities. Any control mechanism would be quite distinct from the possession of nuclear weapons, which could only be strictly confined to existing nuclear countries and would have to exclude the West Germans totally. Under such a system the firing of an allied deterrent could only occur if Britain and France agreed.

In a situation where the Americans were not in agreement, they would only be able to veto the use of their own national forces, which they had committed to joint targeting with the French and British forces. There would, however, be no European veto on the use of the American deterrent. The substantial gain for the Americans from such alternatives would be the considerable safeguard of the major European nations agreeing a policy for the use of nuclear weapons. This runs counter to the present situation, where two nations have theoretically complete independence, and where in the case of France there is no joint targeting or consultation machinery.

The gain for the Europeans would be the attainment within NATO, or linked to NATO, of a proven deterrent force for the 1980s, without having to carry the burden of the formidable research-and-development costs. The European element within such an allied deterrent would be a small force, if it continued to be based on four French and four British missile-carrying submarines. Yet with Poseidon missiles and MIRVs, it would possess a much enhanced capability and would certainly be sufficient to offer a credible second-strike deterrent force. It would be necessary for Britain to start on a programme of fitting Poseidon missiles, such as the United States is already embarked on. In the case of the French, this could present insuperable technical difficulties and might therefore need to be started while their third and fourth submarines are still building and could be extensively adapted. For the British Polaris fleet it would mean a rather more extensive long refit than is at present planned for the Polaris boats, but this would need to be done only at the time of the currently planned refits, and the total extra cost in 1970 prices would be approximately £340 million spread over six years, or only some 2 per cent of the yearly defence budget. It would be necessary for the British and French existing forces to rely on their current missile technology for an interim period of six to seven years. But the two forces would need to be targeted jointly immediately, so that the delay in refitting and building the French submarines and in refitting Britain's existing Polaris submarines would be covered. This would mean that throughout the 1970s there would never be less than one British or French submarine on patrol, and so the European contribution to the allied nuclear deterrent force would be viable throughout this period of preparing for a second-generation capability for the 1980s – a fact probably of more importance to the French than to the British.

It will be argued – mistakenly – by some that the third alternative would ensure a German 'finger on the nuclear trigger'; in fact it would only be a 'finger on the safety catch'. It may be that the West Germans would not put as great a stress as they have in the past on their wish to participate in the decision-making process, for this would almost certainly damage their promising Ostpolitik initiatives. But if West Germany did wish to participate, and a Christian Democrat government probably would, this proposal – even if strongly resisted – would be the least objectionable to the Warsaw Pact countries. The West should certainly not underestimate Soviet fears, and any agreement would have to be so tightly drawn that it would not infringe the Non-Proliferation Treaty. In essence, the effect of this special arrangement would be to ensure a mechanism whereby the use of Europe's existing nuclear forces independent of America would have the added safeguard of guidelines agreed by non-nuclear powers. In the case of all three alternatives, use of the deterrent would depend on the decision of a NATO member-nation.

The NATO Nuclear Planning Group as a wider forum would remain to ensure that the United States was able to influence, through inter-locking membership, the development of the guidelines for the use of all Allied nuclear weapons.

These proposals are of necessity controversial. Many people will strongly condemn the whole concept, but it is presented in the strong belief that the dangers and risks of continuing with the present situation are seriously underestimated. The cause of peace is not promoted by wishful thinking or by the avoidance of unpleasant facts. We have lived for too long in Europe with policies which do not stand up to serious examination. The French may well find many of these proposals initially unacceptable, for they will force them to take a rather more realistic view of their existing nuclear forces than hitherto. There is at present still a wide gulf between the strategic concepts accepted by NATO and those accepted by France. However, if European politicians will seriously examine the facts, it will be hard for them to escape the conclusion that under present policies the British and French nuclear deterrent systems will not remain viable systems. Given limited financial resources, the sensible choice is to follow the American practice of refitting existing submarines rather than rebuilding anew. The time for making such a choice, if it is to have effect during the 1980s, is the middle 1970s. Timing will be of the essence if any second-generation weapon system is to be installed at reasonable cost without in the process critically weakening the effectiveness of the current deterrent by having too many missile-carrying submarines out of commission at any one time.

It would be absurd to pretend that the French government is as yet seriously willing to consider integration of its nuclear deterrent with Britain as part of a European contribution to an allied deterrent. While strong Gaullists such as Michel Debré control the French Ministry of Defence, the demand for complete autonomy of action may well preclude any such arrangement. Debré's belief that defence policy 'is only valid as a function of a nation's patriotism'[9] leads him to the conclusion that 'the very nature of the nuclear weapon restricts it to the national arsenal for a long time to come.' He defines his concept of patriotism as being rooted in a collective consciousness. 'Without this European patriotism there can be no political unity. And without political unity, no European nuclear strategy is possible.'

It is hard to quarrel with Debré's analysis, but defence interests have strong common elements – and arising from such mutual interests it may be possible to forge a degree of political integration that has not yet been achieved through the European Economic Community. The full development of European patriotism will take decades, but its achievement will come only when individual nations are prepared to face up to the realities of their own defence policies. Present French defence policy is an expensive illusion, but there are signs that President Pompidou wishes to re-establish links with the United States. Now that France's nuclear status is assured, any agreement will be easier to negotiate. The overriding need is to develop a greater European identity within NATO.

Such an identity will not be developed merely by collaborating over mundane military hardware, but it might be attained through collaboration on the central issue of nuclear deterrence. A European identity depends as a minimum on a common strategy and operational control for the French and British deterrent forces. Failure to achieve such collaboration within Europe will seriously undermine the effectiveness of a defence alliance that is at present far too heavily dependent on the

United States. The political pressure on successive American Administrations for unilateral troop withdrawals from Europe has been steadily increasing. The 1971 Senate Resolution from Senator Mansfield for a 50 per cent unilateral reduction showed that the strength of feeling even among the more responsible Senators had been only temporarily abated by discussions on mutual and balanced force reductions. The American nuclear guarantee covering Europe likewise cannot for all time be assured, and for some it will always remain the subject of some doubt. It is admittedly far easier to see a British and French government responding to a threat to Bonn or Brussels, simply because any such development is a far greater threat to Paris and London than to New York or Chicago. But any theoretical nuclear scenario has an air of unreality and it is difficult to see any government acting unless its own territory is threatened. To this extent, the more limited warning coming from the use of tactical nuclear weapons is a more credible response, and on this there must be a common European view.

These are desperately difficult issues. Too many people advocate the so-called independent European deterrent in horrifyingly naive terms. Its evolution has tended to be linked too often in the past with British entry into the EEC. It is absurd, however, to envisage a small number of British and French missile-firing submarines as being in any real sense an independent third force. An effective third force could not, as has been stressed previously, be sensibly developed even with American support and collaboration, save at a crippling cost. It can be argued that the hostility of the Warsaw Pact to the creation of a third force would also apply to the development of a more effective allied nuclear deterrent and would threaten the emergence of sensible policies for détente in Western Europe. This might be the result and it would undoubtedly at the present time be far preferable for the West Germans to limit their involvement in nuclear matters, as now, to participation in the NPG within NATO, and to forgo any direct voice in a multinational control mechanism. This would be the likely decision of Willy Brandt and the German Social Democratic Party.

The central issue, however, remains. For better or for worse, Europe is already a nuclear Europe, and there are inherently more dangers within the existing divisive framework than in the development of an integrated command and control system of the existing nuclear powers. It is easy to dismiss too readily the feasibility of developing multinational control systems. Admittedly, the precedents of the MLF and the ANF do not provide much grounds for optimism, but these proposals were, particularly with the MLF's emphasis on mixed-manning, not based on the real world. The United States has already 'two-key' control systems for nuclear deterrent forces based in other countries, and a 'three-key system' with a built-in two-key European option is quite compatible with the state of existing communication technology.

The difficulties certainly exist, but to ignore them now is a certain recipe for an unsatisfactory and even dangerous situation in the 1980s. By the end of the 1970s the British deterrent system will be either obsolete or obsolescent, and the French system obsolescent. If past behaviour is any guideline, the politicians in Britain and France will then face a choice to develop an allied nuclear force with a European identity, to develop an independent European deterrent, or to opt out of nuclear deterrence completely and to rely on the United States. The alternative of opting for independence is either to develop an independent Anglo-French deterrent or for the French and the West Germans to pursue, without the United States or Britain, the nightmare logic of the 1958 Strauss–Chaban-Delmas agreement. To choose the policies of independence will be to opt for European nuclear forces conceived as a third force; it will be to opt deliberately for total nuclear independence of the United States. Such a choice would be no less than an act of political folly. It is probably unwise in present circumstances to rely solely on the United States, without maintaining any nuclear deterrent capability within Europe. Politicians have, however, a social responsibility not to duplicate defence expenditure, which needs to be kept to the necessary minimum at all times. Europe cannot develop the super-power nuclear deterrent system which the United States already has without a massive diversion of resources away from important domestic social expenditure and at the expense of its conventional defence forces. These are real choices, and ones which many politicians, particularly those on the left in Europe, have sought to avoid discussing. In government, politicians, on the left and the right have pursued policies of nuclear independence, whereas in opposition the tendency has been to fall back on genuine but rather wistful hopes for future détente and mutual force reductions.

It is time Europe faced reality. In 1962 Britain faced a clear-cut choice, whether to develop a nuclear deterrent to replace the V bombers. At the time, many believed that Britain should have opted out completely from building the Polaris nuclear deterrent force for the 1970s. In the early 1970s, circumstances are very different. Britain should use the existence of her nuclear deterrent forces in a genuine political initiative aimed to coincide with American troop reductions so as to bring about trilateral discussions and an integrated allied nuclear force within NATO in the 1980s. If, by 1975, sensible collaboration with the French and the Americans has not been achieved, then Britain should not attempt to develop second-generation deterrent forces for the 1980s, and it would be better to stop spending money on perpetuating what would inevitably be an inadequate deterrent system. The challenge is to persuade not only an American Administration but also the all-important Joint Congressional Committee on Atomic Energy that for France to continue developing a nuclear deterrent system, without access to American technology and completely outside the Alliance, is wasteful and seriously weakens the effectiveness of the overall European defence effort.

France as a non-signatory to the Non-Proliferation Treaty is in an exposed position, and Congress would hopefully demand her signature to the Non-Proliferation Treaty and the Partial Test Ban Treaty as essential steps in any agreement to share nuclear information. Though the Non-Proliferation Treaty is quite specific in not prohibiting the transfer of information on nuclear weapons to existing nuclear states, this interpretation could run into difficulties with Congress. The Senate Committee on Foreign Relations did see the treaty as representing

> a potential cost to the United States in its alliance relationships. Heretofore, it was a national decision whether the United States would use its nuclear assets in helping one or more countries to develop nuclear weapons. Admittedly, this was an option the United States never used except in the case of Great Britain; but it was an option subject only to a decision of the executive branch and the Congress. Now we have all but given up that option in the sense that this treaty imposes a formidable barrier to the United States assisting other countries in the development of nuclear-weapons programs.[10]

It will be necessary to persuade the United States that, as her contribution to Western European conventional defence is reduced, so she has a responsibility to reinterpret the McMahon Act and make available to Britain and France, not only nuclear delivery vehicles or delivery systems, but also the information on nuclear weapons technology that will help bridge any gap in the credibility of their existing nuclear guarantee. Many strong supporters of the concept of European integration mistakenly believe that there is a logical necessity to develop not only a European defence community but a specifically independent European nuclear deterrent. It is essential to convince them that there is no merit in divorcing Europe from the existing Alliance with a friendly super-power merely in order to pursue the fanciful charisma of an expensive and probably unobtainable total nuclear independence.

Chapter 14. The Control of Defence Decisions

Effective control of the nation's defence force must be one of the highest priorities of any democrat. Yet it is clear from this brief study of actual defence decisions taken in the 1960s that the existing pattern of controls is insufficient and in many areas ineffective. To highlight the problem is not enough. Solutions are desperately needed; yet, as is so often the case, the most important changes are the least dramatic. Changes must start by attempting to alter basic attitudes.

The first priority must be to try to end existing inter-service rivalries. This can be achieved only by pursuing the elusive goal of greater unification of the three services. It is commonplace to pay lip service to this goal, but its achievement necessitates a greater determination than politicians in most countries have so far displayed.

Any radical reform must start with the educational process to which the serviceman is exposed, for this holds the key to unification. The attainment of a broad-based educational background from the outset will allow the individual serviceman, irrespective of rank, to see his own service within the wider framework of national objectives and of a national defence effort and strategy. The first essential is to widen a young officer's education from an early age. A purely service training is far too narrow an educational background. Officers should be recruited wherever possible from graduates who have been educated outside service institutions. Where manpower problems impose the need to recruit from non-graduates, every effort should be made to provide a service education which does not relate solely to a service career and involves mixing with other non-service higher educational students. A broadening of the educational curriculum should be the first stage. The second stage is consistently to supplement any specifically one-service educational programme with tri-service educational courses and lectures. At present, the tri-service educational process is too frequently introduced only at the mid-career point. It is then necessary to devote a substantial effort to breaking down the all-pervading single-service identification which has already been inculcated.

It is some measure of the importance of military education that those politicians and senior servicemen who have been interested in reforming defence decision-making have almost without exception laid great stress on the need to start with educational reform.

Yet the objective of educational reform is not easily achieved, for it strikes at the very root of single-service attitudes. As with most attempts at unification, educational reform has been bitterly resisted by senior serving officers, and progress has been painfully slow. In Britain, for example, whether one looks at in-service degree courses, tri-service staff colleges or even the establishment of tri-service senior officer courses, the single-service educational system still predominates. In the United States there has been a similar resistance and slow progress.

It is worth stressing once again that the aims of unification are not necessarily promoted by the concept of a total abolition of single-service identities. Exactly similar uniforms, ranks and status are not necessary if the more pragmatic and evolutionary approach can result in the total defence effort being seen as a whole, not as fragmented single-service contributions.

It is, however, almost certainly necessary for the more senior defence posts to have an integrated career structure, and to achieve this it may well be necessary to impose some changes in titles. In order to achieve an integrated command structure at the planning and strategic levels it is vital to ensure that decisions are being made irrespective of single-service identities. The present manner of allocating senior jobs as tri-service appointments and then filling the vacancies on rotation between the three services is wholly unsatisfactory. It is necessary for a senior serving officer to see his higher career prospects in terms of a central defence career structure, not merely relating his advancement to his own service with occasional central defence appointments interspersed somewhat haphazardly. In order to sustain an integrated career structure for senior officers, the extent of functionalization inside the defence field will have to be extended and the concept of single-service self-sufficiency abandoned.

The interdependence of the three services, which has already been emerging in fields such as food, transport and accommodation, could become far more marked than hitherto and the gains would come not necessarily always in financial terms or even with greater efficiency, though these should be achieved, but in the development of an overall defence philosophy that would cut right across the present divisive tripartite structure.

The central organization of defence would inevitably become even more functional in form. The major divisional breakdowns would run across service identities and form management units which as far as possible reflected central defence interests. These and similar changes have already been introduced in many countries over the last two decades. But, all too often, the single-service stranglehold remains behind the new titles and format. In order to achieve effective central control this single-service stranglehold must be broken, and bold decisions are needed if the evolutionary approach is to have any chance of forestalling the impatient advocates of sweeping revolutionary changes involving complete integration, as has happened in Canada.

Once the serviceman sees his role as contributing towards an integrated defence policy with an allegiance to the wider view of defence, then the need for the present level of civilian participation within the defence departments of most countries could be reviewed. Provided the serviceman accepts a position within the decision structure which is more comparable to the position of civilians working in other departments, then the role of the civilian defence department officials acting as a bridge between the politician and the military will lose much of its importance and this will result in an easier and more efficient working relationship. At present, while many servicemen still have wholly unrealistic attitudes towards the financial and political constraints within which a defence policy can operate, civilian intermediaries make a vital contribution, particularly at times when the political leadership of the defence policy may be weak.

The overall aim must be to establish a system in which the service adviser is as capable of dealing with the policies of détente, disarmament and financial control as advising on military threats and a particular weapons system. With the high level of intelligence of most senior servicemen, such an objective is easily attainable. What bedevils its attainment is attitudes conditioned and fostered by a military milieu which is still hopelessly out of touch with present defence needs and objectives. No politician who has attempted to reform service discipline or service education can be unaware of the appalling insularity of many basic service attitudes. Organizational changes, new commands, new names can all be imposed, but unless the underlying attitudes of the services are changed any reform is doomed before it starts.

To assert effective control it is essential that the existing pattern of decision-making by committee in the defence field should be drastically curtailed. The plethora of committees in defence ministries is the inevitable result of having to balance the interests of the three services, but it also reflects the underlying imbalance between the politician and the military adviser and the politician and the civilian adviser. The military are unwilling to give up the special relationship whereby wherever possible they see themselves jointly making decisions with the politician in the defence field. The status and presumed power of the military adviser can be largely illusory, but in terms of efficient decision-making it is even then a costly illusion. It breeds delay, disagreement and compromise. A defence decision-making structure should spell out the lines of responsibility with decision points culminating in individuals not in committees. The decision-maker's position should be held by the individual on the basis solely of ability.

These and similar criticisms have been made many times before, particularly in the field of the defence industrial complex and in matters relating to military procurement. The criticism has arisen out of a whole series of disastrous projects in most major countries, which have concentrated public awareness on the deficiencies in the system. It is much harder for the public to see and to realize that just as many disastrous decisions have been made in the areas of military and strategic defence decision-making. The defects in the decision-making process are similar and are inherent in the organization o. most defence ministries. The public, however, hears more about the industrial defence mistakes because the cost is measured in money terms and public vigilance in this area is well developed. It is also not possible to cloak such failures in the all-embracing security cover which envelops most mistakes in the military and strategic areas of defence decision-making. Yet the consequences of errors in this area are potentially of far more importance.

A significant start on abolishing committee decision-making inside defence ministries would be to abolish the Joint Chiefs of Staff Committee in the United States, the Chiefs of Staff Committee in Britain, and their counterparts in other countries. The politicians should be advised by the Chief of Defence and his staff on all military planning and strategic issues. The individual heads of each service should cease to have responsibility for overall national security.

Operational command of combatant forces should be delegated by the Chief of Defence to the relevant area or regional commander. The heads of the individual services should have overall responsibility for the management of their service, but should not be involved in operational control of combatant forces or in central military and strategic planning. They would, however, be responsible for the efficient execution of decisions taken by the Chief of Defence and his staff. It is worth recognizing that this is a major task, rivalling in scope and complexity the responsibility of the head of the largest international corporation. It will be impossible to achieve an integrated career structure for senior serving officers until they see the Chief of Defence holding an executive role in his own right, not merely acting as the compromised voice of a committee of service chiefs.

The service arguments against such changes lay stress on the importance attached to retaining the individuality of the services, the need for specialization and the dangers of vesting too much authority in one man. They tend to ask why, since most of the highest democratic political decision-making bodies are in effect committees, they should have to adopt a different format. In practical terms, the committee nature of most Cabinet-type decisions is probably over-emphasized, but even so the problems they face are very different. It is essentially a question of balancing expenditure priorities on such completely different subjects as defence, health, pensions and schools.

Such choices are difficult to make in any forum and, for all the problems inherent in Cabinet decision-making, are probably best assessed collectively. Yet no government department other than the defence department feels it necessary to make its internal decision-making process so heavily dependent on committee decisions. Priorities within departments are settled by specific individuals on a fairly well-established decision structure.

The emergence over the last decade of such strong defence ministers as Robert McNamara, Denis Healey, Michel Debré and Helmut Schmidt has done a great deal to weaken the committee decision-making structure, but it still predominates over all but the most important issues. These small decisions taken together and compounded can have a formative role that it would be foolish to underestimate.

Reform of defence departments, though of great importance, must be accompanied by substantial changes in the political area of defence decision-making. The greatest single control exerted by politicians is through limitation of the defence budget. It is inevitable that within government the politician who heads the department of defence will have the major role in determining priorities within the budget, and so outside the government it should be the responsibility of elected parliamentary bodies to scrutinize defence expenditures. It is only by insisting on a more rapid movement towards accountable management with well-defined responsibilities that the politician will be able to come to grips with the totality of defence decision-making.

In the United States, the Armed Services Committee in both the Senate and the House cover the activities of the Defense Department. Two other committees, the Joint Atomic Energy Committee and the Joint Committee on Defense Production, have special areas which cover the Department of Defense. In addition, the Senate Foreign Relations Committee and the House Foreign Affairs Committee frequently call for evidence from the Secretary of Defense and his officials. These committees traditionally question individual servicemen and officials on defence policy decisions as much as expenditure decisions, and provide a public debate on American defence policies and priorities which is unequalled anywhere in the world for its open discussion of military affairs.

In Britain, where the executive and the legislature are not separated, the method of public scrutiny is by comparison sadly underdeveloped. The Public Accounts Committee has had a very important retrospective analytical role and has revealed many of the most disgraceful military procurement mistakes, but this committee has little impact on policy matters. Policy discussion is almost entirely confined to the formal defence debates, usually taking up six days of parliamentary time a year. These set-speech debates only serve to highlight the basic ignorance of most MPs about defence matters. In 1970 the new Expenditure Committee was established to replace the old Estimates Committee, and a Defence and External Affairs Sub-Committee was formed. The remit of the new Defence Expenditure Committee covers forward expenditure and it must, therefore, involve itself in defence policy. It must be hoped that this committee will start the process of an informed public debate within Britain about future defence policy, which has so far been totally missing. A lot will depend upon the readiness of the Ministry of Defence to come out from behind its all too convenient security cover and put forward facts and arguments of equivalent security classification to the evidence given before Congress by the Department of Defense.

Political scrutiny of defence policy must by the very nature of defence have its greatest impact within government. The American President's National Security Council and the Defence and Overseas Policy Committee of the Cabinet in Britain are the two main forums for the highest defence decision-making in the two countries, and it is here that most major decisions are made. It is here also that the judgment of individuals and their abilities is the crucial determinant. In a country where open public debate of defence policy is the rule rather than the exception, there is a reasonable chance that these individuals will not have reached their position without some knowledge and understanding of defence policies. Education of the politician, as with the serviceman, holds the key to sensible decision-making. In the United States, for all the mistakes in policy, there is an informed debate, but Congress will have to win back some of its powers if the executive is to become more responsive to public feelings.

The fact that senior members of the American Administration misled Congressional committees during vitally important Vietnam hearings ensures that the relationships between Congress, the State Department and the Defense Department will never be the same again. A far greater stringency and scepticism will henceforward be the dominant attitude within Congress. To some extent, the facts revealed in the Pentagon Papers have shown a major weakness in the American system. The President is insulated to a far greater extent than a British Prime Minister from dissenting pressures within his country. In the United States all the President's senior appointments are his own, the result not of party position, pressure or balance, but of a freely taken presidential choice. The men appointed are in consequence the President's men. They do not have a position of their own in any way comparable to that of the individual British Cabinet minister, who often has an independent power-base which, though not rivalling that of the Prime

Minister, ensures a greater freedom for dissent than is held by his American counterparts. With access to the same information sources as the Prime Minister when their views represent that of a significant section of the party, British ministers can dissent and not always lose their posts. It is arguable that a British Prime Minister could never have maintained a position similar to that of successive American Presidents on Vietnam. Instead, parliamentary pressures would have ensured greater exposure of the facts and a radically different posture in a far shorter time-scale than occurred in America.

It is, for example, extraordinary how little influence McNamara was able to exert from 1966 when he first began to be seriously disenchanted by the course of the Vietnam war. To some extent his reticence on the subject even when he left the Administration reflected his own personality, but it is also a commentary on the peculiar position in the United States where such a major figure can have no independent power-base from the President. The importance of individuals in the decision-making process, for all the new techniques of quantitative analysis, cannot be overestimated. McNamara, the Secretary of State who was the epitome of the quantitative approach, despite his praiseworthy stance during the Cuban missile crisis, ended his period in office judged a failure because of his Vietnam policies. Ironically, it was first Clark Clifford and then Melvin Laird, previously the supposedly hawkish Chairman of the Senate Armed Services Committee, who grasped the essential fact that a nation cannot be forced to wage war against its will.

The essential task of the politician is to know when to cut his losses, to know when for all the short-term problems it is in the long-term good to change direction. It is the gift of choosing the right moment which is so crucial to the successful politician. A sense of timing is frequently of the essence in any analysis of democratic leadership.

If it is a question of firing nuclear weapons or some other major initiative, the President of France, the President of the United States or the Prime Minister of Britain will always be the final arbiter for the Western Alliance. Without their authority, no decision will be implemented. It is far better, therefore, for any multinational integration to take place at the highest level. President Kennedy was fond of quoting the lines of Domingo Ortega:

> Bull fight critics ranked in rows
> Crowd the enormous plaza full
> But only one man is there who knows
> And he's the man who fights the Bull.[1]

In the last analysis it is not the patriotism of nations, or groups of nations that is the conclusive factor; it is an individual, perhaps joining together at the time of decision with leaders in other nations, who decides the fate of the world.

Under Stalin and Khrushchev, the Soviet Union has had authority vested in one man as well as periods of collective leadership with authority vested in a few individuals in the Politburo. There is some evidence that after Khrushchev the influence of the military increased. More is known about the actual workings of Soviet defence decision-making than many people seem to realize. Professor John Erickson, one of the most authoritative writers on Soviet military affairs, wrote as recently as 1971 in a commentary on the character of the Soviet leadership:

> Should the military, nevertheless, become excessively nervous about Soviet 'security' or the Party leaders entrenched in the Politburo too seignorial in implementing their newly-won status – and here in practical terms Yugoslavia is probably of much greater immediate moment than the Indian Ocean – or yet again should either party mislead or misconstrue each other in what is essentially a devious game, then the outcome could be calamitous.[2]

No one who studies the political-military complex, whether in the East or the West, can be unaware of the dangers and frailties of defence decision-making. The sustained focus of public attention could do much to eradicate some of the deficiencies, and if this book serves to stimulate any such attention then it will have achieved its primary objective.

For those on the outside it may appear a hopeless task to influence this highly complex decision-making structure. Yet it is vital to realize that the structure is sensitive throughout its course to a myriad of small decisions at every level, whether made by servicemen, civilians or politicians. To create a climate in which defence decision-making operates sensibly, sensitively and objectively is in the interests of every citizen. It will not be achieved by avoiding the difficult moral and humanitarian issues that any defence policy inevitably raises. It can be achieved only by a far deeper public involvement in the discussion of military affairs than exists today.

References

CHAPTER 1: THE SMELL OF BURNING

1. Justice Hugo Black, *New York Times*, July 1st, 1971.

General Reference

Stockholm International Peace Research Institute Yearbook of World Armaments and Disarmament, *1969–70* (Stockholm, 1970).

CHAPTER 2: THE MACHINERY OF DEFENCE DECISIONS

1. Blue Ribbon Defense Panel, *Report to the President and Secretary of Defense on the Department of Defense* (US Government Printing Office), p. 1.
2. *Ibid.*, p. 33.
3. David Owen, *The Times*, July 27th, 1970.
4. McGeorge Bundy, 'To Cap the Volcano', *Foreign Affairs*, October 1969.

General References

William P. Snyder, *The Politics of British Defence Policy, 1945–1962* (London, 1964).
Franklyn Arthur Johnson, *Defence by Committee* (Oxford, 1960).
C. W. Borklund, *The Department of Defense* (New York, 1967).
David Holloway, 'Technology Management and the Soviet Military Establishment', Adelphi Paper 76 (International Institute for Strategic Studies, 1971).

CHAPTER 3: THE CUBAN MISSILE CRISIS

1. *Aviation Week and Space Technology*, October 1st, 1962.
2. Select Committee on Export Control, House of Representatives, 87th Congress, 2nd Session, p. 907.
3. Robert Kennedy, *Thirteen Days* (New York, 1969).
4. Elie Abel, *The Missile Crisis* (New York, 1966).

5. USIF, December 17th, 1962 (President Kennedy, television interview).
6. USIF, October 23rd, 1962 (Proclamation).
7. Statement of the Soviet government by Tass, October 23rd, 1962; *The Times*, October 24th, 1962.
8. *Daily Telegraph*, October 24th, 1962.
9. USIF, October 26th, 1962.
10. *The Times*, October 27th, 1962.
11. Report of President Kennedy's speech of November 2nd, 1962, *The Times*, November 3rd, 1962.
12. Tass, October 23rd, 1962.
13. *Soviet News*, September 12th, 1962.
14. USIF, December 18th, 1962.
15. Kennedy, *op. cit.*, p. 108.
16. Abel, *op. cit.*
17. USIF, October 22nd, 1962 (President Kennedy, broadcast to the nation).

CHAPTER 4: THE GULF OF TONKIN INCIDENT

1. Joint Resolution (HJ Res. 1145), *Congressional Record*, Vol. 110, Part 14, p. 18471.
2. Senator Fulbright in *ibid.*, p. 18399.
3. *The Pentagon Papers* (New York, 1971), p. 245.
4. *Ibid.*, p. 283.
5. *Congressional Record, loc. cit.*
6. Senator Morse in *Congressional Record, loc. cit.*, pp. 18134–5.
7. Senator Fulbright in *ibid.*, p. 18407.
8. Senator Morse in *ibid.*, p. 18424.
9. John Gerassi, *North Vietnam: A Documentary* (London, 1968).
10. Defense Secretary McNamara at closed session of Senate Foreign Relations Committee, *New York Times*, February 21st, 1968, p. 12.
11. *Pentagon Papers*, p. 265.
12. *Congressional Record, loc. cit.*, p. 18403.
13. *Baltimore Sun*, January 25th, 1968, p. 4.
14. *Congressional Record*, Vol. 114, Part 3, p. 3817.

15. *Pentagon Papers*, pp. 261–4.
16. USIF, August 4th, 1964 (President Johnson, television statement).
17. Jean Lacouture, *Vietnam: Between Two Truces* (New York, 1966), p. 259.
18. Gerassi, *op. cit.*, Appendix B, p. 158.
19. John Finney, 'Tonkin Gulf Attack: A Case Study in How Not to Go to War', *New Republic*, January 27th, 1968.

CHAPTER 5: THE 1967 ARAB-ISRAELI WAR

1. Randolph S. Churchill and Winston S. Churchill, *The Six-Day War* (London, 1967), pp. 30–31.
2. *Ibid.*, p. 32.
3. *Guardian*, May 25th, 1967 (Nasser's speech in Sinai, May 22nd).
4. Tass, May 23rd, 1967.
5. *Financial Times*, May 24th, 1967.
6. *Al Ahram*, May 24th, 1967.
7. *Observer*, June 4th, 1967.
8. *Guardian*, May 31st, 1967.
9. Churchill and Churchill, *op. cit.*, pp. 48, 49.
10. *Facts on File*, Vol. xxvii, No. 1389.
11. *Newsweek*, May 6th, 1968.
12. *Washington Post*, June 30th, 1967.

CHAPTER 6: THE 'PUEBLO' INCIDENT

1. *Report of the Special Subcommittee on the USS 'Pueblo' of the Committee on Armed Services* (US Government, 1969), p. 1619.
2. *Ibid.*, p. 1639.
3. *Ibid.*, p. 1656.
4. *Ibid.*, p. 1673.

POLITICAL ISSUES

1. Kennedy, *op. cit.*, p. 51.
2. *Pentagon Papers*, p. 432.

CHAPTER 7: EAST OF SUEZ

1. Defence Review, February 1966 (Cmd 2901), Ch. II, para 24.
2. *Ibid.*, February 1967 (Cmd 3203), Ch. I, para 26.
3. Supplementary Defence White Paper, July 1967, Ch. III, para 7.
4. *Ibid.*, Ch. III, para 9.

CHAPTER 8: THE AFRICAN CONTINENT

1. *Hansard*, January 27th, 1966, Vol. 723, Col. 396.

CHAPTER 9: MARITIME STRATEGY

1. *The Times*, January 29th, 1971, p. 15.
2. *Stockholm International Peace Research Institute Yearbook*, 1969–70, p. 307.
3. USIF, August 4th, 1964 (Secretary McNamara's statement to Senate Committee).
4. Finney, *op. cit.*

General Reference

L. W. Martin, *The Sea in Modern Strategy* (London, 1967).

CHAPTER 10: INTERNATIONAL MARITIME LAW

1. *Survey of International Affairs, 1936* (Oxford, 1937), p. 596.
2. Convention regarding the Regime of the Straits (with protocol), Montreux, July 20th, 1936 (HMSO, 1937).
3. *Financial Times*, May 27th, 1967. From Article 16(4) of 1958 Geneva Convention on the High Seas in the Contiguous Zone.
4. *Guardian*, June 1st, 1967.
5. *The Times*, May 31st, 1967.
6. *Guardian*, May 24th, 1967.
7. USIF, May 23rd, 1967 (President Johnson).
8. *The Times*, May 25th, 1967 (Quoting Sir Alan Noble, British delegate of the Conservative Administration to the General Assembly, March 1st, 1957).

9. Senator Humphrey in debate on the Gulf of Tonkin Resolution; *Congressional Record*, Vol. 110, Part 14, p. 18420.

General Reference

Rosslyn Higgins, 'International Law, Rhodesia and the UN', *The World Today*, Vol. XXIII, 1967.

CHAPTER II: THE EVOLUTION OF NATO'S NUCLEAR STRATEGY

1. Henry Kissinger, *Nuclear Weapons and Foreign Policy* (New York 1957), p. 244.
2. Evidence Senate Foreign Relations Committee, April 21st 1959, p. 10.
3. Kissinger, 'The Search for Stability', *Foreign Affairs*, July 1959.
4. Pierre Gallois, *Orbis*, Vol. VII, No. 2 (summer 1963).
5. Maxwell D. Taylor, *The Uncertain Trumpet* (New York, 1959), pp. 145–6.
6. Kennet Love, *Suez, The Twice-Fought War* (New York, 1969), pp. 610–16.
7. Abel, *op. cit.*, p. 96.
8. Kissinger, *Problems of National Strategy* (New York, 1965), p. 12.
9. Robert McNamara, Posture Statement to Senate Armed Service Committee, February 2nd, 1968.
10. Alain Enthoven and K. Wayne Smith, 'What Forces for NATO? And From Whom?', *Foreign Affairs*, October 1969.
11. Denis Healey, 'Thinking About the Unthinkable', *Listener*, April 23rd, 1970.
12. Helmut Schmidt, *Defence or Retaliation?* (Edinburgh, 1962), p. 169.
13. *The Czechoslovak Crisis, 1968*, ed. Robert Rhodes James (London, 1969).
14. John Erickson, *Soviet Military Power*, Royal United Services Institute, 1971.
15. Bruce Reed and Geoffrey Williams, *Denis Healey and the Policies of Power* (London, 1971), p. 169.

16. Defence Estimates, February 1972 (Cmd 4891), Ch. I, para 4.

CHAPTER 12: NATIONAL DETERRENTS

1. Bertrand Goldschmidt, *The Atomic Adventure, Its Political and Technical Aspects* (Oxford, 1964), pp. 226–67.
2. John Newhouse, *De Gaulle and the Anglo-Saxons* (London, 1970), p. 70.
3. USIF, June 16th, 1962 (Robert McNamara, Ann Arbor).
4. USIF, December 18th, 1962 (President Kennedy, television).
5. USIF, December 21st, 1962 (Nassau communiqué).
6. USIF, January 11th, 1962 (President Kennedy, interview).
7. *The Economist*, June 11th, 1966.
8. Report of speech, École Militaire, November 3rd, 1959: *The Times*, November 6th, 1959.
9. Kissinger, *The Dimensions of Diplomacy* (New York, 1964; quoted from 1967 edn), p. 32.

CHAPTER 13: EUROPEAN DEFENCE

1. F. Roy Willis, *France, Germany and the New Europe, 1945–1967* (Oxford, 1968), p. 134.
2. France, Conseils de la République, Débats Parlementaires, October 27th, 1953, pp. 1640–47.
3. Edward Heath, *Old World, New Horizons: Britain, the Common Market and the Atlantic Alliance* (Oxford, 1970), p. 73.
4. Treaty on the Non-Proliferation of Nuclear Weapons (HMSO, Cmd 3683, June 1968).
5. *The Military Balance, 1971–1972* (International Institute for Strategic Studies, 1971).
6. Ian Smart, 'Future Conditional: The Prospect for Anglo-French Nuclear Co-operation', Adelphi Paper 78 (International Institute for Strategic Studies, 1971).
7. *Ibid.*
8. *Ibid.*

9. Michel Debré, 'France's Global Strategy', *Foreign Affairs*, April 1971.
10. Congress Executive Report, 91st Congress, 1st Session, Treaty on the Non-Proliferation of Nuclear Weapons, March 6th, 1969, p. 16.

CHAPTER 14: THE CONTROL OF DEFENCE DECISIONS

1. Domingo Ortega, translation by Robert Graves, *Encounter*, December 1951.
2. Erickson, *op. cit.*

Index

Abel, Elie, 38, 48
Acheson, Dean, 154, 193
Aden, 24
Africa, 109–24
Ailleret, General, 185
aircraft: European technological co-operation, 213–14; F-111, 103–4; Jaguar, 214; multi-role combat (MRCA), 199–213; variable geometry (AFVG), 213
aircraft carriers, 103, 106
Albania, 140
Anatolia, 138
Anderson, Admiral, 19, 48
Anglo-American nuclear collaboration, 17, 169; see also Polaris agreement
Anglo-French nuclear collaboration, 19, 148, 169, 172, 182, 186–7, 196–7, 209
Anglo Malaysian Defence Agreement, 101, 104–5
Anguilla, 20
Antarctic demilitarization, 11
anti-ballistic missile (ABM) system, 30, 182, 202–7, 210; see also Safeguard system
Arab-Israeli conflict, 16, 24, 64–75, 92–93, 140–41
arms race, 9, 13
'Athens guidelines', 160
Atlantic Nuclear Force (ANF), 180, 211, 214, 222
Atomic Weapon Research Establishment, 203

Bahrein, 106
Balkan Pact, 138
Ball, George, 37, 175
Bay of Pigs invasion, 18, 20, 35, 49
Beira patrol, 114–24
Berlin, 44, 48–9, 136, 193
biological weapons, 12
Black, Justice Hugo, 18

Black Sea Straits, 136–9
Blue Ribbon Defense Panel, 25, 27–8
British nuclear force, 19, 168–82, 207, 216, 218, 222–3; see also Polaris submarine force
Brown, George, 67–8
Buchalet, General, 185
Bucher, Lloyd M., 77–8
Bulganin, N.A., 154
Bundy, McGeorge, 30

Cabinet: decisions, 230; Defence and Overseas Policy Committee, 232; maritime intervention, 70
Canada: European force levels, 156; integration of services, 28, 227
Castro, Fidel, 35, 42–3
Central Intelligence Agency (CIA), 55, 91
Chaban-Delmas, Jacques, 171, 222
Chafee, John, 77
chemical weapons, 12
Chief of Defence, 229–30
Chiefs of Staff Committee, 229
China, 147, 199
Churchill, Winston, 193
committee decisions, 228–9
communications, military: see military communications
computer simulation, 29–30
Congo, 109
conscription, 90
Convention of Law at Sea (1958), 57, 84, 140
conventional forces, 151, 156, 208
Corfu Channel case (1949) 140, 143
Cuba: American embargoes, 35, 37; Bay of Pigs invasion, 18, 20, 35, 49; missile crisis, 15, 20, 35–51, 92, 122, 154
Czechoslovakia, 12, 17, 49, 92, 158, 164, 191

'D' notice procedure, 18
Debré, Michel, 185–7, 195, 219
Defence White Papers: 1966, 98; 1967, 101
Department of Defense (US), 78
Department of the Navy (US), 78
devaluation of the pound, 101–2
disarmament, 10–13, 189
disengagement of forces, 148–9
Dobrynin Anatoly, 50
Dominica, 20
Dulles, John Foster, 141, 151, 170, 172

East African mutinies, 109–11
East–West relations, 12, 148–9
East of Suez: British military presence, 94, 108
Eban, Abba, 68–9, 71
Eisenhower, Dwight D., 153–4, 169, 173
electronic information, 133–4
Enthoven, Alain, 157–8
Erhard, Ludwig, 180
Eshkol, Levi, 67
Euro Group, 199
Europe: American force reductions, 148, 158, 191, 214, 221; British offer to Europeanize her defence, 195; defence of, 193–224; disengagement of forces, 148–9; force levels, 151; force level reductions, 157–8; military expenditure, 212–13; super-power status, 149–50; third force concept, 212, 221
European Coal and Steel Community, 193
European Defence Community, 193–5
European Defence Improvement Programme, 199
European Economic Community, 169; British entry, 147, 189, 192, 195–6
European Nuclear Planning Group, 217
European Security Conference, 148–9, 165
European unity, 19, 192
expenditure, military, 9, 165, 190, 208, 212–13

F-111 aircraft, 103–4
Far East: East of Suez policy, 94, 108
Finney, John, 62, 133
force levels: see mutual and balanced force reductions fractional orbital bombardment systems (FOBS), 11

France: conventional orces, 208; joint targeting of missiles, 17, 173, 189, 217; military expenditure, 190, 208; NATO policy, 150, 156, 164, 172, 183–4, 190, 196, 198, 214, 219–20; nuclear deterrent, 16–17, 19, 166, 170–172, 182–91, 208–9, 222–3; Polaris missiles, 177–8; submarine force, 19, 188–9, 208
Franco-American collaboration, 172–3, 185–7, 216
Franco-German collaboration, 170–71, 222
Franco-German Pact (1963), 180
Fulbright, Senator: Pentagon Papers, 17; Gulf of Tonkin incident, 53–4, 56, 60, 62; Pueblo incident, 81

Gaillard, F., 183
Gallois, General Pierre, 153
Gaulle, General Charles de: Cuban missile crisis, 154–5; European Defence Community, 195; Gulf of Tonkin incident, 55; nuclear policy, 171–3, 178, 182–91
Geneva Conference, 55
Germany, West: nuclear weapons, 148, 217–19; Ostpolitik, 162–3; rearmament, 193, 195
Gilpatric, Rosewell, 37
Goldschmidt, Bertrand, 169
Greece, 117
Gromyko, Andrei, 50
Gulf of Aqaba, 64–70, 139–40
Gulf of Tonkin incident, 15, 52–63, 133, 142; text of Senate resolution, 52–3

Hammarskjöld, Dag, 66
Harlech, Lord, 39
Headquarters Organization Committee, 27
Healey, Denis, 103, 156, 159, 164
Heath, Edward, 195–6
Herter, Christian, 153, 179
Hong Kong, 100–101
Hoover Commission Task Force, 24
Humphrey, Hubert, 142
Hungary, 12, 49
Hussein, King, 71

Indian Ocean: American naval presence, 135; British naval presence,; 111
Russian naval presence, 111–13

Indonesian confrontation, 94–9, 106–7
Indo-Pakistan war, 19, 135
intelligence ships: *Liberty*, attack on, 72–5; *Pueblo* incident, 76–85
inter-continental ballistic missiles (ICBMs) 130–31, 134–5, 202
inter-service rivalry, 24–5, 225–6
intermediate-range ballistic missiles (IRBMs), 152, 202
International Court, 140
interventionist military policies ;70 ;97
Italy, 138, 217

Jaguar aircraft, 214
Japan, 147
Jenkins, Roy, 102–3
Johnson, Lyndon B.: Arab-Israeli conflict, 67, 69, 72–3, 141; British East of Suez policy, 100; French nuclear policy, 189; Gulf of Tonkin incident, 15, 52–63; Pentagon Papers, 91; *Pueblo* incident, 82–4
Joint Chiefs of Staff (US), 23, 26–7, 74, 80, 229
Joint targeting of missiles, 17, 173, 189, 217

Kennedy, John, F., 234; Bay of Pigs invasion, 18; Cuban missiles crisis, 35–51; nuclear collaboration with France, 173, 216; Polaris agreement, 174–9
Kennedy, Robert, 37–8, 47–8, 50–51, 91
Kenya, 110–11
Kenyatta, Jomo, 110
Khanh, General, 55
Khrushchev, Nikita, 26, 164–5, 234; Cuban missile crisis, 15, 40–51
Kissinger, Henry, 152–3, 192
Korea, 193; *Pueblo* incident, 15, 76–85
Kutchuk-Kainardji Treaty, 137
Ky, Marshal, 59

Lausanne, Treaty of, 137–8
Lavaud, General G., 173, 185–6
League of Nations, 137–8
Lebanon, 20
Lee Kuan Yew, 100, 102
Liberty, attack on, 72–5
limited war, 127, 155
Love, Kennet, 154

McMahon Act (1946), 168, 170, 224
Macmillan, Harold, 169, 173–6, 178–9

McNamara, Robert: Cuban missile crisis, 40, 48; deterrence, 201; flexible response strategy, 82, 156, 179; French deterrent, 173; Gulf of Tonkin incident, 57–9, 61, 133; national deterrents, 174, 177; NATO forces, 157; Pentagon Papers, 91; Vietnam, 233
McNaughton, John, T., 91
maritime law, international, 136–43
maritime strategy, 127–35; American quarantine of Cuba, 38–50, 122; Beira patrol, 114–24; sanctions policy, 116–24
Mediterranean, 92, 97
medium-range missiles, 202
Messina Conference (1955), 169
Messmer, Pierre, 173
Middle East, 20, 70
military communications, 75, 79, 82–3
ministries, decision-making processes in, 22–3, 28, 229–30, 232–3
Ministry of Defence, 24, 27–8, 231
Minuteman missiles, 201–2, 205
Mirage IV bomber force, 185, 188–9
Mollet, Guy, 183
Montreux Convention, 136, 138–9
Morse, Senator Wayne, 52, 56–9
Mudros, Armistice of, 137
multi-role combat aircraft (MRCA), 199, 213
multilateral nuclear force (MLF), 160, 178–9, 189, 222
Multiple Independently Targetable Re-entry Vehicle (MIRV), 201, 205, 214, 218; moratorium, 202–4
Multiple Re-entry Vehicle (MRV), 202
mutual and balanced force reductions (MBFR), 157–8

Nassau agreement (1962), 174–8, 181
Nasser, President, 65–71
National Security Act (US), 24
National Security Agency (US), 79, 81
National Security Council (US), 38, 232
Newhouse, John, 172
Nigeria, 109
Nixon, President Richard, 100
Non-Proliferation Treaty (1968), 11–12, 162, 191, 196–8, 219, 233–4

North Atlantic Treaty Organization (NATO), 19, 148–50, 194; American troop withdrawals, 148, 158, 191, 214, 221; Arab-Israeli conflict, 70; 'Athens guidelines', 160; Beira patrol, 117; British deterrent, 177; Canadian policy, 156; concept behind, 192; conventional forces, 151, 156; European deterrent, 216–24; European identity, 220; force levels, 157–8; French policy, 150, 156, 164, 172, 183–184, 190, 196, 198, 214, 219–20; integrated command structure, 211–12; joint targeting of missiles, 17, 173, 189, 217; maritime strategy, 128–35; nuclear decision-making, 16, 160–67, 198, 214, 219, 221; nuclear strategy, 151–67, 189, 198–9, 214, 219; organizational changes, 149; third-force concept, 212, 221; tri-directorate, 178, 216–17
Nuclear Defence Affairs Committee (NATO), 160
nuclear free zones, 11
Nuclear Planning Group (NATO), 160–63, 198, 214, 217, 219, 221
Nyerere, Julius, 110

Obote, Milton, 110
Official Secrets Act, 17–18
Organization of American States, 47
Ortega, Domingo, 234
Outer Space Treaty (1967), 11

parity in weapons, 9, 36, 45
parliamentary accountability, 21–2, 231
parliamentary committees, 231
Pentagon Papers, 16–18, 54–7, 60–61, 91, 232
Persian Gulf, 24, 99, 105
Pleven, René, 193
Polaris agreement (1962), 175–7, 181
Polaris missiles, 200
Polaris submarine force, British, 177, 181–2, 218
political decision-making, 10–13, 16, 20–21, 228–9
Pompidou, Georges, 197
Portugal, 117, 119–20, 123
Poseidon missiles, 200–201, 207–8, 218
press censorship, 18
procurement policies, 230–31

Public Accounts Committee, 231
Pueblo incident, 15, 76–85

Quebec Agreement (1943), 168

radar early warning systems, 207
Red Cross, International, 42
Rhodesia, 109; Beira patrol, 114–24; economic sanctions, 115–24; military force, 118–19; South African support, 116–17; 121
Rome, Treaty of (1955), 169
Rusk, Dean, 59, 84, 91, 100, 106, 175
Russia: see Soviet Union

Safeguard system, 205; see also anti-ballistic missile system
sanctions, 114–24
Schmidt, Helmut, 162
Schuman, Robert, 193–4
Sea Bed Treaty 11
Seas, law relating to the, 136–43
second-generation missile system, 182, 214–15
service unification, 22, 27–8, 225–6
Sèvres, Treaty of, 137
Short Range Attack Missile (SRAM), 204
Simonstown Agreement, 112–13
Singapore, 94–6, 98, 100–101
Skybolt missiles, 176
Smith, Ian, 114, 120–21
South Africa, 96, arms supplies, 109, 111–13; navy, 116; Simonstown Agreement, 112–13
South-East Asia Treaty Organization (SEATO), 99–101, 104–5
Soviet Union: American violation of air space, 42; Cuban missile crisis, see Cuba; decision-making process, 23, 26, 29, 234; flexible defence policy, 92–3, 164–5; maritime forces, 111; military expenditure, 165; missile force, 202; naval forces, 45, 111–13, 128–35, 137; nuclear strategy, 44–5, 164–5; SS9 missile, 205; Short Range Attack Missile (SRAM), 204; submarine force, nuclear, 201
SS9 missile, 205
Stevenson, Adlai, 41, 49
Straits of Tiran, 64–70, 140–41
Strategic Arms Limitation Talks (SALT) 12–13, 29–30, 134, 163, 165, 191, 202, 206–7, 214

Strauss, Franz-Josef, 171, 180, 222
submarine fleets, 130–31; British, 177,
  181–2, 218; French, 19, 188–9, 208;
  nuclear propulsion, 170, 172; Russian
  201; United States, 200
Suez Canal, 139–41
Suez crisis (1956), 20, 69, 153–4, 169
Sukarno, President, 95
Syria, 65

tactical nuclear weapons, 152, 159–61,
  211
tanks, 213
Tanzania, 110–11
Taylor, General Maxwell, 47, 153
territorial waters, 139; Arab-Israeli
  conflict, 72–3, 140–41; Beira patrol,
  119; Gulf of Tonkin incident, 57–8;
  Pueblo incident, 84; warships' passage
  through, 140, 142
Test Ban Treaty (1963), 11, 185, 189,
  223
Thant, U, 40, 55, 65, 67, 71
Thor missiles, 170
Truman, President Harry S., 168, 193
Turkey, 137–8; missile bases in, 44, 49,
  154

Uganda, 110–11

United Nations, 117; Charter, 46–7, 65,
  123; Emergency Force, 64–6; peace-
  keeping role, 121–2; Security Council,
  40–41, 52, 68, 71, 113–14, 120, 123;
  Special Committee on Colonialism,
  119
United States: decision making process,
  23–5, 78, 232–4; isolationism, 147,
  210; Polaris fleet, 200
uranium: American supplies to France,
  183; enrichment technology, 197

V bomber force, 176–7, 223
variable geometry aircraft (AFVG),
  213
Vietnam, 20, 22, 89–91, 106–8, 232;
  see also Gulf of Tonkin incident

Warsaw Pact: centralization, 164;
  Czechoslovakia, 191; decision-making
  process, 23; flexible response, strategy,
  165; force levels, 157–8; maritime
  forces, 129; nuclear strategy, 209–10
West Germany: see Germany, West
Western European Union (WEU), 187,
  198
Wilson, Harold, 68, 117, 141, 197

Zorin, V. A., 41

POLITICS OF DEFENCE
David Owen

Is there effective control over the military? How hazardous are many of our modern defence activities? How long will it be before a combination of accident and ineptness, risk and chance, sets off a nuclear response which could threaten our very existence? David Owen, who, as Minister responsible for the Royal Navy from 1968 to 1970, was the youngest member of Harold Wilson's government, has conducted a searching inquiry into recent defence decision-making, its deficiencies, complexities and dangers.

Dr. Owen points to the lessons to be learnt from such incidents as the Cuban missile crisis, the Gulf of Tonkin incident, the Pentagon Papers affair, the *Pueblo* incident and the Arab-Israeli conflict. Drawing on his first-hand knowledge of the British Polaris Submarine Force, he examines fully the controversial issues behind the development of a rational European defence policy for the 1970s and beyond. He discusses the possibility of Anglo-French nuclear collaboration, placing this sensitive question in its historical perspective.

Convinced that American involvement in NATO will decline, Dr. Owen believes it will be necessary to persuade the United States that, as its contribution to Western Europe conventional defence is reduced, so it has a responsibility to reinterpret the McMahon Act and make available to Britain and France, not only nuclear delivery vehicles or delivery systems, but also the information on nuclear weapons technology that will help bridge any gap in the credibility of their existing nuclear guarantee.

The Politics of Defence was written to stimulate greater public interest in, and scrutiny of, defence decision-making. The control of the military is ultimately the public's responsibility, Dr. Owen contends; the failure to exercise that responsibility could be fatal.